Praise for the Previous Edition

"This concrete, easy-to-use guide is designed to help anxious parents support and understand their newly fledged children. Johnson and Schelhas-Miller possess decades of professional experience as college counselors and their easy expertise is obvious. Situations are discussed in level, clear language designed to help parents allow their children to cope. Both a useful guide and a literary security blanket . . . good, solid, clear, consistent, and grounded advice."
—*Kirkus Reviews*

"College may look like a great investment, but don't let your children hit the quad without first making purchase of this wise, advice-filled book. From helping your child prepare the dorm room through your child's postgraduate years and the first job, this comprehensive book will provide the reason and reassurance you're looking for."   —*Denver Rocky Mountain News*

"In addition to humorous dialogues that permeate each chapter, this book is chock-full of sound, practical tips for reshaping relationships between parents and their emerging adult offspring and for coping with the challenges families face during this crucial time."
—*The Christian Science Monitor*

"*Don't Tell Me What to Do, Just Send Money* is down-to-earth, sensible, and wise. The book offers firm direction, yet it is also full of warmth, humor, and hope. It is brilliantly organized, useful, and fun."   —Russell Muirhead, Robert Clements Associate Professor of
Democracy and Politics, Dartmouth College

"Helen Johnson and Christine Schelhas-Miller have done us all a great service. This book is well grounded in the psychological and practical challenges of college life—for parents and students. As a college professor and the father of college students, I welcome this book with open arms. I wish it had been available to my parents!"   —James Garbarino, Ph.D.,
author of *Lost Boys* and Maude C. Clarke Chair in
Humanistic Psychology, Loyola University Chicago

"*Don't Tell Me What to Do* . . . has been an invaluable guide for thousands of University of Denver families. Of all the books available for parents, this is our favorite. Each year parents of upperclassmen recommend it to parents of the incoming class for its insight, advice, and reassurance."   —Laura Stevens, Director of Parent Relations, University of Denver

"This wonderful guide leads nervous parents through one of the most difficult transitions of their lives. I wish a copy of this book could be sent to every parent who's sending a child to college."
—Susan Murphy, Vice President for Student and Academic Affairs, Cornell University

"This indispensable book provides practical advice to parents navigating the rough water of letting go of their children. The authors honest dialogues and meaty analysis also guide parents who are sending their children to boarding school or summer camp."
—Thomas Hassan, Principal, Phillips Exeter Academy

Also by Helen E. Johnson and Christine Schelhas-Miller

Don't Tell Me What to Do, Just Send Money. First Edition

Don't Tell Me What to Do, Just Send Money

The Essential Parenting Guide to the College Years

Revised and Updated Edition

Helen E. Johnson *and*
Christine Schelhas-Miller

 St. Martin's Griffin ♏ New York

DON'T TELL ME WHAT TO DO, JUST SEND MONEY. Copyright © 2011 by Helen E. Johnson and Christine Schelhas-Miller. All rights reserved. Printed in the United States of America. For information, address St. Martin's Press, 175 Fifth Avenue, New York, N.Y. 10010.

www.stmartins.com

Library of Congress Cataloging-in-Publication Data

Johnson, Helen E.
  Don't tell me what to do, just send money : the essential parenting guide to the college years / Helen E. Johnson and Christine Schelhas-Miller.—2nd St. Martin's Griffin ed.
       p. cm.
  Includes bibliographical references.
  ISBN 978-0-312-57364-5
  1. College students—United States—Psychology.   2. Parenting—United States.   I. Schelhas-Miller, Christine.
II. Title.   III. Title: Do not tell me what to do, just send money.
  LA229.J55 2011
  378.1'98—dc22

                                                                          2011018079

First Revised and Updated Edition: July 2011

10 9 8 7 6 5 4 3 2 1

To Travis and Jennifer and Jay and Page who are raising the next generation of college students: Annabel, Jonah, Oliver, Hayes, Hampton, and Bowen

—H.E.J.

To Jim and my favorite college students, Alexis and Laura

—C.S.M.

Contents

Contents

Contents

Contents

Acknowledgments

In addition to the many generous people who contributed so much to the first edition, we would like to thank the hundreds of college parents and students who provided us with real inspiration and wonderful feedback as we prepared this revised version.

This revision would not have been possible without the enthusiasm and extraordinary skill of our editors, Alyse Diamond and Daniela Rapp, at St. Martin's Press. We would also like to thank our agent, Jill Kneerim, and her assistant, Caroline Zimmerman.

I (Helen) would like to thank several special people. My sons, Travis and Jay, whose college experiences yielded rich material for this book and whose postcollege accomplishments have made me proud indeed. Moreover, they have provided me with two lovely daughters-in-law and six beautiful grandchildren. To my dearest friends, Virginia Nelson and her partner Nancy Busch, my deepest gratitude for your steadfast love and support. I would also like to thank other friends, colleagues, and family members who have cheered and inspired me in countless ways: Joan and David Brumberg, Patricia Owens, Jane Sims, Emily Votruba, Anne Brodie, Jeri Vargo, Jeffery Beam, Stanley Finch, Susan and Richard Neulist, Carolyn Holt, Bob Weston, Peg Palmer, Chris McLeod, Irene Defotis, Leigh Berry, and Laura Stevens.

A number of people supported me (Chrissie) during the work on this second edition of the book. My husband, Jim Miller, was the rock of stability and love that he has always been for me. My children, Alexis and Laura, contributed their enthusiasm and college experiences, which found their way into the book. Peter Bloom generously offered his expertise about technology, while Janet Greenfield and other friends shared their experiences as "iConnected" college parents. Many friends and colleagues listened to me and provided encouragement, including Peggy Ulrich-Nims, Marjory Rinaldo-Lee, Bonnie Buettner, Bob Sullivan, Lisa Stankus, Lynne Metzger, Elaine Wethington, Bonnie Biata, Marianne Arcangeli, Joe Myer, Zoe Klemfuss, and Ryan Mitchell.

Introduction

Congratulations! You have made it through eighteen years of parenting and your child is ready to embark on the grand personal odyssey called the college years. This journey will be an adventure for you as well; you are not alone if you feel a mixture of excitement and dread as you prepare to launch your son or daughter into the next step. Over the next few years, as you observe your son or daughter making that often circuitous passage to fully independent adulthood, your job will be fascinating and at times frustrating. While you will always be your child's parent, the college years signal a fundamental change in that relationship—a change that this book will help you to understand and even to celebrate.

College life today is remarkably different from what it was when you were young. It has also changed significantly since we published the first edition of this book in 2000. When you deliver your child to college, you will encounter a wired campus; online registration and course offerings; gender-integrated residence halls (sometimes with gender-integrated bathrooms and often with in-house technical support); dining halls that are open continuously twelve to fifteen hours a day and cater to special diets; orientation, and special programs for parents throughout the year; and an exceptionally diverse group of students toting smartphones and laptop computers.

Moreover, when you return home, you will have the capacity for continuous connection to your son or daughter, thanks to cell phones, e-mail, Skype, texting, and Twitter. It's difficult to believe that just a few years ago, worries about staying in touch were tantamount among college parents! Now that you can easily communicate with your child all day, every day, it's more important than ever that you consider how this involvement might affect your child's progress toward developing his or her own identity and autonomous decision-making. The college years represent a unique phase in human development; this is the time when your child needs to explore and master the challenges of life without your constant engagement and reassurance. While this is rarely a smooth journey, it is a critical period in which you, too, can learn to shift your approach and become a trusted guide and consultant as your child navigates the path to independent adulthood.

This may be a particularly difficult shift because your generation (whether you are a baby boomer or a Gen Xer) has been more involved in your children's education and development than any generation in American history. You have been dubbed "helicopter parents" and have been scrutinized in the popular press for the zeal with which you have nurtured your children from infancy to emerging adulthood. You likely enjoy a close relationship with your son or daughter, and your child no doubt admires you, relies on you, and wants to stay connected to you.

As your child heads to college, you may wonder: What does it mean to be the parent of a legally adult college student today? What influence can I or should I have from afar? How can I be an effective guide as my child faces adult choices and responsibilities? What *is* my role now?

This book will help you understand your evolving role during the college years. Through the use of real-life scenarios and dialogues that illustrate the challenges of college life, you will have an insider's view of the academic and social scene on campus. The practical, straightforward advice we offer will give you the tools you need to address those challenges appropriately and effectively. Our perspective, grounded in sound developmental theory and research, as well as in years of professional work with college students and parents, also reflects our personal experiences in parenting our own college-aged children.

Chapter 1

From Supervisor to Consultant

Laying the Groundwork for a New Kind of Relationship with Your Child

When our son called from college, we were confused about what he needed from us. Was he asking for our opinion? Did he want us to make decisions for him? Did he simply want a sounding board? Or did he need us to guide him through a decision-making process? As parents, we've come a long way this year. We've learned to step back and allow him to make mistakes, knowing that our love, support, and guidance are still vital in his life, and looking forward to a new and developing adult-to-adult relationship.

One of the most difficult parts of being the parent of a college student is observing from afar as your child makes the often bumpy transition from dependence to independence. After years of being a responsible, caring, and "in-control" parent, this change can be frightening, rewarding, and nerve-wracking—sometimes all in the same week!

Let's face it: once your child has gone to college, you have very little control. The college or university will treat your child as a legal adult, even though you know your child is far from independent. While you are no longer in a position to regulate, supervise, or direct your child's life, you do have a unique opportunity to *influence* your child's decisions and behavior. Your child will experiment with taking on fully adult responsibilities and privileges. What better time for you, too, to try out new ways of relating to and communicating with your child?

The healthiest adult-to-adult relationships we've seen in families with grown children develop when the parents begin to adopt a consulting/coaching role during the college years. One wise new college parent told us, "I realize now that my job is to shift from being a supervisor to being a consultant."

Becoming a Consultant: Adding a New Dimension to Your Parenting Role

The word *consultant* comes from the Latin word *consultare,* which means "to discuss." While you have no doubt played many roles—caregiver, teacher, nurturer, adviser, provider, confidant, rule setter and enforcer, disciplinarian, and counselor—in raising your child to this stage of development, the college years present unique challenges in that you are now the parent of an emerging adult. While it is true that you will always be your child's parent, now is the time to add a new dimension to your parenting role. As your child begins to encounter adult responsibilities and choices, you can become a trusted consultant, assisting your child in making wise decisions and becoming fully independent. The shift to a consulting style of parenting does not happen overnight, but you will find many occasions in which it will be useful during the college years.

Although we strongly believe that parents need to act as consultants, rather than as supervisors, when interacting with their college-aged children, we recognize that this approach may not fit every situation. You know your child; trust your instincts. If you sense that your child is in danger or is calling out for help, you may need to intervene. While it is important that you respect and trust your child and encourage independent problem-solving, there are times when you need to act. Chapter 10 will help you assess when it's appropriate for you to get involved in the problems and crises that can occur during college.

In typical situations, however, a consulting approach based on trust, respect, and clear communication will be most effective.

Essential Skills for Consultants

What skills does a consultant employ? A consultant must communicate effectively so that he or she can teach, advise, and challenge in a way that offers support while encouraging practice in the development of problem-solving and decision-making skills. A consultant offers guidance based on experience and encourages an exploration of alternative approaches to problems and decisions. A consultant facilitates discussion by employing effective communication strategies.

Communicating Effectively

Listening, combined with skillful questioning, can help you become a valued consultant to your child as he or she navigates the path from teenager to adult.

Listening

The key to effective consulting is active and reflective listening. For some of you, this approach will come naturally. For others it may seem awkward and artificial at first. You may be thinking, "Why shouldn't I just tell my child what to do?" or "Doesn't my child need to know what I expect?" While you may want to give advice and make your expectations clear, this approach usually stops the process of investigating alternatives and puts your child in the position of either accepting or rejecting your advice. If you start by really listening to your child, the outcome is more likely to be satisfying to both of you. Effective listening requires that you:

- Make a sincere commitment to listen without evaluating or judging.
- Wait patiently, even if your child struggles to express feelings and thoughts.
- Take notice of verbal and nonverbal behaviors.
- Check your assumptions and responses to make sure they reflect what your child is feeling.
- Listen without trying to "fix" the problem.
- Above all, try not to judge, moralize, manipulate, or "catastrophize" the situation.

Some roadblocks that can hinder effective listening, include:

- warning, threatening
- providing solutions or "shoulds"
- disagreeing, judging, criticizing, blaming
- moralizing, preaching
- interpreting, ridiculing, shaming
- questioning and probing instead of listening

These roadblocks strengthen the power imbalance between you and your child. Through consulting, you can empower your child to make decisions and act responsibly. This approach may seem tedious and drawn out, especially for those who like to come up with solutions and get things done. But it is important for parents to acknowledge that it is not their responsibility to solve their children's problems. If you take over, you're sending the message to your child that you don't feel he or she is competent. Your role as consultant is to provide support, encouragement, and information so that your child can explore alternatives and learn to solve his or her own problems.

Closed and Open Questions

A critical component of effective communication is to understand the difference between closed and open questions. Closed questions usually stop the flow of dialogue while open questions encourage continued dialogue. Few parents have escaped the frustration of the following kind of dialogue:

> PARENT (noticing your teenager putting on his coat): Where are you going?
> CHILD: Out.
> PARENT: When will you be back?
> CHILD: Later.

This is a good example of asking closed questions. Not much information was shared because closed questions do not call on the responder to think. What if the parent had tried using open questions, as in the following example?

> PARENT: Tell me about your plans for tonight.
> CHILD: Well, Jason and I are going to the mall and then to a movie.
> PARENT: Can you tell me around what time you'll be back?
> CHILD: Oh, probably about midnight.

Here are two dialogues. The first example uses closed questions, while the second uses open questions.

> DAD: How's school going?
> JEFF: Good.
> DAD: Do you like your classes so far?
> JEFF: Yeah.
> DAD: Did you get into that biology class you wanted?
> JEFF: Yup.
> DAD: So, do you have a lot of work?
> JEFF: Yeah, tons.
> DAD: Are you getting enough sleep?
> JEFF: Ha! Are you kidding? Nobody sleeps here.
> DAD: Are you having any fun?
> JEFF: Oh, yeah.

DAD: What did you do last weekend?

JEFF: Just hung out with friends.

DAD: What did you do?

JEFF: Nothing much really, we just hung out.

DAD: Well, it's been great talking to you. I'll call you next week, okay?

JEFF: Okay, Dad, catch ya later.

You can see the difference in the following dialogue, which uses open questions.

DAD: Hi, Jeff. How are you doing?

JEFF: Good, Dad. What's up with you?

DAD: Things are fine here. Is this a good time to talk?

JEFF: Yeah, I guess.

DAD: I was just sitting here wondering about what you were doing right now and how your classes are going. Tell me what your day was like.

JEFF: Well, this morning I dragged myself out of bed around eight-thirty to go to my first class and then I had breakfast at the dining hall and just hung around until my eleven o'clock class. Then I came back to my room and crashed until my two-fifteen class. After that, I just hung out with my friends until dinnertime and now I have to study. I usually go to bed pretty late; last night I had to stay up 'til three A.M. to finish my English essay.

DAD: It sounds like a pretty busy schedule. Tell me about your English essay.

JEFF: Oh, we had to write about a childhood friend and describe, you know, his or her qualities that made them a good friend. I wrote about Tim.

DAD: Really? It's been a long time since you've seen him, huh? What do you remember most about him?

JEFF: I wrote about how he always came to our house because Mom baked cookies a lot. I also remember feeling kind of jealous 'cause Mom paid so much attention to him.

DAD: So, how do you feel about your classes so far?

JEFF: They're okay. I really like my biology class, and it's a good thing, because I spend an awful lot of time with class, sections, and labs.

DAD: What is it that makes biology so interesting?

JEFF: Well, we're doing this really cool unit on environmental hazards to wildlife.

DAD: I just read about that the other day in the paper. What does your professor say about that trend?

JEFF: Well, she says there are ways to stop it but it means we'd have to change the way we live and stop using up so many natural resources. It's pretty interesting.

DAD: It sounds like it. What about your social life? How was your weekend?

JEFF: It wasn't that much fun. I did go to a movie Saturday night with some guys on the floor. Oh, Dad, I gotta go—Dan's waiting for me to go to dinner. Talk to you later.

DAD: Okay, Jeff. Take care.

Open-ended questions help you engage your child in more meaningful conversations. If you want to help your child reflect on his experiences and come up with his own solutions to problems, open-ended questions are an essential tool. Parents who use open questions feel more a part of their child's life without coming off like the Grand Inquisitor.

Jeff's father started out the conversation by showing respect for Jeff's schedule. He asked if this was a good time to talk. This set the tone for the conversation. It also meant that he could expect a few minutes of Jeff's undivided attention. There is nothing more frustrating than trying to carry on a conversation with your child when he is preoccupied or has a room full of friends unwinding from a day of classes.

After making sure that this was a good time to talk, Jeff's father proceeded to show genuine interest in his son's experiences by asking a series of open questions. His open questions prompted much more than yes or no responses from Jeff and helped him get a deeper sense of Jeff's life at school. Moreover, this type of conversation allowed Jeff's father to model useful communication skills. It's helpful to remember that this dialogue represents an ideal conversation. Your child may not be as chatty as Jeff or may not feel comfortable opening up in this way. Still, it's worthwhile to practice using open questions in all of your important relationships. You can be a role model of an effective and respectful communicator.

"Why" Questions—Communication Stoppers

You may have noticed that Jeff's father did not use any questions that started with "why"—even though there were many instances in the conversation when he might have wanted to ask why! "Why don't you get up a little earlier so you have time for breakfast before class?" "Why don't you start studying earlier in the evening so you can get to bed at a decent hour?"

"Why" questions are inherently judgmental and come off sounding critical. Even if you are genuinely curious and concerned about why your child behaves in a certain way, the "why" question will put your child on the defensive, which means that he won't be open to sharing his experience with you for fear of being judged. Instead of asking "why" questions, you can ask questions about feelings. His father could have asked Jeff, "How do you feel about your schedule?" or "It must be hard to feel so sleep-deprived."

If your child is struggling with a problem, you can also try asking him how he would like the situation to be different. For example, let's say your son is someone who needs eight to ten hours of sleep every night in order to feel okay the next day. You're alarmed that he's talking about going to bed late every night and dragging himself out of bed in the morning for class. Try putting the ball back in your child's court where it belongs by asking, "If you could wave a magic wand and create the perfect schedule, what would it be like?"

"I" Statements—Beyond Blaming

It's a rare parent who isn't tempted to jump in with solutions to dilemmas, especially when the child's college career or health may be in jeopardy. But usually the parent's response comes in the form of a warning or an ultimatum, such as "You're never going to get through college if you can't get up for class in the morning!" or "You'd better figure out a way to get your sleep or you're going to be a wreck when finals come around!"

It's very difficult to express concerns without sliding into "you" messages, such as "You haven't done your work," or "You party too much and therefore you have rotten grades." Try to express "I" messages, such as "I worry about you when I hear that you're not eating properly or getting enough sleep," or "I'm concerned that you're spending so much time partying during the week." When a parent avoids blaming and expresses sincere and honest concerns through "I" messages, a child is drawn into the conversation in a fundamentally different way. The parent is able to communicate concerns without immediately putting the child on the defensive.

The first year of college, in particular, can be pretty chaotic for students. As they experiment with their new lifestyle, the last thing they want to hear from home is that they're not doing it right. Although they may appear cool and in control, chances are they are as worried as you are about whether they can cope. But they will never admit it if they are confronted with a judging, blaming parent. Although it's frustrating to observe your child going through these adjustments, it's really important to do everything you can to reinforce your faith in your child's ability to manage life at school. At times, this requires a giant leap of faith in your child and a sincere commitment to trust that your child has the resources to deal with the consequences of his behavior.

Acting as a Consultant

A consultant teaches, challenges, and supports. Inherent in the consulting relationship is an underlying trust and respect for the student as an emerging adult who is capable of learning how to manage his or her own life. The college years are a structured in-between period for most students in which they are treated as quasi-independent adults. Parenting a college student requires that you set aside many of your traditional parenting behaviors in favor of learning ways to teach, coach, and advise your child through the sometimes rocky transition from child to adult.

This can be done in several ways. Using the communication skills outlined above, you can listen carefully, ask open questions, suggest alternatives, and encourage your child to take responsibility for finding solutions to problems. As a parent, you don't have to have all of the answers for your child.

Encourage your child to take advantage of the many relationships that can be developed during college. Professors, staff members, work-study supervisors, coaches, and other students can also act as consultants to your child on campus. Plus, you can connect your child to people in your professional setting, your social group, or in the wider community at home.

It is ironic that, by giving less advice and allowing your child to have ownership of decisions, your child will more likely seek your involvement in future decisions. And this, we assume, is your goal: to be involved in your child's life as a loving and helpful parent. In accepting a consulting role, you don't give up your role as a parent, you merely expand it in preparation for an adult-to-adult relationship with your child in the years to come.

The following scenarios further demonstrate ways in which parents can use consulting skills to lay the groundwork for a new kind of relationship with their college-aged child.

Missing Home

The first few weeks at college have been hard for your daughter, Rachel. She calls home often and appears to be having trouble adjusting. She was home for fall break and seemed fine, but a week or so after she returned to school, you had the following conversation with her:

MOM: Hello?

RACHEL: Hi, Mom. It's me.

MOM: Oh, hi, Rachel. How are you doing?

RACHEL: Not so great.

MOM: What do you mean?

RACHEL: I just hate it here. I want to come home.

MOM: What's the matter, honey?

RACHEL: I don't know. I just don't like it here.

MOM: You seemed to be okay when you were home last week. What happened?

RACHEL: Nothing in particular. I just don't feel like I belong here. I'm so lonely and depressed all the time.

MOM: Don't you think you should give it more time? You've only been there two months or so.

RACHEL: I know, but it seems like forever.

MOM: Are you making any friends?

RACHEL: Not really. Everybody seems like they're loving school so much. It's sickening, really. I can't relate to anybody.

MOM: Your roommate seemed like a nice girl.

RACHEL: Well, she may seem nice to you, but all she cares about is guys and going to frat parties.

MOM: Why don't you go with her?

RACHEL: Mom! I hate frat parties. It's just a bunch of stupid people getting wasted every weekend.

MOM: You mean there's drinking? I thought the college had rules about that.

RACHEL: Mom, you just don't understand. That's *all* people do here.

MOM: What about your classes?

RACHEL: I don't understand why they make us take all of this introductory stuff—it's so boring.

MOM: What's so boring?

RACHEL: Everything!

MOM: But, Rachel, you were so excited about going to college. What happened?

RACHEL: I just hate it here. Can I come home?

What's on Your Mind

I don't know what to do.
I wonder if Rachel can make it at college.
Should I let her come home?

What's on Your Child's Mind

I'm miserable.
I don't fit in here.
I'm scared about what will happen to me if I quit.

What's Going On

The first few weeks, and often months, of college are a big adjustment for new students. Everything is different, and many students miss the predictability of home and their high school friends. Even for children who are wildly enthusiastic about going to college, the reality of college life can be overwhelming and scary. It's difficult for parents to understand what is really going on with their child when they get a phone call like this one. Your own fears can make it hard to listen to your child's fears and unhappiness. It's tempting to want to fix things for your child when you hear this kind of pain.

What to Do

- Try to listen to your child's anxieties.
- Express your empathy for her situation.
- Let her know that you sympathize with the difficulties of adjusting to college.
- Express your confidence in and love for her.

What to Avoid

- Letting your concern about her situation dominate the conversation.
- Judging her ability to deal with college.
- Dismissing her fears and telling her everything will be okay if she just sticks it out.

Missing Home: The Replay

Let's look at how this conversation could have gone if the parent had adopted the role of consultant with her child.

MOM: Hello?

RACHEL: Hi, Mom. It's me.

MOM: How are you doing?

RACHEL: I'm feeling awful. I hate it here. I want to come home.

MOM: Oh, Rachel, I'm sorry you're feeling so sad. Tell me what's going on.

RACHEL: I'm just so miserable and lonely.

MOM: You sound really unhappy.

RACHEL: I am. I just don't fit in here.

MOM: So, you're feeling pretty out of it, huh? Are you kind of homesick, too?

RACHEL: Yeah, I really miss Jen and Chris. I don't have any real friends here.

MOM: It's pretty hard to try to get used to all the things you have to deal with there, and meet other kids you can relate to.

RACHEL: All the girls on my floor are so into the fraternity scene. All they can think about is going to frat parties on the weekends.

MOM: That must make you feel pretty alone, huh?

RACHEL: Yeah, I just feel so out of it.

MOM: I guess you're wondering if you'll ever fit in.

RACHEL: What if I don't? What if this isn't the place for me?

MOM: Well, you can always change your mind and go to college somewhere else, you know.

RACHEL: Yeah, I guess I could. But it would be such a hassle to start all over.

MOM: Yes, it might be, but the most important thing is that you feel comfortable and are able to do your work in college.

RACHEL: It's hard to feel good about my classes when I'm so depressed. It's really hard to get used to this.

MOM: I know it must be, and I can understand how hard this is for you. Is there anything I could do to be helpful?

RACHEL: No, not really. I guess I just have to cope, huh, Mom?

MOM: I think you'll know what to do and I trust that you'll figure it out. You know that your dad and I want to do what we can to help you get through this tough period.

RACHEL: I know. Thanks, Mom. I guess I'd better start studying for my test tomorrow. I'll talk to you later. Okay?

MOM: Okay. Do you want me to give you a call tomorrow to see how you're doing?

RACHEL: I guess so. Call me after eight o'clock though.

MOM: Okay. Well, take care and good luck on the test.

What's on Your Mind

I'm really worried that Rachel is so unhappy.
I wonder what I can do to help.
If she quits college now, what will she do?

What's on Your Child's Mind

I'm so miserable here.
I really want to quit, but what would I do then?
Maybe I wouldn't be happy anywhere.

What's Going On

Rachel is experiencing normal adjustment issues. She hasn't found a social group that fits her temperament and therefore feels different from everyone. She also feels the stress of the first college-level exams ahead. It's normal for her to want to quit, but she's worried about what she'll do if she does quit. Rachel needs to share her worries with her mom and, once she's done that, she probably feels much better about her situation.

What to Do

- Remember that this is your child's life and your child's dilemma.
- Empathize with her feelings of loneliness and depression.
- Let her know that you care and ask if you can be helpful.

What to Avoid

- Coming up with solutions ("Why don't you join the Habitat for Humanity group? You loved that in high school.") before you've really listened and responded to her feelings.
- Warning, threatening, or moralizing: "If you don't make friends soon, you're really going to feel left out later. All the kids there can't be jerks. You just need to try harder to meet some nice kids."

What You Need to Know

We know how hard (and time-consuming) it can be simply to listen to your child and allow her to feel what she's feeling without jumping in with solutions or "shoulds." In the second dialogue, Rachel's mother reflected the basic attitude that fosters a relationship with an emerging adult child. She listened and resisted the impulse to come up with solutions to Rachel's problems. This can be a particularly difficult shift for both of you if your child has relied on you to solve her problems. If she has, you need to make this shift with compassion, but also with the resolve to help your child mature so that she can manage her daily life without your constant assistance.

Choosing a Major

Thankfully, not all consulting situations with your child are fraught with worry. Sometimes your child simply needs a rational, practical adviser, or coach, such as in the case below.

When your daughter, Tanisha, was home on vacation during her first year of college, you had the following conversation:

TANISHA: Mom, I'm having a lot of trouble deciding what I should major in. I really like English and history and I'm getting good grades in both. What do you think I should do?

MOM: I'm not sure just how to advise you. Tell me more about what you're thinking.

TANISHA: Well, I've heard that some people do a double major and I'm wondering if I should do that.

MOM: What are the advantages and disadvantages of doing a double major?

TANISHA: I guess if I chose to double major, I wouldn't have to make this hard decision between the two but I might have to stay an extra semester to get in all of the requirements for both majors. And if I double major, I won't have time to take many electives, like the photography course I've been wanting to take.

MOM: It sounds like you might have to give up quite a bit just to avoid making a hard decision, huh?

TANISHA: I guess.

MOM: Have you looked at the upper-level courses in history and English? Do they seem as interesting as the courses you're taking now?

TANISHA: I haven't really checked that out. Maybe I should. I do know that there are fewer requirements for a history major than there are for an English major.

MOM: Maybe if you decided to major in history, then, you'd have spaces in your schedule for quite a few English courses, too. Have you talked to your adviser about this?

TANISHA: No, not yet. I just felt kind of funny about it because my adviser is an English professor. She might be mad if I tell her I like history better.

MOM: What about talking to a history professor?

TANISHA: Yeah, I guess I could. My American history professor from last semester was pretty easy to talk to.

MOM: Having a good adviser in your major seems important. Have you talked to other students who are majoring in history or English? Maybe they could give you some good advice.

TANISHA: Yeah, I know a couple of kids. But what about a job after college? Do you think it matters what I major in?

MOM: Well, from everything I've heard, your major doesn't really matter if you're doing a liberal arts degree. What matters is if you like it and do well in it.

TANISHA: I guess it's not like deciding between painting and premed, is it?

MOM: No, but I know it's a big decision for you anyway.

TANISHA: I think I'll talk to some more kids at school and maybe talk to the history professor again.

MOM: That sounds like a good plan. I know you'll do well, whatever you decide.

What's on Your Mind

I don't see that there's much difference between history and English for Tanisha.
I can see it's hard for her to make this decision.
I wish the professors would do more to help Tanisha make this decision.

What's on Your Child's Mind

I'm really confused.
I have to decide soon.
What if I make the wrong decision?

What's Going On

Choosing a college major is a big decision for most college students, one that many struggle with during their first two years. It's not uncommon for a student to change majors several times before settling on one course of study.

What to Do

- Encourage your child to seek all of the advice available by talking to academic advisers, faculty members in departments, other students, and staff members in academic and career counseling offices.
- Listen carefully to your child's concerns about this choice and ask open questions such as "What are the advantages and disadvantages of each major?"
- Remember that this is a time of great exploration and change and that your child's behavior is normal.

What to Avoid

- Trying to talk your child into a certain major because of its alleged career potential.
- Worrying that your child is hopelessly confused and unable to make a good decision.
- Dismissing this as a trivial decision, especially if your child is deciding between relatively similar majors.

What You Need to Know

You have been an important adviser in your child's life and this remains true during the college years. Tanisha's mother did an excellent job of helping her daughter move closer to making a difficult decision. She did this by asking open questions and by reinforcing Tanisha's ability to research her options and make a choice. So often, what your child needs is a sounding board for her ideas and thoughts and reassurance that you have confidence in her.

Changing Majors

Your son, Scott, has expressed some doubts about his computer science major and now, while home on spring break, he makes an unsettling announcement.

SCOTT: I'm really freaking out about declaring a major. I have to decide by next month and I'm so confused.

DAD: I thought you were going to major in computer science. What's the problem?

SCOTT: Well, I don't think that computer science is right for me, and I'm not doing that well in my computer science classes. But I'm doing really well in my political science class. The professor is so smart and funny; maybe I should major in political science.

DAD: I don't understand. You've been so sure about computer science. You loved everything about computers in high school. Maybe you're just taking the wrong computer science classes. And why aren't you doing well? Maybe you're not putting in the time it takes to get good grades.

SCOTT: Dad, that's not it. I try, but it's just so hard and it's not very interesting. I didn't expect computer science to be like this.

DAD: You know there are a lot of great jobs for computer science majors. I can't understand why suddenly you're so discouraged. You seemed happy about your classes when you were home for break in December.

SCOTT: Dad, you just don't understand. Computer science is really hard, and it's not very interesting, either. It's almost impossible to get good grades. Do you want me to flunk out?

DAD: No, I certainly don't want you to flunk out. I just want to understand why you're so undecided and why you're changing what you always said you wanted to study. Maybe you should try to get some help with your courses. Isn't there anyone who can tutor you?

SCOTT: I don't know, but that's not the point, Dad. I just don't like computer science anymore.

DAD: But, what will you do if you major in political science? I'm not too happy about spending all of this money for you to be unemployed when you graduate!

SCOTT: I'm sure I can get a job if that's what you're so worried about!

DAD: Yeah, like what? I bet there are a lot of political science majors flipping burgers. I think you should just stick with computer science and work a little harder. I know you can do it if you try.

What's on Your Mind

What's going on with Scott? He seems so confused.
I worry about him changing majors.
What will he do with a major in political science?

What's on Your Child's Mind

I feel like such a failure.
What are my parents going to think if I change majors?
I hate my computer science courses.

What's Going On

Scott's father finds it difficult to deal with the confusion that Scott is experiencing. Instead of listening to Scott, he is dominating the conversation with his own concerns. Neither Scott nor his father are really listening to the other person's point of view, hence the conversation ends up being a series of accusations, judgments, and threats. Scott's father has legitimate concerns about how changing majors could affect Scott's future and whether Scott is really making an effort. He may also believe that he has a right to control Scott's choice of major because he's footing the bill for college. He may convince Scott to remain a computer science major, but in doing so he will take away Scott's capacity to make this decision about his own life. It's tempting for parents to jump into the void and take responsibility for decisions when their children are confused.

What to Do

- Listen to your child's worries. Empathize with his confusion.
- Ask for information and respond to feelings before telling your child what you think about the situation.
- Ask questions that will help your child come to his own conclusions.

What to Avoid

- Letting your concerns be most important.
- Criticizing your son for being so indecisive.
- Warning him about the dire future consequences of his decision.
- Forcing your child to stick with a major that you think is more sensible.

Changing Majors: The Replay

Now, see the difference in the same conversation when Dad communicates as a consultant:

SCOTT: Dad, I'm kinda freaked out right now. I'm not sure I want to be a computer science major anymore.

DAD: Really? What changed your mind?

SCOTT: I'm just not doing well in my computer science classes and I have a political science class that I really like. It's so much more interesting than computer science.

DAD: What is it that you like about your political science class?

SCOTT: I'm learning so much about government and the consequence of policy decisions— it's amazing. It's about people's lives, not just numbers.

DAD: So, you're disillusioned with crunching numbers and learning about programming machines, huh?

SCOTT: Yeah, it's just so boring and it's hard, too. No one in my computer science classes is doing well.

DAD: Is it the difficulty of the work or the fact that it's not interesting that disturbs you most?

SCOTT: I guess it's both. I just don't think I'd be happy doing this kind of work forever.

DAD: And the political science course seems interesting and fun right now.

SCOTT: Yeah, my professor is great. He's an amazing lecturer and has a way of making the information interesting. I got an A on my first paper.

DAD: That's terrific, Scott. It sounds like political science really interests you.

SCOTT: But, maybe I'm wimping out because computer science is so hard.

DAD: Do you think that you're going to be a failure if you don't study computer science?

SCOTT: Well, sort of. I mean that's what I came here to study.

DAD: Maybe it would help if you had an idea of what kind of jobs people with computer science and political science degrees have after they finish college.

SCOTT: Well, I guess computer science majors just sit in a cubicle somewhere and program computers all day. I don't know what political science majors do.

DAD: It seems like you're a little worried because you're not doing so well in your CS classes and you also feel the pressure of having to declare a major soon. Is that true?

SCOTT: Yeah, I'm pretty sure I don't want to be a CS major, but I don't know what to do. I've always thought I'd work with computers.

DAD: And you wonder if you should declare a political science major after having taken only one course.

SCOTT: I don't know what to do. I can't believe I have to declare a major in a month.

DAD: What would you like to do?

SCOTT: Well, I'd like to have more time to decide, but if I *had* to decide today, I wouldn't be a computer science major. What do you think I should do?

DAD: It's not my decision, but I'd be happy to try and help you make a choice. Would you be interested in spending a day or two with John Warner, my friend who has the small computer business? Maybe if you saw firsthand what computer science folks do at work it would help you make a decision. Or you could talk to a professor in computer science and one in political science and ask them what their graduates are doing now. I think your mom knows someone at the bank who majored in political science in college. She could introduce you to her.

SCOTT: Well, I guess I could do that.

DAD: Would you like John's number? You can call him to see if he'd let you stop by and observe for a day or two.

SCOTT: Okay, I'll give him a call, but I'm not sure it will change my mind.

DAD: Maybe just having more information will help you make your decision. I have faith in your ability to choose what's right for you.

SCOTT: Yeah. I'll call him tomorrow.

What's on Your Mind

Scott seems confused about his major and that worries me.
This is a good opportunity for Scott to explore his interests.
I hope I can be helpful to Scott as he sorts this out.

What's on Your Child's Mind

I don't want to disappoint my parents but I hate computer science.

Maybe I'm just not willing to invest the time to do well in computer science.

I wonder what I really want to study in college. Political science is so much more interesting.

What's Going On

Parents' expectations can get dashed as college students explore courses of study and seem confused about their direction. It's not unusual for students to change majors—even several times. Scott's father gave him the greatest gift a parent can give—to help his son trust in his own ability to make decisions. Communicating and caring in this way sets the stage for a more satisfying and respectful dialogue that will carry Scott and his father through many changes throughout the college years.

What to Do

- Listen to your child's dilemma openly.
- Check your assumptions by repeating your child's concerns and asking if you're hearing correctly.
- Suggest ways that your child can get more information to solve his problem.
- Remind your child that you have confidence in his ability to make decisions and choices.

What to Avoid

- Criticizing your child for being confused and indecisive.
- Threatening dire consequences if he changes majors.
- Making your expectations more important than his exploration.

What You Need to Know

In our experience, students who feel they must take their parents' advice and direction are ultimately less successful than students who strive to reach their own goals. This doesn't mean that you can't share your feelings about decisions or that you can't take the lead in asking questions, laying out alternatives, and providing suggestions. You do, however, want your son or daughter to take ownership for developing solutions to problems.

While you can't convince your child to approach every decision as you would, you can guide him through a process that will help in addressing problems and making difficult decisions. Letting your child know that you're willing to examine alternatives, try on other points of view, and experiment with your own attitudes and beliefs, teaches him a decision-making process that will be useful throughout his life.

Fall Trip

Your daughter decided to go on a camping trip with her new boyfriend over fall break. She calls you from the Smoky Mountains at eleven o'clock on Saturday night and announces that she hates camping *and* her boyfriend, and wants you to come and get her because she still has three days of fall break to spend at home.

What's on Your Mind

> What's really going on?
> Is my daughter in danger?
> Should I rescue her or let her deal with the consequences of her decision?

What's on Your Child's Mind

> I hate it here. It's cold and there's nothing to do.
> Boy, was I stupid to come on this trip with my boyfriend. He's a real jerk.
> I just want to go home.

What's Going On

Your daughter is miserable and really wishes that you would bail her out of this unpleasant situation. She made a decision to go on this trip without knowing her boyfriend very well. Now she's stuck for a long weekend with him alone in the woods and she's finding out that she doesn't like him very much after all.

What to Do

- Find out if she is safe.
- Ask her, "What changed your mind about this trip?" and "What are your thoughts about getting out of this situation? How would you like me to help?"
- Be frank with her about what you're willing to do to help her, once you've determined that she's not in danger.
- Help her brainstorm her options: She could ask her boyfriend to drive her home, she could ask him to get her to the nearest bus station, or she could decide to stick it out.

What to Avoid

- Jumping in the car and going to get her.
- Feeling that it's your job, as her parent, to get her out of this situation.
- Criticizing her for going on the trip in the first place.
- Blaming her for ruining your weekend and making you worry.

What You Need to Know

Once you've determined that your daughter isn't in danger, you can be an effective adviser, helping her to brainstorm solutions to her dilemma. In asking her how she would like to resolve her problem, you reinforce her ability to evaluate her situation and take action. It's not appropriate, or helpful, for you to simply approve or disapprove; it *is* your role to listen and support your child in examining her options and recognizing the consequences of her behavior. While fall break may be ruined, she will also have learned something about herself—that even though she made a poor choice, she is in charge of her behavior and decisions. Parents who rob their children of experiencing the consequences of their actions impede their progress toward responsible adulthood. Better a wasted fall break than a child who learns that someone else has to take responsibility for her actions and choices.

Even though consulting often seems like an inefficient exercise, it's helpful to remember that consulting is like teaching and coaching. No one is born with these skills fully developed. As you try out these new skills, you need to be patient with your child who is also confronting new situations that demand he or she take on adult responsibilities.

Academic Probation

You're visiting campus for a special spring weekend and your son, Brian, seems nervous and preoccupied. You finally ask what's wrong.

BRIAN: Well, it's bad news. I was put on academic probation. I failed a course last semester and didn't do too well in the other courses, either.

DAD: When did you find out? Why didn't you tell us?

BRIAN: I just got the letter from the dean this week. I thought I could do better this semester.

DAD: Well, are you doing better?

BRIAN: Not that much.

DAD: What do you mean, "Not that much"?

BRIAN: Well, I'm having trouble with chemistry, and I'm getting way behind in a couple of my other courses, too.

DAD: I can't believe this. Do you know how much money it's costing me to put you through college? I know you have the ability. Why aren't you applying yourself?

BRIAN: I am, Dad. It's just so hard.

DAD: Of course, it's hard. What did you think it would be? You have to work hard in college. It sounds like you've just been goofing off. You'd better straighten out your priorities and get off of probation.

BRIAN: I'm not sure I can. I'm already so far behind and my midterm grades haven't been so hot.

DAD: What do you mean you're not sure you can? Of course, you can. You just need to try harder. You were such a good student in high school. What is going on here?

BRIAN: I don't know, Dad. I guess I'm just a loser.

DAD: You *will* be, if that's your attitude.

What's on Your Mind

I can't believe how hard I'm working to keep Brian in college and he's just screwing off. I'm really mad at him.

I'm so disappointed in Brian and his attitude stinks.

He'd better not be partying all the time.

What's on Your Child's Mind

> I feel lousy. Maybe I can't handle college work.
> My dad is really mad at me. But he doesn't understand how hard this is.
> What if I flunk out? What will I do?

What's Going On

It's not unusual for the first year of college to present real challenges and disappointments to students and parents alike. Even the student who has done well in high school may find college work overwhelming, especially when he has to be in charge of every aspect of his life away from home. Parents are usually shocked when their child is put on academic probation and angry that their tuition money is being wasted.

What to Do

- Try to put your feelings on hold and listen to your child.
- Tell him that, while you're disappointed in his performance, you have confidence in his ability to do the work.
- Ask if he's thought of any ways he might salvage this semester's work.
- Suggest that he get help, either by asking his professors, going to the learning skills center, or getting a tutor to get him through this semester.

What to Avoid

- Blaming him for being in this mess. He knows he's screwed up.
- Warning him that you're going to cut off financial support.
- Moralizing and preaching about what he could have done better—the point is, he didn't!
- Issuing ultimatums: You'd better get it together, or else!

Academic Probation: The Replay

Your consulting skills will come in handy when your child faces a serious situation and you're a bit baffled about what to do. In this replay, Brian's dad demonstrates an ideal response, which we realize is hard to do in such an emotionally charged situation.

BRIAN: Well, it's bad news. I was put on academic probation. I failed a course last semester and didn't do too well in the other courses, either.

DAD: What does academic probation mean?

BRIAN: It means that I'm outta here if I don't get at least a 2.0 GPA this semester and it doesn't look too good right now.

DAD: When did you find this out?

BRIAN: I just got the letter this week. I guess I should have told you, but I thought this semester would be better. It's just that the work here is so hard.

DAD: I've been wondering why you seemed so edgy. You must be feeling pretty rotten about this.

BRIAN: Well, what am I supposed to feel? I'm flunking out of school. I just don't know what happened. I guess last semester I fell too far behind and couldn't catch up when finals came around. Maybe I should just take a year off like they suggested and try to figure out what to do next.

DAD: Tell me more about what you've been thinking.

BRIAN: I'm thinking you and Mom must be really upset with me. I don't know, maybe I need to go home and take some courses at the community college. I'm sure I could do okay there.

DAD: Have you decided what you'll do for the rest of the semester here?

BRIAN: I don't know. What do you think I should do?

DAD: What I think isn't really important. You need to decide what you're going to do.

BRIAN: You *always* say that! Sometimes I just wish you'd yell at me and tell me what to do.

DAD: Well, I could yell at you to work harder and get better grades. Would that make it happen?

BRIAN: I guess not.

DAD: Your mom and I aren't around every day to make sure you study. It's your responsibility now. We'll be disappointed if you don't try, but we can't *make* you do what it takes from home.

BRIAN: I know. It's just so hard.

DAD: It sounds like you want to stay here and try to finish. Is that right?

BRIAN: I guess I should. After all, you and Mom have spent so much money on this year. Maybe I could leave with a few credits anyway.

DAD: Do you see any way that your mother or I can help you right now?

BRIAN: Well, I should have done it before, but I could hire a tutor if you guys want to spring for it.

DAD: I think that would be a good investment. I'd be willing to pay for it if you think it will help.

BRIAN: I guess I just need to try to get it together and see what happens.

DAD: That sounds like a good plan. I have a lot of confidence in your abilities. You'll know what's right for you. And you know we'll love you no matter what, don't you?

BRIAN: Yeah, Dad. Thanks.

What's on Your Mind

Brian is in a lot of trouble.

I wish we had known about his failing grades.

I'm not sure he has the resilience to get through this.

What's on Your Child's Mind

Boy, are my parents going to be pissed at me.

I can't believe this has happened to me.

Maybe I'm not smart enough for college.

What's Going On

Students learn a lot about themselves during the first year of college, and not all of the lessons are easy ones. Many are asked to take time off to reassess their goals when they are failing courses or are unable to maintain an acceptable grade point average. Some students need extra time to mature into the responsibilities of college life. If Brian had been assertive and taken the initiative to get help in his first semester, he may not have been asked to take a leave. This may seem like the end of the world for your child or for you, but it can also serve as a wake-up call that your child needs extra help in handling college work.

What to Do

- Listen to your child's feelings.
- Empathize with his experience and try to keep your ego out of it. You may find it's easier to do this if you can imagine advising the son or daughter of a friend.
- Ask for clarification when needed. Ask for his point of view and then listen, without evaluating it.
- Reinforce your confidence in his ability to manage this difficult situation.
- Help him problem-solve, encouraging him to make short-term and long-term decisions when he is ready.

What to Avoid

- Coming up with hasty solutions that will make you feel better.
- Dwelling on how upset you are.
- Punishing him: Having to leave school will be punishment enough. He'll learn more from the real consequences of his behavior.

What You Need to Know

In this replay, Brian's father exhibited superior consulting skills in a difficult situation. Becoming this skillful doesn't happen overnight and this response may not feel comfortable for you in the beginning. You will be on the way to being an effective consultant, however, just by taking the first steps: trying to focus on your child rather than on your own feelings of anger and disappointment, and recognizing that your role is to help your child solve his problem, not to solve it for him.

As parents, we have little control over what happens to our children in college, but we do have control over how we respond to the situation. Keep your eye on the end goal—the issue here is to get through this crisis and help your child land on his feet again. This doesn't mean that you can't express your fears and desires to your child. It's just that this isn't the time to do it. This situation calls for empathy and a reasoned response, not panic. It might be helpful, however, if you share a story from your life in which you felt like a failure and describe how you felt and what you did about the situation. Children need to know that their parents have weathered storms in the past and that these experiences, although tough, are ultimately manageable.

If you feel, after some time has elapsed, that your child is still floundering and not able to be productive, it may be the time to express your concerns. It may be that your child doesn't have the necessary level of maturity at this time to manage life in college or it may be that he or she has just ignored work in favor of partying. Or it may be that your child has a serious problem—drug or alcohol abuse or depression—that needs your attention. We offer help in assessing a range of problems in Chapter 10. Remember, though, that you should avoid using "you" messages, such as "You haven't done your work," or "You're just lying around all day when you should be studying." Try to express "I" messages, such as "I don't feel I can continue to support your education if you're not willing to put in the time to get decent grades," or "I'm concerned that you're not motivated right now to do college work."

When your child fails at something, he or she is the first to recognize that failure. It's not necessary to criticize or blame. Doing so doesn't change the failure into a success; it only serves to make your child feel more helpless. An effective consultant sees a problem or crisis and responds as Brian's dad did—listening, reflecting, empathizing, suggesting, and supporting. This takes time and patience, but it is well worth the effort on your part.

One of the greatest joys of parenting is witnessing your child take on the responsibilities, rewards, and challenges of fully independent adulthood. The college years present a unique opportunity for you, as a parent, to begin to relate to your child as an emerging adult and to adopt behaviors that will serve you well in the years to come.

Helicopter Parenting

The term "helicopter parent" was first used in 1977 by Jim Fay and Foster Cline, cofounders of the Love and Logic parent education center in Golden, Colorado. In recent years, the label has been widely used to describe parents who "hover" over every aspect of their children's lives, from conception through the college years and beyond. In *A Nation of Wimps: The High Cost of Invasive Parenting,* Hara Marano, an editor-at-large of *Psychology Today,* argued that 60 to 70 percent of all parents today are helicopter parents.

There are many reasons for the rise of helicopter parenting, but most observers agree that it gained real traction in the early 1980s when events conspired to create an environment in which parenting became a fundamentally different activity than it had been in earlier generations. At that time, the mid- to late-wave baby boomers (those born between 1950 and 1963) began having fewer children and having them later in life. They gave birth to the new Millennial Generation, children born into the Era of the Child. They were the parents who hung BABY ON BOARD signs in their mini-vans, complete with the latest, legally mandated baby car seats. This was the beginning of a national preoccupation with child health and safety and the baby boomers, rejecting their own parents' hands-off parenting style, became the most involved generation of parents in American history. They began planning their kids' lives when they were still in utero. They stuffed their preschoolers' schedules with enrichment activities and continued to obsess over their trophy kids through every developmental stage from nursery school through the college years and beyond. The boomers, infamous when they were students for profoundly changing the face of higher education in the late '60s, had changed it again as parents of college students.

Raising children had become the most vital endeavor of their lives. Parenting went from being a natural life event to becoming a professionalized enterprise, with children the objects of constant scrutiny and transcendent meaning. At the same time, new brain research supported the idea that parents could affect their child's intellectual development even before they were born. Who doesn't remember the tummy packs playing Mozart to the fetus in order to stimu-late brain activity? Parents came to believe that their extraordinary efforts in raising their chil-dren could result in superior children. Add to that the increasing competition for spots at the best universities, due to the population boom that characterized the Millennials, and you have a "perfect storm" of events, resulting in the type of hyperparenting that has set the standard for parenting behavior and led many parents to become "helicopters."

So, Are You a Helicopter Parent?

If we're honest, we could all admit to a bit of hovering; naturally we want our kids to be happy, healthy, and successful in life. We probably all know someone who goes a little overboard in the parenting arena, micromana-ging everything that happens and taking an active role in making sure that every possible obstacle to a child's success is removed.

This phenomenon has become so perva-sive that the College Board, which oversees the Student Achievement Tests (SATs) and Advanced Placement (AP) programs, devel-oped a survey for parents of high school stu-dents to determine if they were helicopter parents with regard to the college admissions process. Here are some questions we've devel-oped for college parents to help you decide if you fall into that category:

1. Are you in constant contact with your child?
2. Do you feel bad about yourself if your child does not do well?
3. Do you make academic decisions for your child?
4. Do you "take over" when your child is in distress?
5. Are you likely to intervene if your child has a problem with a class or a roommate?

The baby boomers, often on the cutting edge of so-cial change, changed the practice of parenting and influ-enced the next generation of parents—the X Generation. Although the X Generation, children of the first wave of baby boomers, were arguably the least protected—they were the latchkey kids whose parents divorced in unpre-cedented numbers and whose mothers eagerly entered the full-time labor force in the 1970s—they have contin-ued and even escalated the parenting behaviors initiated by the mid- to late-wave baby boomers.

One interesting outgrowth of this type of parenting has been the extraordinarily close relationships between parents and kids. In overwhelming numbers, today's col-lege students report that they genuinely like and respect their parents. This is quite a departure from previous generations. While on the surface this appears to be a positive development (and in many cases it is), the flip side of this closeness can be an unhealthy dependence on par-ents. Despite parents pumping their kids up with con-stant support and positive regard, many children in this generation are remarkably fragile, especially when con-fronted with adversity. They haven't developed the capac-ity to face the bumps in the road and work out problems independently.

Let's look at this from the child's point of view. If your parents are obsessed with your achievement, you are not allowed to fail. If every sports team you've played on results in a trophy for every kid, you have never expe-rienced the disappointment of losing and learned how to deal with those feelings. If your parents insist on every accommodation for you and never let you out of that

protective bubble, it's likely that you feel pretty helpless facing adult problems and responsibilities on your
own.

Here are several reasons why helicopter parenting a
college student is detrimental.

- The college years are widely acknowledged to be
  a crucial time in the development of late adolescents. Crucial because this is the time in which
  young adults need to become increasingly independent in order to transfer their primary intimate attachment from parents to peers.
- Repeated and continual reliance on parents at
  this stage of development inhibits the capacity
  for dealing with challenges, facing new experi-
  ences, and finding the real happiness that comes through a search for meaning and
  purpose that entails personal struggle and reflection.
- Students need to learn to manage decision-making and rely on their own judgment.

6. Have you ever talked to a faculty member about your child's grades?
7. Have you ever confronted a coach about
   your child's performance in a sport?
8. Have you ever edited or rewritten an academic paper for your child?
9. Do you see your child's successes or fail-
   ures as a reflection on you?
10. Do you do everything possible to make
    sure your child does experience the nega-
    tive consequence of his or her behavior?
    If you answered yes to all of these ques-
    tions, you may actually be a Black Hawk
    helicopter parent!

Here are some questions to reflect on as you contemplate parenting a college student:

- What capabilities do I want my student to have when they receive their diploma and
  begin their first job?
- Does my son or daughter really need my help to solve this problem or do I just need to
  be needed? If so, what need am I getting met by keeping my son or daughter dependent
  on me?
- What message am I conveying to my child by "taking on" and trying to fix all of his or
  her problems? (*Hint:* You're essentially telling them that you don't feel they are capable of
  handling their own life.)
- At what age do I see my son or daughter able to make decisions independently and in
  what ways can I support that process now?

In recent years, there has been a lot of talk about "letting go" when a child goes to college. Rather
than letting your child *go,* we believe that you need to focus on letting your child *grow.* In fact, parents
can play an incredibly important role as their children go through college, especially during the first
year. Many positive outcomes for students are associated with the quality of their relationship with
their parents. Researchers have discovered that high levels of academic performance and self-esteem

and low levels of depression were associated with a specific style of parenting that provides warmth and support while encouraging independence and autonomy in college students.

In our years of working with parents and students, we've found that the most successful relationships occur when parents are able to step back from being a controlling parent and shift their parenting style to that of being a consultant. This style of parenting means guiding your child through a process that will assist him or her in addressing problems, making difficult decisions, and, one day, becoming fully independent.

You know and we know that your parenting days are not over and that your college-aged child still needs your wise counsel and support. Parenting an emerging adult can be a tumultuous ride; we trust this book will help you navigate this new and rewarding journey.

Chapter 2

The Electronic Umbilical Cord

Is This TEOTWAWKI or Just WTMI?*

(*IS THIS THE END OF THE WORLD AS WE KNOW IT
OR JUST WAY TOO MUCH INFORMATION?)

When I helped my college-bound daughter pack up her array of digital devices, I couldn't help but reflect on my own trip to college in 1978, toting what I thought was a very sleek new portable typewriter. Back then, I was very excited that the college had just installed landline phones in every residence hall room. Now I'm transporting a college student with enough electronic equipment to run a small business!

The 24/7 Connection

Just a few years ago, the biggest concern for most parents was how they'd stay in touch with their college students. You may recall the college days of yore when there was a pay telephone at the end of the dorm hallway and students made the obligatory phone call home to parents on Sunday night. My, has this changed! Whether you have adopted these new technologies enthusiastically or are still struggling to understand and use them, there is ample evidence that communication between students and their parents is dramatically different from what it was when you were in college.

Can you even imagine a scenario in which you could not contact your child 24/7 via cell phone, text message, or Skype?

Keep in mind, though, this electronic umbilical cord that provides you constant access can be seductive and it can facilitate an unhealthy involvement in every aspect of your child's life in college. For example, you can now be privy to your son's or daughter's daily ups and downs and be tempted to step in, make decisions, and solve problems for your child. Due to the fact that you *can* be constantly in touch, you need to be more cautious than ever to ensure that you are not getting in the way of the important developmental tasks that your child needs to accomplish during the college years. Struggling with daily problems and developing independent decision-making abilities are valuable skills that your child needs to learn in order to grow and become fully adult.

Now that the capacity for continuous electronic connection exists, it's evident how profoundly this phenomenon has affected the relationship between parents and college students. In this chapter, we'll ask you to reflect on the implications and possible consequences of constant connectivity. We'll also explore how technology is changing the landscape of college life and raising questions about the effect of digital technologies on brain development and behavior.

WTMI (Way Too Much Information)

Ashley's mom is beginning to wonder what's going on with her daughter. She's in her second semester of college and she often calls several times a day. The following are phone conversations between Ashley and her mom within the span of one day.

8:45 A.M.
MOM: Hello.
ASHLEY: Hi, Mom. I just got up and thought I'd say, "Hey."
MOM: Did you have a good sleep?
ASHLEY: Yeah, okay, I guess. I'm trying to decide if I have the energy to go to my nine o'clock.
MOM: Don't you feel well?
ASHLEY: No, it's not that; I'm just tired.
MOM: Honey, I'm sorry to cut you off but I have a meeting in five minutes.
ASHLEY: Okay, I'll talk to you later. Bye.

11:30 A.M.
MOM: Hello.
ASHLEY: Hi, Mom. Just wanted to let you know that I decided to go to class after all.
MOM: Well, that's good. How was it?
ASHLEY: Pretty interesting. Pam and I went out for coffee afterward and talked about her lame boyfriend.
MOM: Really.

ASHLEY: Yeah, he's really not her boyfriend, I guess, but she likes him a lot.

MOM: What's up this afternoon?

ASHLEY: Bio lab and then I'm going to crash. I'm so tired.

MOM: Sounds like you're not getting enough sleep.

ASHLEY: I guess four hours isn't enough, is it?

MOM: No, it's not. Maybe a nap will help.

ASHLEY: Hope so. Mom, I've got to go. I have a call waiting.

MOM: Okay. Bye.

4:30 P.M.

MOM: Hello.

ASHLEY: Hi, Mom.

MOM: Hi, Ashley. Did you get a nap?

ASHLEY (yawning): Yeah, I'm kind of groggy but I've got to get some homework done before I go out tonight.

MOM: What's happening tonight?

ASHLEY: There's a frat party I'm going to with a bunch of other girls. It should be fun.

MOM: What's the party for?

ASHLEY: Just to celebrate Thursday night and only one more day of class this week. Maybe I'll actually eat dinner tonight if I get my reading done for class before seven.

MOM: I guess you'd better get to it, huh?

ASHLEY: Yup. I'll call you later.

6:30 P.M.

MOM (sees it's Ashley calling again): Hi, Ashley. What's up?

ASHLEY: I got my reading done so I'm on my way to dinner. Let's hope there is something edible.

MOM: Indeed. Don't they always have a salad bar at least?

ASHLEY: Yeah, but I'm really hungry. Maybe I can grab a pizza.

MOM: Sounds good. Speaking of dinner, I'd better get something going here for your dad and Betsy.

ASHLEY: What are you going to make?

MOM: Probably just pasta and a salad. It's quick.

ASHLEY: I wish I were there. That sounds good.

MOM: Well, you'll be home before long. Have fun at the party tonight. Get some sleep!

ASHLEY: Okay. Catch you later!

MOM: Bye.

What's on Your Mind

Why is Ashley still calling me several times a day?
Do I really need to know every detail of her daily life?
I don't want to appear insensitive, but isn't this a little much?

What's on Your Child's Mind

It's great to talk with my mom; we've always been so close.
No one here understands me like my mom does.
Sometimes I miss home.

What's Going On

In the summer of 2000, when this book was first published, about 25 percent of new college students had cell phones. Now it's clear that virtually every student in America will come to college with a cell phone and computer.

Ashley is behaving similarly to many new college students. While she likes the independence of college life, she has a cell phone and, therefore, the capacity to speed-dial her family and friends whenever she wants. One of the fascinating characteristics of this generation is that, in large numbers, they actually want to stay closely connected to their parents and often rely on their parents for daily reassurance and support.

What to Do

- Begin the process of stepping back from multiple daily phone calls.
- Talk to your child about checking in a couple of times a week when you both have time for an in-depth conversation.
- Let your child know that you expect him or her to manage life on campus but that you're available if problems or emergencies arise.
- Be honest with yourself. If you're feeling good that your daughter calls you several times a day, it may be time to wean yourself!

What to Avoid

- Thinking that it's critical for you to be available 24/7 for "check in" phone calls.
- Impatiently asking your daughter why she keeps calling you all the time.
- Confronting her with how much time she's spending talking on the phone.

What You Need to Know

The good news is that cell phones can be a reassuring way to stay in touch with your college student. The bad news is that this technology makes it possible to be in touch 24/7! You may have provided a cell phone to your child in high school and viewed it as a valuable tool to keep tabs on her and to manage busy family schedules. Moreover, most parents see cell phones as important safety devices, knowing that their children can call in an emergency.

Students are never without their cell phones and assume that they can get in touch with anyone at any time. But the downside is that when Mom and Dad are constantly available, a student never has to figure out what to do without input or reassurance from parents. This hyperconnectivity between parents and new college students is actually making it more difficult for students to attain the skills they need to manage their own lives, such as developing self-reliance and resilience in the face of adversity and asking and negotiating for what they need.

In their book, *The iConnected Parent: Staying Close to Your Kids in College (and Beyond) While Letting Them Grow Up,* Barbara Hofer and Abigail Moore report that the average college student and parent have contact with each other thirteen times a week, and whether it's the parent or student who initiates the contact is fairly evenly split. The number of contacts a week was nearly the same whether the child was a freshman, sophomore, junior, or senior. No differences were found based on family income, ethnicity, race, distance from home, or whether the student had attended boarding school. Only the gender of the child made a difference in the amount of communication, with girls talking on average 14.5 times a week and boys talking 11.3 times. On average, both male and female students talked more with their moms than with their dads. Approximately 75 percent of students were satisfied with how much they talked to their parents, and those who were dissatisfied were more likely to want to talk more, rather than less. About 70 percent of parents were satisfied with how much they talked with their children and most did not want more contact. The authors, in exploring the possible effects of this capacity for constant connection, reinforce much of the advice we present in this book.

Here is a scene that plays out on virtually every college campus in the country today:

Class is dismissed and students rush out of buildings with their cell phones on their ears. Often they are calling Mom or Dad for the second or third time that day. They may be simply checking in; they may be reporting on a difficult exam; or they may be seeking advice on how to solve a roommate problem or choose a major. This provides Mom or Dad with an opportunity to assist them in managing college life and deprives them of seeking support from a friend or talking with a classmate about the ideas presented in class. Just because you can be connected 24/7, doesn't mean it's a good idea.

E-mail

Your son e-mails you Web links half a dozen times a week, but never sends a personal message. Sometimes he sends links to news articles, sometimes photos, and sometimes Web sites. When you reply with a one sentence response to thank him, he never responds.

What's on Your Mind

Why is he sending me these links so often?
Why doesn't he ever include a personal message or respond to my e-mails?
How does he expect me to respond to this?

What's on Your Child's Mind

It's great to find these articles that I know will interest Mom.
Why does she complain that I never e-mail her? I send her e-mails every week.

What's Going On

When your son reads something that reminds him of you, he sends it to you. Sometimes he sends things that interest him to provide you with more information about them. He feels as if he is contacting you frequently; you feel like you haven't heard anything personal from him for weeks.

What to Do

- Continue to send him short e-mail responses to thank him and comment on what he's sent you.
- Don't expect to get replies to these thank-you e-mails.
- Send him links to things that you come across that you know will interest him.
- Enjoy the fact that he's thinking of you.

What to Avoid

- Nagging him to send you personal e-mails.
- Complaining that he doesn't respond to your thank-you e-mails.
- Asking him why he's sending you all this junk e-mail.

What You Need to Know

The good news is that your son thinks of you often and goes to the trouble to send you electronic links to items he thinks will interest you. By sending these links your son is able to make contact with you without acknowledging that he *needs* contact. He's in control of this interaction with you and can regulate it. This is similar to when he calls you on his cell phone and after two sentences says, "I have to go now," or "I'm going into an elevator and am going to lose you now." He gets to hear your voice, but he also gets to control the contact. Rather than asking why he called you when it wasn't a good time to talk, you can recognize that he has gotten what he needed from this call.

Social Media: Facebook

Your son, Brad, insisted that he will not "friend" you on Facebook. He's been in college now for a year and one of your friends (the mother of one of your son's friends) called to tell you that there are some disturbing photos of your son on his Facebook page. When he came home for the summer, you confronted him about this.

> MOM: I've been worried about you since Irene told me that she saw your Facebook page. She said that it had photos of you and your friends, half naked, drinking, and carrying on at a party. Is this true?

BRAD: Mom! What are you doing? Spying on me? I told you I didn't want to friend you on Facebook.

MOM: And I respect your choice, but now I'm not sure you are using Facebook appropriately.

BRAD: What do you mean? Everyone has photos on their Facebook page! It's no big deal.

MOM: But photos of you barely dressed and acting drunk?

BRAD: We were just having fun! We go to parties, we drink, and we do silly things. So what? These are my best friends. I can be myself with them.

MOM: I just don't understand why you have to put those photos up. They aren't a very flattering way to present yourself.

BRAD: Who cares? Facebook is just a bunch of friends having fun.

What's on Your Mind

What is Brad thinking?
I guess he's not thinking.
I'm so embarrassed and I haven't even seen the actual photos yet.

What's on Your Child's Mind

What's the big deal?
My mom is so out of it.
Facebook is fun; everybody puts up stupid photos.

What's Going On

Facebook is now a staple of college life, and is the largest and most popular online social networking site in the world. Most college students have a history of using Facebook or other social media sites in high school. When students go to college, they may want to exert their right to privacy in many areas. Ironically, they may use a very public medium, such as Facebook, to express their right to privacy and independence from parents.

What to Do

- Acknowledge that your son has the right to privacy on his Facebook page.
- Express your concern about the long-range consequences of his postings online and remind him that many people have access to it.

- Accept that this is his issue to deal with, and be reassured that you have pointed out the possible negative repercussions.

What to Avoid

- Demanding that he stop using Facebook.
- Imploring him to remove the photos and clean up his page.
- Chastising him for poor judgment.

What You Need to Know

Facebook was founded in 2004 by a couple of Harvard undergraduates as a way for students to keep tabs on one another and to contact their classmates on the Web. This was an outgrowth of the "freshman face-book" that many universities created to help students get to know each other in the summer before classes began; the original face-book consisted of small photos and short biographies that were printed in yearbook-style format and sent to incoming students.

Facebook has become a major Web superpower, currently boasting over 600 million users domestically and internationally, and that number is likely to keep growing. The foundation of Facebook's appeal is the opportunity to quickly and easily share stories, photos, and experiences with friends and family in real time. This is an extremely seductive medium and it's not only college students who spend many hours each week connecting with friends on Facebook.

Nearly everyone has experienced, heard about, or been affected by social networking sites. Private businesses and not-for-profit organizations alike are joining the Facebook phenomenon, posting news, selling products, and gathering valuable demographic information in the process. In fact, our obvious fascination with sharing details of our personal lives with others has resulted in Facebook's users becoming not just customers but products themselves for sale to corporations.

Recognizing that Facebook users freely share (and overshare!) their private and most intimate information online, businesses have been eager to mine that data to enhance their bottom line. This has led to serious concerns and investigations regarding the use and privacy of personal information on the Facebook system.

The disturbing fact that most college students (and others) fail to recognize, however, is that the information they post online is extremely difficult (and maybe impossible) to ever remove. An added cause for worry is that individuals have *no* control over what their "friends" post about them on their Facebook wall; a student may find an unflattering photo of himself or herself on a friend's Facebook page. While e-mail messages are also difficult to remove from Internet servers that store vast amounts of information, the addition of photos and personal details—not routinely shared in e-mails—makes Facebook and sites like it of greater concern. This means that your child's photos and postings will be available forever to anyone with the technical capacity to access them, unless steps are taken to securely remove these items.

In response to these troubling privacy concerns, researchers at a number of universities are working to develop technologies that could make messages and posts on the Web "self-destruct" after a certain period of time. And consulting businesses are springing up that promise, for a fee, to clean up an individual's online image. While these efforts to expunge online data may bear fruit in the next few years, currently the best solution to maintain a positive online reputation is to be vigilant about the information shared in public forums.

A study commissioned by Microsoft in December 2009, revealed that 79 percent of recruiters and hiring managers surveyed online information about potential hires and that 70 percent of those hiring managers reported that they had rejected candidates based on what they found online. While most students would rather not have to explain their Facebook information to a potential employer or graduate school admissions committee, those (often embarrassing) photos and postings are a part of their résumé even if they have set privacy controls. Add to this technology the fact that we now know adolescents' brains are not fully developed in the areas of impulse control and planning, and you may have a recipe for some pretty unpleasant consequences.

There are some enterprising and creative students who use their Facebook profile to highlight their interests and career aspirations and to network with alumni and others who can provide professional advice. These students use their Facebook activity to bolster their career prospects, rather than to derail them.

As with many areas of your child's college life, you may not have control but you still have influence. Talk to your child about the possible repercussions of some forms of Facebook use. Discuss the dangers, such as cyberstalking and cyberbullying, which can result from impulsive and thoughtless sharing of private information. You might ask, "How would you feel about having your profile, photos, and posts appear on the front page of your college newspaper?"

To be fair, social networking sites can connect individuals in very positive and useful ways as well. Students can easily gather groups with common interests, get involved in campus organizations, become activists for social justice, participate in public service activities, make rewarding new friendships and even become more familiar with their international counterparts, thanks to the ubiquity and speed of these tools. Through the Internet, students who may not have interacted socially with those of different backgrounds can find themselves working on a project together, thereby creating a deeper sense of community and understanding on campus.

More Facebook

You looked up your son's roommate on Facebook and found out he's gay. Your son is straight. You don't think your son should have to share a bedroom with a guy who is attracted to males and you want to talk to your son about it.

What's on Your Mind

What if this roommate is attracted to my son?
What if the roommate brings all his gay friends around and my son starts acting gay to fit in?
What if my son's roommate forces him to have sex with him? What if he has AIDS?

What's on Your Child's Mind

Why is my mom spying on my roommate?
I already know that my roommate is gay and it's not a problem.
If it's not a problem for me, it shouldn't be a problem for my mom.

What's Going On

You have looked up your son's roommate on Facebook and are now worried about something you found out. You don't have any friends who are gay and you assumed your son didn't, either. You imagine that your son would be uncomfortable—or even be in danger—with a gay roommate. You think it's important to warn your son about his roommate.

What to Do

- Don't assume that your son doesn't know that his roommate is gay or would be uncomfortable with a gay roommate.
- Keep this information to yourself and let your son manage his relationship with his roommate.

What to Avoid

- Jumping to conclusions about what having a gay roommate will mean for your son.
- Panicking and frantically telling your son that his roommate is gay.

- Calling the university and demanding that they give your son a new roommate.
- Telling your son that you're willing to pay for an apartment, so he doesn't have to live with a gay roommate.

What You Need to Know

Just as the university would not move your son if you didn't like his roommate's race or religion, they will not move him because of his roommate's sexual orientation. Before snooping around, think about the burden it will place on you if you find out private information. Should you tell your son about information you learn and how you learned it? Before you create issues between your son and his roommate, let your son have his own experience. Just because private information is available electronically, it's not always wise to try to find it. It's a bad idea to stalk your children or their friends on Facebook.

Skype

Your daughter is often on Skype when she's sitting in front of her computer. When you go on Skype and check your buddy list, you can see that she's on. Whenever you see that she's on, you ping her and start Skyping with her.

What's on Your Mind

I love Skype; it's like being in the same room.
I am so lucky to have this free way to have a conversation with her.
Sometimes it's annoying when she just disappears without even saying good-bye.

What's on Your Child's Mind

I don't mind Skyping with Mom, but she wants to do it several times a day.
Sometimes when I've pulled an all-nighter, I don't want her to see how tired I look.
It's annoying when Mom interrupts me when I'm Skyping with friends.

What's Going On

Mom feels like she's on *The Jetsons* when she's Skyping. When she watched that TV cartoon show as a kid, she never imagined that she would be able to see and talk to her daughter in real time on a computer. She likes to be able to see her daughter and to assess her health and the condition of her room: Is she losing or gaining weight? Does she look tired? Is her room a complete mess with clothes and pizza boxes all over the floor? Skyping can be a way for Mom to not rely only on what her daughter chooses to tell her.

What to Do

- Restrain yourself and wait for your child to Skype you.
- Give your child some privacy.
- Consider text chatting and/or using Skype without the video activated.

What to Avoid

- Being annoyed if your child just disappears without saying good-bye, and bugging her until she gets back on with you.
- Nagging her about how she looks or the appearance of her room.
- Skyping so often and for so long that it's as though she never left home.

What You Need to Know

Skype is a software application company that was founded in 2003 and is headquartered in Luxembourg. Users can make free video and voice calls, send instant messages, and share files with other Skype users. Users can also make low-cost calls to traditional landline telephones and mobile phones. Wherever your child is, but especially when she studies abroad, it allows you to make free calls as often as you want. Your child can show you her room while she is abroad and introduce you to friends over Skype. More than any other of the new technologies, Skype allows you to feel that you are with your child.

Texting and Tweeting

Mom feels like she's encountered a foreign language when she gets the following text from her daughter:

@*$, ru@wrk? hand ilu b4n

Translation: At Starbucks, are you at work? Have a nice day. I love you. Bye for now.

What's on Your Mind

I hate texting! It's impossible to understand.
Why can't she use real words?
Whatever happened to good old e-mail?

What's on Your Child's Mind

I *love* texting. It's so quick.
I can send my mom a message when I don't have time to talk.

What's Going On

It's hard to believe that e-mail is practically a relic to college students today. Texting and tweeting are keeping thumbs tapping away at an alarming rate. Young people idolize new media and quickly adopt new digital communication tools. A recent Pew Research Center study shows that text messaging isn't just on the rise, it has exploded in recent years, and now is outpacing all other communication methods used by young people. Half of those surveyed sent more than fifty texts messages a day, and one in three sent more than one hundred a day.

Twitter is a social networking and microblogging service, enabling users to send "tweets," which are small messages limited to 140 characters. This is essentially an information network (news organizations, in particular, have adopted this service in order to receive instant feedback on newscasts); college students use it to record and send short accounts of their daily activities to their network of fellow tweeters, called "followers."

The Pew study also revealed that while students prefer texting with their friends (it's more efficient; they don't have to go through the preamble and niceties of a phone conversation), they are more likely to use the phone when connecting with their parents. Although 71 percent of parents say they know how to text, they complained about the text lingo that young people use to keep their messages to peers below the radar of parental scrutiny. This text lingo developed with Instant Messaging (IM, as it is called), an AOL text-chatting Internet service, which has been replaced for many college students by texting, Skyping, and Facebook. IM was popular during the middle of the first decade of the twenty-first century. It may be that the use of text lingo will fade as more students have smartphones with keyboards, making it easier to write out whole words in a message.

What to Do

- Try texting or tweeting; it's a fast, convenient way to share information.
- Insist that she never text or tweet while driving.

What to Avoid

- Telling your daughter to stop texting you.
- Responding to a text with a phone call. As Chrissie, this book's coauthor, relates: once, when she phoned her daughter, she was told, "If I wanted to talk to you, I would have called."
- Feeling pressure to adopt a medium you don't want to use.

What You Need to Know

Students wander around campus staring down at their phones as they text; they are always on and always in response mode. It takes time to manage this endless flow of texts and tweets, and this is stressful activity, enticing users to engage in and respond instantly to boundless stimuli.

We'll describe later in the chapter what this media enmeshment might mean for their brains. What is it doing to the social well-being of individuals? And what could students be doing instead if only they weren't spending hours every day gazing at screens, distracted from their immediate surroundings and the other human beings that inhabit it?

Instead of communicating in sound bites, they might engage in an actual face-to-face conversation, notice the beauty of the majestic trees lining their campus quad, or simply observe their classmates emerging from a campus building under an imposing gothic archway.

In *Distracted: The Erosion of Attention and the Coming Dark Age,* author and journalist Maggie Jackson suggests, "The way we live is eroding our capacity for deep, sustained, perceptive attention—the building block of intimacy and wisdom, and cultural progress."[1]

The college years have traditionally been the time when students engage in learning and activities that support their quest to shape a unique identity and prepare themselves for independent adulthood. Today, students are facing these crucial tasks embedded in a fast-moving and hard-to-control online environment that consumes many of their waking hours. While texting can be a convenient way to share information, you need to be aware of how this constant communication can facilitate your being overly involved in your child's life on campus.

Laptops on Campus

Your son, a freshman at the state university, is never without his laptop computer. He carries it around campus in his backpack every day. He uses it to take notes in class, to receive e-mail updates from his professors, to do research for his papers, to log on to his Facebook page, and to check the weather during the day to see if his afternoon baseball game will go ahead as planned.

When he was home over the winter holidays, he announced, with obvious distress, that one of his professors had banned laptops from class beginning in the spring semester. He's obviously angry, and you're a bit confused, about this new rule.

What's on Your Mind

We just got him this new computer, why can't he use it?

I don't understand the reasoning behind this new rule.

Technology is the future; don't these professors get that?

What's on Your Child's Mind

I can't believe I'm not going to be able to use my computer in class.

How will I take notes?

My professors are so behind the times.

What's Going On

In the late 1990s, universities rushed to adopt the latest technologies. But, as with many innovations, these digital tools presented unforeseen challenges in the classroom. Imagine being a professor and standing in front of a class in which students are focused on their laptops, clicking away on their keyboards. The noise is distracting enough, but add to that the reality that many of those students are actually surfing the Web and checking their e-mail instead of attending to what the professor is saying.

Understandably, faculty members can feel frustrated as they try to engage preoccupied students in topics that matter to their education. The result, for some teachers, is that they have decided to limit the use of computers in classrooms in the interest of engaging their students' full attention to the material being presented.

What to Do

- Listen to your son's frustrations with empathy.
- Help him brainstorm ways to adapt to this new rule.
- Remind him that you expect him to be attentive in class.

What to Avoid

- Blaming his professors.
- Discounting his concerns.

What You Need to Know

Although most campuses are now fully wired for technology, learning institutions are still scrambling to understand and keep up with the way young people access and absorb information. Faculty members are confronting the fact that some of the teaching methods used in the past are now obsolete, and they grapple with how to preserve the positive aspects of the traditional classroom in which young people learn through dialogue and the exchange of views, and professors preside over in-depth discussions of the material they have presented. Many faculty members who have witnessed a dramatic shift in the way students approach learning are convinced that students are channel-surfing through their education, unable to pay attention to the topics at hand for any sustained length of time.

While some faculty members eagerly embrace these new technologies (in fact, there are numerous courses taught online and others focused on technology as the sole subject matter) and see them as tools that enhance their teaching, others feel that technology is being forced upon them and that it does nothing but distract students.

After six weeks of instituting a ban on laptops in his classroom, a Georgetown University professor surveyed the class. Four-fifths said they were more engaged in class discussion and 95 percent admitted that they had used their laptops for "purposes other than taking notes."[2] Some students support these bans, arguing that they are paying a lot of money to be in class and really shouldn't spend the time gaming, checking their e-mail, or reading blogs.

Regardless of whether individual faculty members are willing to embrace and accept new technologies, students will continue to adopt the latest digital devices. The laptop ban, for example, may not be as big an issue as the increasing use of the small, less obtrusive smartphone: iPhones, BlackBerrys, and other Internet-ready cell phones are becoming more prevalent than laptops in college classes.

As we begin to more deeply understand the impact of technology on the educational environment, we may find that students benefit from having to turn off their laptops and smartphones to more fully concentrate on the class. At its most basic level, learning requires that a student is focused and aware enough to choose what to pay attention to; this may be an admirable skill to foster in our distracted world.

Multitasking and Overload

You marvel at your son as he watches TV while texting his friends on his cell phone and listening to music on his iPod. He seems perpetually connected to multiple gadgets and screens, and appears to be fully capable of keeping them all going at once.

What's on Your Mind

Does he ever "unplug"?
Maybe when he's sleeping!
He's always been a multitasker, but now he has so many more screens to attend to.

What's on Your Child's Mind

My new iPhone is awesome!
I can do so many different things at once.
Who just sits and watches TV anymore?

What's Going On

Those of us who are "digital immigrants" (people born before the explosion of digital technology) often find our children's preoccupation with screens baffling. Multitasking is the way of life for most college students and they appear to manage these tools with impressive skill.

What to Do

- Learn about the consequences of multitasking and overload. (Check out the references section at the back of this book.)
- Talk with your child about multitasking and overload.

- Act as a role model by turning off your screens and engaging in face-to-face interactions with others.

What to Avoid

- Blaming your child for being a scatterbrain.
- Threatening to remove the screens if he doesn't pay attention to you.
- Just accepting that this is the way it is and there's nothing you can do about it.

What You Need to Know

Recently researchers at the University of Maryland asked two hundred students to "unplug" from social media and cell phones for twenty-four hours. When the students were asked to describe their experiences, they reported withdrawal symptoms similar to those experienced by individuals addicted to alcohol and other substances.

Although the idea of "Internet addiction" may sound hyperbolic, even the study's director was surprised by the number of students who reported that they were "incredibly addicted" to media. One student explained, "Texting my friends gives me a constant feeling of comfort. I felt quite alone and isolated; the fact that I was unable to communicate with anyone via technology was almost unbearable."[3]

Multitasking, once an engineering term applied to a computer's apparent capacity to perform multiple tasks through its central processing unit, has now become a term applied to human behavior. While it's not technically true that computers can multitask, it appears that many of us think we can. However, recent research points to the fact that multitasking is a myth; we really cannot pay attention to and focus on two or more things at once.[4]

The New York Times recently reported the results of a research study that illustrated an age-old conflict in the brain, a conflict that the use of technology seems to be intensifying.[5] Researchers at Stanford have found that multitaskers have more trouble filtering out irrelevant information than non-multitaskers. From an evolutionary perspective, it may have been helpful to pay attention to any new information which could indicate that danger was near; but today, students writing a paper will have trouble completing the task if they pay attention to every text and tweet that comes along.

Scientists have argued that "the depth of our intelligence hinges on our ability to transfer information from working memory, the 'scratch pad' of consciousness, to long-term memory, the mind's 'filing system.' Our 'scratch pad' or working memory can hold only a relatively small amount of information at a time and that 'scratch pad' storage is fragile. A break in attention can sweep it from our minds. However, when facts and experiences enter our long-term memory (our filing cabinet), we are able to weave them into the complex ideas that give richness to our thought."[6]

Digital media serve up multiple stimuli, bombarding our "scratch pad" of short-term memory with information—the scroll that runs across the bottom of your television screen, the pop-up advertising online, the snippets of information contained in side bars, hypertexts that divert attention in the middle of an article, the increasingly shorter articles (which read more like headlines) in print media. All of these, and more, reinforce the need for individuals to be constantly taking in multiple pieces of information. Our media tools prompt us with pings, rings, flashing alerts, and blinking icons, grabbing our attention and distracting us from the task at hand.

This relentless appeal for attention to incoming information often results in cognitive overload, making it harder to retain information, to focus on deeper meanings, and to draw connections with other memories. In this media-saturated world, the chime of incoming e-mail or the ringtone on a cell phone can override a student's goal of studying for an exam or writing a paper. Attempting to perform multiple tasks at the same time, these so-called multitaskers are continually distracted and, yes, scatterbrained.

How does a young person, bombarded by a torrent of texts, e-mail, Web sites, and tweets distinguish between quality information and merely available information? And what does a student gain from attending to a constant flow of trivial information from a network of friends?

What would it feel like if you had to "unplug" from all media for a day? Before we "tsk-tsk" the behavior of young people, it's useful to acknowledge that all of us are now inextricably enmeshed in digital technology and the screens and devices that deliver it to us instantly and insistently all day, every day.

More urgently, we might ask, what is this constant connectivity doing to human beings and human interaction? Some experts believe that technology use is slowly reshaping personalities, causing us to be more impatient, impulsive, forgetful, and narcissistic. Stanford University has become an important center for research on multitasking. Clifford Nass is a professor at the university, and he has said that the brain's ability to be diverted to pay attention to new sights, sounds, and information had evolutionary value when a person might have been focused on building a hut and a lion was suddenly lurking behind a bush. In today's world, the ring of an incoming text message or e-mail might distract a student from writing a paper, or a mother from writing a business plan, and a father from playing with his children. Being alerted to danger when you are engrossed in a task is one thing, but being distracted from an important activity because you are unable to resist checking whenever you are alerted to a message on an electronic device is another thing entirely. Nass believes that the biggest risk of heavy technology use might be the fact that it decreases how much people engage with each other, even when they are in the same room. This could decrease empathy, which is essential to the human condition. "The way we become more human is by paying attention to each other," Nass says. "It shows how much you care."[7]

This constant connectivity can also lull a parent into a false sense of intimacy with a college student because text messages, Facebook entries, or e-mails provide only a snippet of what that student may be feeling. Voice tone and depth of emotion are missing when using these media, and it's important to be aware that intentions can be easily misinterpreted.

What can you, as the parent of a college student, do to understand and respond to these media challenges?

- You can learn more about these technologies and engage your student in a discussion about the advantages and disadvantages of media usage.
- You can model a different approach by turning off your screens and engaging in actual face-to-face conversations and interactions with your family and friends.
- You can institute "no cell phone" times in your home and make a point to eat meals with your family without cell phones and other devices present.
- You need to have a discussion with the whole family about developing your own positive social norms around online life. For example, make it clear that you do not condone or approve of "sexting"—sending sexually explicit images or messages via text or e-mail.
- Talk to your child about the possible effects of playing violent video games, putting up personal photos on Facebook, uploading personal videos to YouTube, viewing pornography, or engaging in hate speech or bullying through blogs or social networking sites. Make your values clear and ask your child to share his or her thoughts on these issues.
- Stop yearning for the days when you thought you had total *control* over your child's behavior—start talking now so you can be the best *influence*.
- Examine your need to be in constant contact with your college student and think about how you can support his or her progress in becoming independent and self-directed.

Technology and the Brain

We are in the midst of a lively public debate about the effects of technology use on the brain. Scientists at the forefront of research on the impact of Internet use on the brain are reporting intriguing findings. No doubt, this subject will receive increasing attention in the years to come as we move more deeply into a technology-saturated mediated world.

There is already compelling evidence that Internet use is changing the structure of our brains and the way we think and process information. Gary Small, professor of psychiatry at UCLA argues, "The current explosion of Internet technology is not only changing the way we live and communicate but it is rapidly and profoundly altering our brains. The daily use of computers, smartphones, search engines, and other such tools stimulates brain cell alteration and neurotransmitter release, gradually strengthening new neural pathways in our brains while weakening old ones."[8]

Michael Merzenich, the research scientist who pioneered our understanding of the plasticity of the brain in 1968, recently stressed that heavy use of online tools has neurological consequences. It has only been in the last fifteen years that scientists have discovered that our brains are almost infinitely plastic—meaning that they continue to grow and change over time—and are not fixed in development after childhood.

On one side of the debate about technology's effect on the brain is Nicholas Carr, author of *The Shallows: What the Internet Is Doing to Our Brains,* who believes that we are at a moment of transition in our history between two very different modes of thinking. "The linear mind (calm, focused and undistracted) is being pushed aside by a new kind of mind that wants and needs to take in and dole out information in short, *disjointed,* often overlapping bursts."[9] We are being trained in how to communicate within technology's structure—a fast, interactive, and immediate structure confined to various digital screens.

Carr explains, "If, knowing what we know today about the brain's plasticity, you were to set out to invent a medium that would rewire our mental circuits as quickly and thoroughly as possible, you would probably end up designing something that looks and works a lot like the Internet. . . . [t]he Net delivers precisely the kind of sensory and cognitive stimuli—repetitive, intensive, interactive, addictive—that have been shown to result in strong and rapid alterations in brain circuit and functions." Carr argues that "even as the Internet grants us easy access to vast amounts of information, it is turning us into shallower thinkers."[10] He notes, "Psychological research long ago proved what most of us know from experience: frequent interruptions scatter our thoughts, weaken our memory and make us tense and anxious."[11]

On the other side of the debate, some imaging studies have shown that the brains of Internet users become more efficient at finding information and players of some video games develop more visual acuity. Other research indicates that some people can more easily juggle multiple information streams. Scientists at the University of Utah say that these "supertaskers" make up about 3 percent of the population. Gary Small at UCLA found that Internet users showed greater brain activity than nonusers, perhaps indicating that they were growing more neural connections. "The bottom line is, the brain is wired to adapt," said Steven Yantis, a professor of neuroscience at Johns Hopkins University. "There's no question that rewiring goes on all the time," he added. But he believes it is too early to say whether the changes caused by technology were materially different from others in the past."[12]

The debate among scientists over whether technology's influence on behavior and the brain is good or bad, and how significant it is, will continue as long as neuroscience research studies continue to examine technology and the brain. Just as we have had an explosion in the use of technology in recent years, we have also had an explosion of new forms of research on the brain. As Nicholas Carr has conceded, "We still await the long-term neurological and psychological experiments that will provide a definitive picture of how Internet use affects cognition."[13]

A Balancing Act

Notwithstanding the somewhat unsettling realities of these changes and certainly not eager to be labeled Luddites, we recognize that the Web and other digital tools have done much to shrink our planet and provide opportunities for increased interconnectedness and understanding. Technology has also made it possible to more deeply explore and develop life-saving and life-enhancing scientific advances.

Moreover, through an array of digital technologies, people are able to work remotely, escape the office cubicle, and add hours to their day that they formerly spent commuting. Few would argue that the release from the mundane tasks that the computer performs is a bad thing. Online work through the use of electronically facilitated conferences and meetings can shrink the distance between coworkers and reduce the cost of communicating with colleagues across the country and around the world.

Who doesn't marvel at the ease of gathering information instantaneously on the Web? Who doesn't appreciate being able to "Google," to use a GPS to navigate unfamiliar territory, or to listen to music downloads on an iPod? And who doesn't value the ability to be in touch often with family and friends?

But just try to separate from your cell phone, Internet, or e-mail and you'll be amazed at the power these media wield over your daily life. Our obsession with digital technology doesn't have to signal TEOTWAWKI (The End Of The World As We Know It). Perhaps the most daunting challenge we face is maintaining "balance"—the ability to celebrate progress and innovation, while remaining alert to their profound effects on us as thinking, feeling human beings.

Chapter 3

Getting Them Off to College

Preparing Yourself and Your Child for the Transition

I never understood the meaning of the word inevitability *until I was wheeled into the delivery room to give birth to my first child. The responsibility of caring for a helpless child was awesome indeed. Then, about two minutes later, he was eighteen years old and we were packing the car to take him to college. Again, the word, "inevitability," came to mind, but in a different way. This time, I knew in my heart that he would never really come home again.*

With the flurry of activity surrounding the college choice and admissions process, you haven't had much time to think about how *your* life is going to change when your child actually leaves home for college. This chapter will help you deal with many of the logistical and emotional challenges you'll face in the weeks leading up to his or her departure. You may be surprised by the intensity of your feelings about having your child (whether he or she is the first or the fifth!) go off to college.

Before You Leave Home

What can you do to prepare yourself (and your child) for this major change? First, you can take pride in the job you have done as a parent. The years of caring, chauffeuring, nursing, listening, empathizing, supporting, and, yes, sometimes just coping with your child on a daily basis are nearly over. The last year of high school is usually a challenging one. High school seniors typically are more than ready to move away from the family and they have a way of making that clear. After the stresses of applications, test-taking, and acceptance decisions are over, most high school seniors find themselves in an ambivalent place—still at home but ready to move on. Parents complain that their high school seniors are hard to recognize as the children they've known and loved. Some feel this is nature's way of preparing you to say good-bye. In fact, at some points, you can't wait to say good-bye!

Getting Organized

As the excitement of anticipating college acceptance letters and the relief of having made the choice wears off, you'll notice a gradual shift in your child's behavior which usually intensifies in the weeks just before he or she leaves for college. Just as parents are ambivalent about this event, their children are often experiencing conflicting emotions, too. They are nervous, excited, sad, and confused, all at the same time. And this can make for some intense family interactions.

It's two weeks before you make the car trip to deliver Mary to college. She has finished up her summer job and is doing an impressive imitation of a young woman without a care in the world. At the dinner table one night, you finally confront her.

MOM: Do you realize that in just two weeks from today we're driving you down to school?
MARY: Yeah, I guess so.
MOM: When are you going to start getting ready to leave? You have a million things to do.
MARY: Mom, chill. I have plenty of time. I just finished my job and I want to hang out for a while.
MOM: But, Mary, you can't wait until the last minute to get it together.
MARY: I just have to pack up my clothes and stuff.
MOM: Speaking of stuff, what do you plan to take? Have you read the information from school on what you should bring? Have you talked to your roommate yet about what she's bringing?
MARY: *Mom,* stop it! I'm not a baby. I can handle getting ready to go to school.
MOM: I just don't want to deal with the last-minute panic that I see coming if you don't get organized now.
MARY: Yeah, well, I gotta run. I promised Jess I'd meet her at the mall at seven o'clock. See ya!

What's on Your Mind

Mary is driving me crazy. She can't seem to do anything but sleep and hang out.
I'm going to get stuck with getting her ready for school at the last minute.
She seems so lukewarm about going to college now—she was so excited a couple of months ago.

What's on Your Child's Mind

I wish Mom would stop bugging me about getting ready to go to school. She acts like
> I'm twelve and going to summer camp.

I can't wait to get away from here, but I'm really going to miss my friends.

I wonder what my roommate is like. Maybe I should text her, but I'm not sure what to say.

What's Going On

You're surprised that Mary appears so disinterested in preparing to go to school. You wonder if she's having second thoughts about going at all. Mary seems to be withdrawing from the family scene, but not getting ready for college, either. This behavior is natural for a student entering college. As the day she leaves for school draws nearer, the "what if" fears and thoughts emerge for both parents and children. You may find yourself arguing with your child over seemingly trivial things, a common occurrence before a separation. You're most likely trying to deal with this situation on two levels at once—logistical and emotional.

What to Do Logistically

- Recognize that these are normal precollege jitters on your child's part and that it is important for her to spend time with her high school friends in order to make the break with them.
- Many colleges have Facebook or other social networking sites targeted at new students; ask your child if she's investigated this possibility. It can go a long way toward helping her connect with other incoming students and allowing her to feel more comfortable when she eventually arrives on campus.
- Ask if there is something you can do to be helpful (while not taking on the whole project yourself).
- Ask your child to set aside a couple of hours on a specific day to go out for lunch with you to talk about plans for the move. Make a list of things that you feel need to be accomplished, and ask her to do the same.

What to Do Emotionally

- Take care of yourself. Recognize that you may be expressing your own precollege jitters in trying to be hyperorganized when what you really need to do is deal with your feelings about your daughter leaving home. Commiserate with a friend who's in the same situation.

- Ask your child, "What are your hopes, fears, and expectations about being a college student?" Then simply *listen* without judging or dismissing anything she says.
- Let her know *your* hopes, fears, and expectations. Make it brief and try to build on what she said instead of lecturing. You may be most concerned about safety, grades, drinking, drugs, the social scene, eating habits, and basic adjustment. It will be interesting for you to hear your child's concerns. *Warning:* Your child may not be eager to do this. That's okay. Expressing some of your feelings will make *you* feel better.
- Remind your child that she may be on an emotional roller coaster for a while, but that you are confident that she is ready for this new life away from home.
- Reassure her that she can always call on you for support.

What to Avoid Logistically

- Taking on the packing and organizing yourself.
- Giving her the third degree or nagging her every day about getting ready.

What to Avoid Emotionally

- Ignoring your own feelings or projecting them onto your child.
- Taking on your daughter's tasks and emotions as your own. This will only make you feel frustrated and angry.

Helping Your Child Decide What to Bring

Most colleges send entering students a list of things they will need to set up their rooms, including personal items. Ask your child to review this list with you. We have suggested some of the most common items to consider.

Electronic Equipment/Appliances/Furniture

College students often arrive on campus with a room-clogging array of electronic equipment in addition to mini-refrigerators, microwave ovens, and even furniture! Most dormitory rooms are small and cannot accommodate all of this stuff. It's a good idea for roommates to discuss what they're planning to bring to avoid having two or three of everything. Dormitory rooms typically have the basics: a bed, a desk, a dresser, and a closet. Things like small refrigerators, coffee/tea makers, toaster ovens/microwaves, irons, extra bookshelves, laundry hampers, drying racks, and fans can take up a lot of room. Most residence halls have group kitchen facilities, so many of these things are not necessary in each individual room. Moreover, local merchants usually rent small refrigerators and sell residence hall-sized rugs and other room furnishings to incoming college students.

Decoration for the Room

We've noted a remarkable difference between males and females in approaches to "decorating" dorm rooms. Girls often want to coordinate bedspreads, rugs, curtains, and wall decorations, and boys usually don't. Your daughter may want to wait to decorate her room until she confers with her roommate so that their things will match. Your son will probably take very little interest in things like room furnishings and will not want to coordinate with his roommate. Either way, you and your child can decide whether to purchase these items before leaving home or to take extra cash to buy them at school. It's a good idea to remember that many residence hall mattresses are not high quality. The beds are often extra long and regular fitted sheets may not work. You may want to bring extra mattress padding or even a piece of plywood to help firm up the mattress.

Computers/Phones

Most students heading for college these days have their own personal laptop computer. If your son or daughter wants to buy a new laptop or smartphone, many colleges sell these through their campus stores and may offer significant discounts. Although most campuses today are totally wired for technology, it's a good idea to check with your college to know what to expect with regard to network capability and compatibility. It's usually essential that every student has or has access to a computer and cell phone, as so much of the communication about courses, campus events, and safety issues is handled through the Internet.

Cars on Campus

Many colleges do not allow students to bring cars to campus during the first year; some discourage having a car at all. Find out the school's policy before you agree to allow your child to have a car.

Most campuses have limited parking space and will charge your child a hefty fee for parking. In general, it's not a good idea to have your child bring a car to campus during the first year. It adds a level of complexity to a new student's life that is easily avoided. If your child is going to bring a car to campus, check on the regulations beforehand. It's also a good idea to review basic car maintenance and service needs with your child—simple things like checking the oil or adding antifreeze and coolant may need to be covered, especially if you have taken responsibility for those things in the past.

Bicycles

Bicycles can be a terrific, inexpensive way for your child to navigate the campus and get some exercise as well. Check ahead of time to ensure adequate, safe storage for the bicycle in the residence hall. Few rooms can accommodate a bicycle, unless you install special hooks to hang it from the wall or ceiling. It's important to have a high-quality lock to discourage theft—bicycles in college towns are often prime targets for thieves.

When Your Child Is Attending College Near Home

With an increasing number of students attending community colleges and state universities to save money, many students are attending college in or near their hometown. With your child so close to home, it is particularly important to discuss your expectations before the semester starts. Will the child be able to borrow the family car? If so, how will they make arrangements to borrow the car? May the child come home to do their laundry? Do you expect them to let you know before they drop by? Will you let them know before you drop by? Is it okay if they show up for dinner unannounced? May they bring friends to dinner unannounced? Different families will have different answers to these questions, but many conflicts can be avoided by sharing your assumptions and having your child share his before he begins the first semester.

Money

Have a frank conversation with your child about finances before he leaves for college. For most people, talking about money is somewhat difficult, but being open with your child about what resources you have (or don't have!) to commit to her college expenses will help her to understand and appreciate your point of view. It's important to try to do this in a straightforward way—you don't want your child to feel guilty if you are making great sacrifices to send her to college, but you also don't want your child to expect support that you aren't able or willing to provide. Don't apologize; just explain what you are willing and unwilling to do. Discussing money openly with your child may be awkward, but it will significantly reduce tension and problems later.

Initial Costs

Room furnishing and set-up costs can be considerable. The first textbook bill can also come as a surprise. It is not unusual for a student's textbooks to cost upward of five hundred dollars for a semester or term. If the student is majoring in architecture, engineering, or art, the additional cost of supplies can be substantial.

Check with your home or apartment owner's insurance carrier ahead of time to ensure that your child's expensive electronic equipment is covered under your policy. Consider getting replacement value insurance coverage, which usually adds very little cost to your policy. It ensures that you will be able to replace this expensive equipment instead of simply getting reimbursed for a used computer, which will be considerably less than you'd have to pay for a replacement.

Spending Money

Many parents expect their children to earn spending money through a summer job or a job on campus. If you agree that your child must earn spending money, make it clear that you will not send more unless there is an emergency. If you're planning to provide spending money, discuss a reasonable amount. If you have a limit, make it clear. You may agree to renegotiate this amount at Thanksgiving break when the actual costs are clearer.

The amount of spending money your child will need can vary a great deal depending on several factors, such as the school's location and its general social culture. If it's an urban school, opportunities to spend money on entertainment and expensive diversions will be greater; if it's a rural school, more time may be spent on campus taking part in college activities and cultural events that are free or relatively inexpensive. It will depend mostly on what kind of social life your child wants. If fraternities and sororities are the main social activity and your child decides to pledge, it can be costly. If your child has an active social life, the need for spending money may be greater than for a student who spends his or her time studying and eating pizza with friends in the dorm or going to a movie occasionally. The ubiquity of e-mail, cell phones, texting, and Skype has dramatically decreased the amount of money students used to spend on long-distance phone calls, but it is a good idea to have an understanding of who will pay cell-phone bills.

If your child spends a lot of money on personal care products, try to buy these things in quantity at home. College stores tend to respond to their captive consumer audience by charging more for basics such as shampoo, toothpaste, soap, tissues, aspirin, cosmetics, and so on. Cleaning supplies for the room will also be necessary, as most residence halls have cleaning services only for public areas and communal bathrooms.

Credit Cards/Checking Accounts

Many college-bound students already have credit or debit cards and checking accounts, although checking accounts are rapidly becoming obsolete. A recent survey revealed that more than 80 percent of college students have credit cards and 47 percent have four or more credit cards. Those students also have an average credit card debt of nearly three thousand dollars. Until recently, it was extremely easy for new students to get one or more credit cards, as companies flocked to colleges and freely handed out credit card applications to students at orientation. This rather risky practice has now been dramatically curtailed so that it may be more difficult for your child to apply for and receive a credit card while in college.

If you want your child to have a credit card, it's important to have a talk about how to use credit responsibly. Too many students get into real debt trouble when they have access to a credit card. For your son or daughter, a first credit card is the beginning of their official credit history, a history that may haunt them for years to come if it is littered with debt that they are unable to manage. A poor credit history can have an impact on many areas of life, including job prospects after graduation. Many companies take credit histories of prospective employees very seriously, as financial responsibility is often a key trait they seek when recruiting new hires.

Sit down and come up with a plan to help your child understand how to use credit responsibly. If you determine the card is only for emergencies, talk about what constitutes an emergency (running out of pizza on Friday night isn't one!). If you want your child to have access to a credit card, you may decide to allow him or her to become an additional cardholder on your credit card account. If that's the case, you'll need to set expectations and limits on its use and monitor the charges carefully. Or you may choose to cosign on a credit card. If you decide to cosign, however, you need to be aware that your own credit history will be affected if your child misuses the credit card. Some parents offer their children a debit card on their credit card account and deposit funds as needed for expenses. This option allows you to monitor the use of the card and it can also help your child learn how to budget for monthly expenses.

Although students today rarely use a checking account, some choose to have a local bank account that offers an ATM debit card. This may mean having a cashier's check prepared before leaving home with funds from an existing account to start the new one or transferring funds electronically from bank to bank.

Many colleges offer credit card-like charging privileges at the campus store with the student ID card. Be clear about what you will pay for if your child uses a commercial or college charge card. You may want to approve charging textbooks and school supplies but not other items.

Learning to handle money is an important step on the path to adulthood. You need to think carefully about how you can help your child become financially literate and responsible during the college years.

Health Insurance

Make sure that your child will continue to be covered under the family health insurance plan. Due to recent changes in national health insurance policy, insurance companies are now required to cover children until the age of twenty-six, regardless of whether they are full-time students. Most colleges and universities offer a health insurance plan for students if your policy will not cover your child. Check it out in time to make the change if necessary.

Extras

If special trips or expensive events come up, talk about who will foot the bill. This will avoid the frantic calls home for more money at the last minute to attend a concert or an out-of-town athletic event. It will also encourage your child to think ahead about which extras are important, instead of simply going along with the gang on spur-of-the-moment adventures that may be costly. This may be the first time your child encounters other students who are much wealthier or much more financially limited. Clear up expectations for "extras" ahead of time, as peer pressure will undoubtedly kick in to attend special events.

Dealing with Special Needs

An increasing number of young people come to college with special issues, challenges, and needs. Some students need regular medications, psychological counseling, and/or help in coping with academics due to a learning disability. If your child has special issues such as these, it is useful to discuss how these needs will be met at college. For example, if your child has an eating disorder, it can be especially frightening to "let go" of monitoring her eating behavior. What can you do? Talk to your child about the challenges she will face at college. While it's not appropriate to enlist the aid of a roommate in getting your child to eat properly, it is useful, with your child's consent, to inform the resident adviser that this is an issue for your child. You might also, with your child's knowledge and consent, help arrange an initial consultation with the campus health service counseling group.

If your child needs special help with a learning disability, check with the college to ensure that the necessary support services are available. Encourage your child to take advantage of these services.

Visiting Your Child

It's good to wait at least a couple of months before you visit your child at school. Many schools have an organized parents' weekend in the first semester when you can visit. Whether you're planning to attend parents' weekend or making your own informal visit to campus, always let your child know beforehand to make sure that it's a good time to come. This can be especially tricky if you live close to the college and are tempted to drop in on your child to see how things are going. This is never a good idea! Just as you wouldn't barge into your child's room at home without knocking, you need to respect his or her new space and privacy.

Orientation/Send-off Parties

Many colleges and universities include a component for parents in their orientation program. If so, it's a good way to have many of your questions answered and meet other parents as well. If you can't attend, or the institution doesn't offer a parents' orientation, check out the college's Web site for orientation information. If it's not available on the Web, call the office of the dean of students on campus and ask for orientation materials to be sent to you. Even materials prepared specifically for students will help you become more familiar with life at college.

In some cities, alumni groups or parents associations give send-off parties for new students and their families in the summer before the college year begins. This is a great way to meet other parents of new students. There are also parents' programs at many colleges through which you can receive information and possibly a listing of parents in your area. Sharing this experience with other parents can help, particularly in the first few months of adjustment for you and your child. See Chapter 7 for more information on parents' programming.

The Dreaded Drop-Off

Whether you say good-bye to your new college student at the residence hall or at the airport, you've anticipated this moment and perhaps dreaded it for months. For years, we have witnessed that most poignant of scenes—arrival day for students with their parents in tow. Families wandering around campus looking confused and concerned. New students trying to distance themselves from their parents and younger brothers and sisters. Families standing around feeling useless after the last box has been carted to the room and the roommate has appeared for the obligatory handshake.

Saying Good-bye

Parents who plan for this unceremonious leave-taking can avoid interactions like in the following example.

MOM: So, Josh, do you want me to make up your bed before we leave?

JOSH: No, Mom, I can handle it.

MOM: Well, maybe we should unpack some of these boxes and throw the empty boxes out.

JOSH: It's okay. I can do it later.

DAD: Well, let's go get some lunch.

JOSH: I'm supposed to go to a hall meeting in an hour. I think I'll just stay here and hang with Jim. His parents have left already.

MOM: Oh, okay. Well, where will we meet you later?

JOSH: I'm not really sure. There's a lot to do here and there's a party later on in the quad for new students.

AMY (Josh's little sister): Can we leave now? I'm so bored. There's nothing to do here.

MOM: I told you, Amy, that we were going to stay until tonight and go to some of the parents' activities.

DAD: Let's go get some lunch and then we can go to the new parents meeting. It's at two o'clock and I've got a map so we can find it on our own. We'll see you later, son.

MOM: When?

JOSH: Uh, I don't know, Mom. Maybe we could meet back here at around five before I go to dinner.

MOM: Aren't you going to go out to dinner with us before we leave?

DAD: Maybe we should just say good-bye now and then Josh can get settled.

AMY: Mom, Dad, I'm so bored! Can't we do something?

DAD: Well, Josh, have a great time and study hard. Let us know how you're doing, okay?

MOM (hugging Josh with tears in her eyes): Bye, hon. Are you sure you're going to be okay? Call us if you need anything. We should be home by ten o'clock tonight.

AMY: Bye, Josh. Have fun!

What's on Mom's Mind

I don't want to leave yet. I'm not ready for this!

Josh is acting like he doesn't even care that we're leaving.

I wish we could just spend the day together.

What's on Dad's Mind

I think it's time to clear out.

Josh seems pretty anxious to get rid of us and get to know his roommate.

What's on Josh's Mind

I wish they'd just go. They're driving me crazy!

I want to get unpacked and hang out with my roommate.

I know my mom is going to cry and make me feel stupid.

What's Going On

Everyone's caught in an emotional bind. The parents' expectations for a last, meaningful good bye are not going to be met, and Josh fears the worst—a tearful scene with his mom that will make him look ridiculous. The family needs to make a quick, dignified exit and allow Josh to begin the process of settling in. The first few hours and days of college are critical for a new student to share the "blending in" with the other new students. If he spends the day with his family, he'll miss those crucial first hours of getting to know other students and participating in planned activities. At this point, he's eager to get on with his new life and is totally focused on himself; your feelings will probably make him extremely uncomfortable. It's the rare student who clings to parents, wishing they would stay a bit longer.

What to Do

- Have the meaningful conversation and tearful good-bye *before* you leave home.
- Make a rapid, graceful exit! A quick hug, preferably when no one else is around, and you should be on your way.
- Tour the campus and attend parents' events on your own.
- Do something fun with the rest of your family.

What to Avoid

- A drawn-out leave-taking. It will only make you and your child miserable.
- Don't be tempted to come back for just one more good-bye before you leave town. It's guaranteed to be an unsatisfying experience for all of you.

Returning Home

As the car pulls away from the dorm parking lot, Josh's dad seems happy to get on the road for home:

DAD: What a great day! Josh's roommate seemed like a good guy, huh?

MOM (her eyes moist with tears): Yes, he does. I just wonder if there's room in that tiny closet for all of his stuff.

DAD: I'm sure he'll be fine. Honey, why are you crying? He's only four hours away. Just think of how peaceful it's going to be at home. Ah, just the thought of being first in line for the shower and finding the car in the driveway makes me smile. Seriously, though, aren't you glad he's at such a good school? I was really impressed with the facilities and the people we met seemed really nice. He's going to be just fine, I'm sure. How about you?

MOM: I feel like I've lost my son. I knew this was coming, but I guess I wasn't ready to say good-bye.

DAD: But just think of all the extra time we'll have together now.

MOM: I know, but what if he doesn't like it, or the classes are too difficult, or he doesn't make any friends? He might be really lonely and we won't be there to help him.

DAD: Hey, honey, be realistic. He hasn't needed, or wanted, us around much for quite a while. He's probably going to love the independence. He never had trouble making friends before, so why should he now?

MOM (sniffling): I guess the truth is that I'm the only one who's upset. I mean, he didn't even seem sad to see us leave.

DAD: He wasn't! I'm sure he's already on his way to some orientation party. He's been waiting a long time to get to college and be on his own. I'm sure he'll miss us, but he's got an exciting year ahead.

MOM: I can't believe you're so happy. It's almost like you're glad to be rid of him!

What's on Mom's Mind

Will I ever get used to Josh being gone?

It's going to feel so strange not having him around the house anymore.

Is he going to be okay?

What's on Dad's Mind

It's great to have this whole getting-into-college hassle over.

All I have to worry about now is paying that tuition bill.

I think Josh is going to love it there. What a great place to go to college.

He's a smart kid. I'm really proud of him.

What's Going On

When we surveyed more than ten thousand parents of new college students, the responses to the question, "How did you feel when your son or daughter went off to college?" all came from mothers. Even though fathers miss their children and care deeply about them, the mothers tended to be more openly expressive about their feelings of loss and sadness. Mothers may, over time, find that the so-called "empty nest" syndrome frees them to do some things that child-rearing had put on hold. Fathers can find the "empty den" tougher to deal with. Many fathers have spent a major portion of their child's growing up years trying to establish a career and respond to a growing family's need for increased income. Because of this, the transition to college can bring strong feelings of loss and guilt for fathers as well.

One of this book's coauthors, Helen, still has vivid memories of crying nearly all the way home from dropping off her first son at college. She recalls, "My husband kept stealing sidelong glances at me, genuinely perplexed at the flood of tears. He seemed to accept this transition as natural and logical; I could only feel the sadness and the loss. He thought about the pride he felt due to our son beginning college at a prestigious university and about how much more freedom we'd have. I worried about whether our son would be safe and happy and wondered if this pit-of-the-stomach feeling of emptiness would ever go away. I was grieving, while my husband was rejoicing."

What to Do

- Ask your spouse about his or her hopes, fears, and expectations as you leave your child at college.
- Try to listen, without judgment, to your partner's feelings, even though yours may differ.
- Realize that change, even though it's essentially positive, can leave you with feelings of loss.

What to Avoid

- Accusing your spouse of being unfeeling or too emotional.
- Expecting your partner to react the same way you do.
- Burdening your new college student with your feelings of loss and sadness.

What You Need to Know

As you begin to contemplate life back at home without your child, your feelings may differ from those of your spouse, partner, or other family members. When a child goes to college, the family changes. Some parents feel guilty that it's great to be rid of their kids and look forward to some peace and quiet at home. Some feel devastated and dread going home. You may have all of these feelings at different times, or all at once. Not everyone experiences major changes in the same way—and this kind of change usually includes feelings of loss as well.

Going It Alone

We were surprised by our friend, Susan, when she gave an account of her husband Dan's experience taking their daughter to college. He set off on the trip with enthusiasm, the van loaded to the ceiling with Jennifer's belongings. Later that day, he called home to talk to his wife.

DAN: Hi, hon. How are things at home?
SUSAN: Fine. How did it go? Is Jennifer all set up in her room?
DAN: Yeah, she's fine, but I feel lousy!

SUSAN: What happened?

DAN: I don't know. I just felt like I was a "fifth wheel," cramping her style all day. I really wish you had been here. Jennifer acted like I was an embarrassment and basically ignored me most of the time. Then, after we'd unloaded all of her stuff, she just took off with her roommate for some new students' barbecue and barely said good-bye to me. She acted like she couldn't wait to get rid of me, so I just left, went into town alone, and found a place for dinner.

SUSAN: I'm sorry that you're all alone. Actually, though, I'm not surprised at Jennifer's behavior. She's acted like we were pretty annoying all summer.

DAN: Well, I guess I just expected her to want to spend some time with me. After all, I'm not going to see her again for a while.

SUSAN: I know it would have been easier for you if I had been there. When will you be getting home?

DAN: I guess I'll start out now. Nothing to do here.

What's on Dan's Mind

I can't figure out if I'm mad at Jennifer for being so rude or sad to see her go.

She didn't even say thanks or really say good-bye.

I don't think she realizes how hard we've worked to get her to this point and how much it's costing us.

This seems like such an anticlimax.

What's on Susan's Mind

I wish I could have been there to see Jennifer's new room.

I feel guilty that Dan had to do this alone, even though he knows I couldn't change my work schedule.

I wonder if Dan would have felt this way if I had been there.

What's Going On

Parents who make the trip to college alone with a child often feel awkward and superfluous. If Susan had been along on this trip, she might have absorbed the feelings of rejection that Dan felt and he might have been the one to remind her that Jennifer was just acting like most new college students. Single parents, who have had to fulfill multiple roles in the family, often feel this separation intensely and have to cope with these feelings alone.

What to Do

- Remember that each person experiences change and loss in his or her unique way. No one way is right or wrong.
- Try to respect your spouse's feelings, even if they are unexpected and uncomfortable for you.
- Listen to the feelings without judging them.
- Talk to a friend who has gone through or is going through the same experience.

What to Avoid

- Assigning blame.
- Making "I told you so" remarks.
- Confronting your daughter about how she treated her father.
- Taking on your spouse's reaction and getting in between your daughter and him.

What You Need to Know

Whether you are a single parent, a divorced parent, or part of a blended or traditional family, you will surely feel the loss of one of your family members. If this is your last child to go to college, you may miss the presence of children in your life.

When parents leave their child at college, they are concerned about safety, adjustment, and what the college culture may do to change their child. Parents who themselves experienced college in a different era may long for the good old days of *in loco parentis* when the college and its staff acted as surrogate parents, setting rules and enforcing them instead of treating students as quasi-adults and providing free condoms. Today's college campuses reflect the problems of the larger culture—including excessive drinking, drugs, sexually transmitted diseases, and crime. College is no longer a cloistered youth ghetto, safely isolated from the larger world. To parents of new college students, there seem to be so many things to worry about, so many things that could go wrong for their child.

It's important to remember, however, that you've laid the groundwork for this change through years of instilling values in your child. Our experience (supported by research on adolescent development) shows that most students finish their college years with most of their family's core values intact. This doesn't mean that they won't try out other values and ideas during the college years—they will. But you can rest assured that the foundation you've provided will remain strong, although you may have to struggle through some disconcerting experimentation with new "looks," taste in music, religious questioning, and lifestyle adventures.

As the columnist Ellen Goodman wrote, going to college is for families "a part of the great American balancing act between independence and connection. And at the end of this long process, if it goes well, parents and children are adults, connected by choice as well as history."[1] In Chapter 6, we will explore, in greater depth, the changes in the family when a child goes to college.

Chapter 4

Roommates, Fraternity Parties, All-nighters, Changing Majors, and Hanging Out

Adjustment During the First Year

I was so naïve when my daughter went off to college. Of course, I had read everything in the newspapers about teenage drinking, sex, and drug use, but I still didn't think college could be so different today from when I was an undergraduate. After all, my generation had started the sexual revolution—sex, drugs, rock and roll, and all that. Wow, was I surprised! When I was in college, if girls had sex at all, it was only with their boyfriends. We had the pill and we didn't have to worry about AIDS. Now it seems that everyone's "hooking up." I'm not sure exactly what that means. In some ways, kids today are much more knowledgeable and sophisticated than I was, but they're faced with decisions that I never had to consider. And the risks seem so much higher.

An exciting, if somewhat disconcerting, process has begun. You wonder how your child will handle the increased academic and social pressures of college. You worry about safety, underage drinking, living habits, roommate problems, and whether he or she is happy. You'd like to know what's going on, even as you realize that your parental role is beginning to change. This chapter will help you understand what to expect during your child's first year of college.

Adjustment Issues

As students begin college, they will be adjusting to taking care of themselves, making new friends, finding a place in the social scene, and handling increased academic expectations.

The following scenarios will help you to anticipate the adjustment challenges that face your child.

Staying in Touch

In the first few days after Megan left for college, your home felt empty and you found yourself lingering at her bedroom door, marveling at its neatness. You've actually missed the mess and chaos that Megan created. Although you've left messages on her cell phone and texted her repeatedly, she's only responded with a quick text of "I'm fine. Catch you later, Mom." You're tired of leaving cheery messages with no real reply. You're a little worried and a little irked.

Finally, on Monday night at 11:30 P.M., your phone rings.

MOM: Hello?

MEGAN: Hi, Mom.

MOM: Oh, Megan, it's you! I'm so glad you called. I've been worried about you and how you're doing.

MEGAN: Oh, yeah, I'm sorry. It's just been so busy here. I've been to lots of cool parties and usually don't have time to call 'til it's too late.

MOM: How late are you staying out?

MEGAN: Oh, I don't know. Late. Anyway, I've met the neatest people from all over and it's really fun. Look, I gotta run. I promised the kids down the hall that I'd come over for pizza later and I have to take a shower.

MOM: But, Megan, I want to know how you're doing. Did you get your classes all scheduled? Did you see your adviser? Did you eat breakfast?

MEGAN: Mom, I'm all set. Everything's cool. Look, I'll call you later, okay? Give my love to Dad and Joey. Bye.

MOM (to herself): Well, at least I know she's alive.

What's on Your Mind

I miss her.
How is she doing?
Is she making friends?
Why is she staying out so late on a school night?

What's on Your Child's Mind

There are so many great people here.
I'm glad I have a good roommate.
I've never been to so many cool parties.
I wonder if that cute guy I met last night will be in any of my classes.

What's Going On

You're looking for a connection and reassurance; your child is so involved in this new life that you are irrelevant (for now!). You need information at this point, and your college student needs to deal with the overwhelming "newness." It's hard to believe that less than a week ago, this same child was sitting at the kitchen table asking your advice about what to pack for college.

What to Do

- Keep in mind that your child is getting used to a totally new place—it's appropriate that social adjustment is consuming a great deal of her time.
- Try to put aside your need for information for the time being and realize that your child is going to be self-absorbed during this period.
- Be open with your child about your need to be in touch. Simply say, "I need to hear from you because I care about you and what's happening."
- Stay in touch—send notes with news from home.

What to Avoid

- Grilling your child for detailed information, such as "Have you seen your adviser?" or "How is your class schedule?"
- Making your child feel guilty: "Why don't you answer my phone calls?"
- Making demands for attention and reassurance; your child can't be expected to meet your needs.

A couple of days later, Mom catches Megan on her way to class.

MOM: Hi, Megan. I'm so glad I caught you. How is everything going?
MEGAN: Great! I love my classes and my roommate is really fun. Did I tell you she's an art

major? She's been all over the world with her parents and she's got the best clothes. Oh, that reminds me, can you send my winter coat? It's really cold here already.

MOM: Sure, I'll get it off in the mail tomorrow. So, tell me about your classes.

MEGAN: Well, my German professor is young and really tough. I mean, he makes us do homework every night, which isn't so easy with my other classes. I'm already so far behind. It sure is different from high school. There's so much time during the day when I don't have class but I don't get any studying done. So I stay up late every night and then have to drag myself out of bed. I never make it to breakfast. I just don't have time.

MOM: Well, maybe you could try to study a bit during the day and then you could get to bed at a decent hour.

MEGAN: Even if I did study during the day, there's no way I can go to bed early. Everyone's up 'til two or three in the morning. After dinner, everyone just hangs out and talks and then we start studying around eleven o'clock when things quiet down on the floor.

MOM: That sounds a little crazy.

MEGAN: No, everything's cool, Mom. So, what's happening there?

MOM: Not much, just the usual. Joey made the JV soccer team.

MEGAN: That's great. How's Dad?

MOM: He's fine; he sends his love.

MEGAN: Well, I have to run. My English essay is due tomorrow and I haven't even started it yet.

MOM: Well, good luck with the essay.

MEGAN: Thanks! Bye.

What's on Your Mind

I miss the long talks we used to have; now she always seems to be in a rush.
I'm a little worried about the late hours and lack of sleep.
Is she taking care of herself—sleeping enough and eating properly?

What's on Your Child's Mind

College is awesome! I already have so many new friends.
I hope I can do the work—it's going to be a lot harder than high school.
I'm so busy, I wonder if I'll ever get a full night's sleep again.

What's Going On

Although this conversation gives the parent a little more information, the child is still "high" on the new experiences, talking a mile a minute and not really eager to spend lots of time on the phone with Mom.

What to Do

- Try to listen, without judgment.
- Avoid leaving multiple, increasingly desperate messages on her cell phone or texting her several times a day.
- Remember that your child's behavior is normal.
- Write letters—you may not get any in return, but your child will love getting news from home, and it may help you to write to her when you miss her.

What to Avoid

- Giving orders: "You need to get yourself on a schedule or you're going to be overwhelmed by all the work."
- Setting unreasonable expectations: "Make sure you get eight hours of sleep and eat breakfast."

What You Need to Know

Students are typically nocturnal creatures and always seem to be on the move. It's hard for parents, who usually keep a pretty predictable schedule, to imagine the frenetic activity that usually characterizes the first few weeks of college. Caller ID has made it possible for students to screen calls from parents; moreover, texting makes it possible to shoot a quick message to Mom or Dad without having to take the time to talk. Although texting is not necessarily a satisfying way to communicate, it can be a way to check in and reassure yourself that your child is still there and okay. With the constant possibility of connection (albeit often superficial), many parents expect to be in touch all of the time, which is not only unreasonable, but can also actually interfere with your child's efforts to make new connections and feel comfortable on campus.

Academic Adjustment

Given Megan's carefree attitude recently, her dad is surprised to get the following phone call from her a few nights later.

DAD: Hello?

MEGAN: Hi, Dad.

DAD: Megan, is that you?

MEGAN: Of course, it's me. Who did you think it was?

DAD: I don't know. It's late. Are you okay?

MEGAN: Well, not really. I got my English essay back today and I got a C. I couldn't believe it. I worked so hard on it and she gave me a C. I haven't had a C since seventh grade! Everyone in the class got horrible grades. I think she's just trying to prove that she's some tough professor or something.

DAD: Well, have you talked to her about your grade? Maybe she could help you learn about what she wants in an essay.

MEGAN: Dad, there's no way I'm talking to her. She's so intimidating, you wouldn't believe it.

DAD: But that's her job to teach English and to help you learn how to write, isn't it?

MEGAN: Dad, you just don't understand. Look, I gotta go. I have this test in bio tomorrow and I've barely started to study for it. Did Mom send my coat?

DAD: I think she sent it a couple of days ago.

MEGAN: Good. I hope it gets here tomorrow 'cause it's really freezing here.

DAD: Well, honey, get some sleep and you'll feel better. Okay?

MEGAN: Okay, Dad. Bye.

What's on Your Mind

I'm worried that she's in over her head.
Can she cope?
Should I do something to help?

What's on Your Child's Mind

I'm overwhelmed—this college stuff is harder than I thought it would be.
Maybe everyone else is smarter than me.
What if I fail?

What's Going On

Within a few weeks of classes, students can become somewhat overwhelmed and wonder if they can meet the challenges of college work. This is alarming for them. You may receive disturbing calls and worry about your child's ability to cope. What you may not realize is that these calls are an early alert that college kids send out when they feel a bit defeated by the workload and have yet to settle into a reasonable study schedule. For many college students, their first C comes in their first semester at college and it shakes their confidence in their abilities. What do they do? Call home, of course. Your child sees home as a haven in a scary new world, although he or she will rarely want advice on how to manage studies more efficiently. Students really want reassurance that they are loved, regardless of how well they do in college.

What to Do

- Reassure your child that you have confidence in her: "This must be really upsetting for you, but I know you've tackled tough situations before and managed to figure out what you needed to do."
- Ask "leading" questions that help her come up with a solution: "Have you thought about what you could do to learn to write an essay that is closer to what your professor is looking for?"
- Ask if a follow-up call would be helpful in a day or so.
- Remind yourself that this is transitory, a natural part of the adjustment process.
- Have faith in your child's ability to cope.
- Call a friend with a college-aged child and commiserate. It can help to talk to someone who is going through the same experience.

What to Avoid

- Solving the problem for your child.
- Getting into an argument about the professor's attitude or competence.
- Offering advice before you have finished listening to the emotional issues.
- Becoming alarmed by a relatively insignificant issue.

Academic Adjustment: The Replay

Let's see how Dad could have helped Megan through this crisis of confidence in her academic ability. Remember, it's your job to be a consultant, not a supervisor.

DAD: Hello?

MEGAN: Hi, Dad. It's me.

DAD: Hi, Megan. How are you doing?

MEGAN: I had a horrible day. I got a C on my English essay.

DAD: I'm sorry. You sound really upset. I can't remember you ever getting a C before. What happened? Tell me about it.

MEGAN: Well, everyone in the class got terrible grades. We were all just freaked out. I think the professor really stinks. How could she give everyone horrible grades like that? There were only like two As in the whole class.

DAD: That must have been pretty upsetting to get a grade like that. You're so used to being a top student.

MEGAN: I don't know. Maybe I'm not smart enough to be here. What if I flunk?

DAD: You sound pretty worried.

MEGAN: I'm behind all the time and everyone else is so smart.

DAD: So, you're feeling pretty overwhelmed.

MEGAN: Yeah, it's just so hard. I can't believe it. There isn't any time to do all the stuff they want us to do. I wish I hadn't come here to begin with. Or, I wish I had been a fine arts major like my roommate. All she does is go to the studio and hang out with her art friends and paint things.

DAD: She has it pretty easy, huh?

MEGAN: I don't know. It just seems too hard, Dad. What do you think I should do?

DAD: Well, that's really up to you, honey. We have a lot of confidence in you and know that you can do the work.

MEGAN: Why? I'm already failing. I just can't keep up.

DAD: Is there someone there you could talk to? Like an adviser or someone?

MEGAN: No, there isn't anyone like that. Look, Dad, I gotta go and get something done on my project for tomorrow.

DAD: Okay, but maybe we could talk tomorrow and see how you're doing then?

MEGAN: Okay. Bye.

What You Need to Know

Chances are that minutes after Megan hung up the phone she felt better. She unloaded her frustrations on you and you reassured her that she was smart and capable. You, however, don't feel so great. If you could have a hidden camera in her residence hall, you'd know that she was fine. A little shaken, but fine. She touched base with you, gave you the reality check that she might not come home with all As her first semester in college, and was reassured that you understood her anxiety and believed in her abilities.

This is a very common occurrence between new college students and their parents. We call it the "stress dump." Students typically call home when they are distressed and dump their anxieties on their parents. It's a good bet that if you had called her the next day to find out how she was, you would be greeted with a cheery response: "Hey, everything's okay." You may have lost a night's sleep, but Megan now feels fine. Her anxieties of last night are ancient history and she may be a little embarrassed that she blew her cool with you on the phone.

Roommates and Residence Hall Living

You find out when your daughter comes home for break that her roommate borrowed one of her favorite sweaters and lost it at a party. The roommate has also borrowed money from your daughter and didn't pay her back when she promised to last week.

What's on Your Mind

> My daughter's roommate is taking advantage of her.
> Why can't she learn to not lend her things to others?
> What is this going to cost?

What's on Your Child's Mind

> I'm really bummed that she lost my favorite sweater.
> Should I confront my roommate, and if I do, will she hate me?

What's Going On

Residence halls are living and learning laboratories in which students learn to get along with people who are different from them and to negotiate touchy situations. Many college students have never had to share a room or possessions. It's important that they learn to be both assertive and respectful of other people's space and things. At the same time, it's really important to them to be liked and not appear selfish or immature.

What to Do

- Remember that this *is* a big adjustment for your daughter.
- Ask your child if she feels comfortable negotiating solutions; if not, suggest getting the residence hall director or adviser involved.
- Be firm in reinforcing that she needs to deal with these issues.

What to Avoid

- Replacing her sweater or sending her extra spending money.
- Blaming the roommate: "I told you I thought she would be trouble. Don't lend her money or let her wear your stuff anymore."
- Calling a college staff member yourself to complain.

What You Need to Know

Residence hall staff members are there to offer support in situations like this. They will not solve the problem for your daughter, but they will help her find the solution. She may want to meet with a staff member before confronting her roommate and get some advice on how to handle the problems. In the end, however, it's up to her to take the initiative.

About two months into the first semester, your son, Andy, calls to unload his roommate frustrations.

ANDY: Hi, Mom. What's happening?
MOM: Oh, not much. How are you?
ANDY: Okay.
MOM: Just okay? You sound a little down. What's going on?
ANDY: My roommate is being a pain in the butt.
MOM: What do you mean?
ANDY: Well, for starters, he has these really disgusting lizards that he loves and he keeps them in a couple of cages under his bed.

MOM: Isn't that against the rules? I thought pets weren't allowed.

ANDY: Yeah, well, he's not the only one who has some kind of animal, but the thing that really bugs me is that his girlfriend is here all the time. They just found out they both have mono and so now they just lie around all day, and it's driving me crazy. I think she's really rude and I can't even walk around in my underwear because she's always here. I spend most of my time down the hall in Ben's room, but they are really becoming annoying.

MOM: That's terrible! Can't you get the dorm director to do something about this?

ANDY: Nah, I don't want to go tattle on them. I just wish he'd get rid of her at least. The animals aren't so bad, but I feel like I don't have a room anymore. Oh, well, maybe they'll decide they don't like each other after all and she'll go back to living in her own room.

MOM: Andy, I think you should do something about this. Do you want me to call the director?

ANDY: No, it'll be all right. Look, I gotta get to work. I have a paper due Friday and I haven't started it yet. So, I'll see you soon. I'll be home for Thanksgiving in a couple of weeks. I can't wait to get home and do nothing but eat and sleep. Talk to you later.

What's on Your Mind

I'm really upset. I'm paying for a room for my son, and his roommate has taken it over with his pets and his girlfriend.

Andy will probably get sick, too.

Aren't there rules in these residence halls and shouldn't the director be enforcing them?

What's on Your Child's Mind

I can handle this, but it's a real drag.

I don't have any privacy—my roommate's a jerk.

If I complain to the RA, I'll look stupid.

I wish this would just go away.

What's Going On

One of the most common complaints in residence halls is the roommate who brings home a boyfriend or girlfriend on a regular basis. It's totally reasonable for your son to insist that the roommate move his girlfriend out of their room, but he needs to do that himself or with the help of the director who can assist through mediation.

For most students, having a roommate is a new and challenging experience. Many college students have never had to share a bedroom with a brother or sister, let alone a virtual stranger.

Dad and Mom may have mediated bedroom-sharing struggles at home; hence, many students are ill-prepared to negotiate a reasonable living situation at school.

What to Do

- Listen and empathize with this unfortunate situation.
- Remind him that he's entitled to half a room with one other person and that he could request a room change.
- Instead of sharing your alarm and anger, ask your son, "What do you want to do about this?"
- Suggest that he ask his resident adviser for help with this situation.

What to Avoid

- Calling the residence hall director, and demanding that the problem be fixed. This action should be reserved for times when you feel there is a real safety or health threat to your child.
- Imposing your cleanliness or basic living standards on the situation. This is your son's home; you can't dictate living standards for him or his roommate. They need to work it out.
- Renting an apartment, so your son can have a single his freshman year and avoid the hassle of dealing with a roommate.

What You Need to Know

There is no doubt that roommate conflicts have escalated in the past few years. Housing officials interviewed in a recent *New York Times* article reported that room change requests stemming from roommate problems have increased dramatically—in some cases ten-fold—in the past five years.[1] They speculate, in part, that reliance on technology to communicate makes it easier for students to avoid uncomfortable encounters. For example, instead of confronting a roommate problem, a student may post criticisms on Facebook or text the roommate with cryptic remarks on his or her behavior.

Moreover, these officials noted an alarming increase in parents getting involved in roommate conflicts. Students who have relied on parents to mediate disputes often lack the ability to negotiate face-to-face; they expect residence hall staff members (or parents) to solve problems for them. While residence hall staff members *are* there to help with these situations, it's also important for students to take an active role in resolving conflicts. As we said before, residence halls are living and learning laboratories in which your student can learn valuable life skills. Parents need to step back and allow their sons and daughters to manage and resolve these situations. While it's usually feasible for your child to request a room change, especially if a roommate conflict is not able to be resolved, it's also critical that he or she learns to confront problems and deal with them. These skills will be invaluable as your child goes through college and eventually enters the workforce.

Stress and Pressure

You are really looking forward to having your daughter come home for Thanksgiving break. She arrives laden with books and announces that she has two midterms next week and a paper to write while she is home. She looks exhausted, but immediately gets on the phone, calls her old high school friends, and makes plans to go out later. You next see her when she drags herself out of bed the following day at noon and begins complaining about how tired she is and how much work she has to do. Later that afternoon, she makes plans to go out with her friends again. By Sunday, when it's time to return to college, she hasn't cracked a book or spent much time with the family, but she's still obsessing about her work and how far behind she is.

What's on Your Mind

> If she had buckled down and done some work, she wouldn't be in this position.
> What if she's really in over her head with schoolwork?
> She didn't even seem that happy to see us or to be at home.

What's on Your Child's Mind

> Panic: I'll never get all of this work done.
> I should have spent the whole holiday working.
> Why are my parents on my case when I'm so stressed out?

What's Going On

Thanksgiving break is often a crisis point in the first semester at college. Early feedback on schoolwork may not look good and papers and exams are looming ahead. Your daughter is exhausted from the personal adjustments she's making to college life, but when she's home, she wants to forget college pressures and see old friends and have fun. She also wants to let you know just how hard this is.

What to Do

- Try to be sympathetic. Let her know that you understand how difficult the adjustment to college can be.
- Remember this is your child's problem, not yours.
- Reinforce that you have faith in her ability to complete her work.
- Relate stories from your own life—perhaps a tough challenge and how you handled your fear about accomplishing it.
- Ask, "Have you thought at all about what you might do to cope with all of this work hanging over you? Is there a way for you to get some help with managing your workload?"
- Make it clear to her what level of involvement you expect from her in the family's holiday plans. For example, "We are all having Thanksgiving dinner together and I expect you to be a part of our celebration from three until about seven o'clock."

What to Avoid

- Taking on her problem and trying to fix it.
- Telling your child what to do, such as "If you'd stay home and study for your exams or work on your paper instead of going out every night, you wouldn't be in this jam."
- Reorganizing your holiday weekend around your child's erratic schedule or nagging her about being involved with the family. This will only make you feel exasperated and resentful, and probably won't get your daughter to change her behavior.

What You Need to Know

Your child may need to come home and recover from the stress and pressure she is under at school. She's still learning to manage her schedule and handle the much more challenging academic work at college. Just the volume of reading alone can be a big shock to new students. There are resources on campus to help students who are willing to take advantage of them. Most colleges and universities have learning-skills centers, time-management workshops, peer tutoring programs, and other support services to help new students adjust to college-level work. The first semester at college demands personal and academic adjustments that test students' confidence and force them to accept the consequences of their actions (or inaction!). This is not a lesson you can teach her; she has to learn it herself by trial and error.

Making the Transition from High School and Home

When you visited your daughter at school for a football weekend, you were surprised that she complained about her lack of social life at school. She talked about how much she missed her high school friends. Although she was a bit shy in middle school, she had several close friends by the time she graduated from high school. She doesn't know anyone other than her roommate at college and feels pretty lonely.

What's on Your Mind

> I'm worried that she spends so much time alone.
> I wonder if she's too shy to get out and meet people.
> There must be social activities at college that would appeal to her.

What's on Your Child's Mind

> I miss my high school friends so much.
> No one here seems like me.
> I don't feel comfortable going to fraternity parties.
> I wonder if I'll ever fit in.

What's Going On

Social adjustment the first few months of college can be hard, especially if your child is a bit shy. It's difficult for some students to leave behind close high school friends and start all over. For many new college students, the social group consists of roommates and others living in their residence hall. It's challenging to find new friends while students are trying to adjust to so many changes, especially when they feel homesick for old friends.

What to Do

- Listen to your daughter's feelings and let her know you sympathize with her loneliness.
- Show that you understand how difficult it is for her to make new friends.
- Remind her of how she survived the middle school years, while empathizing with how hard that was for her.

- Suggest that she look into joining a club or activity so that she can meet other students with similar interests.

What to Avoid

- Suggesting that she have her old high school friends visit her at college.
- Letting her know you're really worried about her.
- Trying to fix it for her by suggesting she come home for weekends more often.

What You Need to Know

Even the most socially skilled students go through adjustments when they arrive at college and have to make new friends. Many students who appear well adjusted socially actually have a hard time fitting in to the college social scene. Although social adjustment is one of the biggest challenges for new students, most find a niche for themselves eventually. On campuses where fraternities and sororities dominate social life, it can be more difficult for students who aren't sorority or fraternity types to find a social group. There are many ways to fit in at college, but students have to be assertive in seeking out alternatives, such as joining clubs, getting involved in volunteer work, signing up for an intramural team, or working on the school newspaper.

It's common for students to feel as if everyone else is happy and well adjusted socially, while they feel awkward and out of place. This usually changes within a few weeks or months. Going through this part of the adjustment process is hard, but it's important to let this evolve naturally. There are few students indeed who haven't made some good friends by the end of the first year of college.

Finding a Social Niche

Ever since you last talked with your son on the phone, you've been worried about his social life at college. He doesn't seem to be making friends. He spends most of his time studying, sleeping, and talking on the phone to his girlfriend at home, who is a senior in high school.

What's on Your Mind

I wonder if he'll ever make friends at college.
I think he's hanging on to her because he's afraid to try to make new friends.

What's on Your Child's Mind

> I'm glad I have a girlfriend or I'd really feel out of it.
> Why should I go out when I'm not interested in meeting girls?

What's Going On

It's hard for some students to leave high school behind when they go to college. The social scene can be intimidating at first, and if your child doesn't get involved in social life in the beginning, it gets harder to break in later in the semester. The process of acclimating to college and letting go of high school often begins for the student by his joining an organization, or having one good friend getting him involved in a club or activity.

What to Do

- Try to be patient and understanding of your child's need to cling to a high school sweetheart.
- Suggest that he join a club or organization that is not completely social in nature.

What to Avoid

- Trying to split up the relationship. It almost always backfires.
- Telling him he can't come home so much to see his girlfriend.

What You Need to Know

It's not unusual for your son to hold on to the security of this relationship. If you are patient with his need to hang on to his high school girlfriend, he'll probably grow out of that relationship in time. Many high school relationships don't last beyond the first semester when one person goes off to college. As long as you see some evidence that your son is slowly beginning to get more involved in college life, you don't need to worry.

The Freshman 15—Weight Issues

When your daughter was home for winter break, you noticed how much weight she had gained during her first semester in college. You've always struggled with weight and you're worried that she's getting fat.

What's on Your Mind

> She was so trim and attractive when she went off to college.
> Her clothes look terrible on her.
> If she keeps gaining weight at this rate, she'll be a blimp.

What's on Your Child's Mind

> I can tell my mother thinks I'm fat.
> What's the big deal? Everyone gains weight freshman year.

What's Going On

Gaining the "Freshman 15" is a common experience for new college students. This may be the first time they have control (or lack of it!) over what they eat and it may take some time for them to settle into a sensible and healthy eating routine. Most colleges offer cafeteria-style dining and some even offer continuous dining around the clock. Students can eat whatever and whenever they want and their days often end with pizza shared with dorm mates.

What to Do

- Listen to your daughter's anxiety about her weight, without preaching.
- Reinforce that her weight and body type do not define her as a person.
- Discuss the cultural pressures related to body image and let her know that your love for her is not based on her looks or her weight.
- Ask if she would like to talk about how to eat sensibly, and suggest that getting some exercise might help her maintain a weight that is reasonable for her.

What to Avoid

- Making this a big deal and trying to shame her into dieting.
- Leaping to the conclusion that she's on the road to obesity.
- Overreacting, thereby emphasizing weight issues over other developmental concerns, such as learning healthy eating habits.
- Imposing your attitudes about weight and body image.

What You Need to Know

The Freshman 15 is a common phenomenon for new students. In trying to adjust to so many lifestyle changes away from home and parental supervision, many students gain weight; it may take a couple of semesters for them to settle into a normal eating routine. Some students get carried away with the freedom of being able to eat whatever and whenever they want and some find food a comfort in a new and stressful environment.

Parents need to be very careful about overreacting to this situation. You don't want your child to begin to obsess about weight and body image. Try to keep your perspective on this and avoid making it a big issue. Although you can no longer control what and when your child eats, you can influence how she views this weight gain and offer helpful advice on maintaining a healthy lifestyle. If you are worried about your child's eating habits and suspect that she may have an eating disorder, you may want to follow the advice we offer in Chapter 10.

Greek Life

When your daughter returned home for fall break, she had just been through rush—a drive by a fraternity or sorority to recruit new members—and did not receive a bid from a sorority. Her two best friends were pledged and she is devastated.

What's on Your Mind

I feel so sorry for her. She's so unhappy.
What can I do to make her feel better?

What's on Your Child's Mind

> Why didn't they like me?
> I'm so embarrassed and hurt.
> I'm going to miss out on all of the fun.

What's Going On

The Greek system, like many other selective systems, is inherently unfair. Choices made on appearances and personality traits are often subjective, confusing, and hurtful. It's a lesson in life that you don't want your child to have to learn.

What to Do

- Listen to your daughter's feelings.
- Sympathize with her pain and tell her you're sorry she's so sad.
- Keep in touch with her, write her notes, and gently reinforce that she's an attractive and likable person.

What to Avoid

- Trying to make her feel better by telling her you think sororities are silly or not important.
- Getting involved by calling the dean of Greek life.

What You Need to Know

Campus culture determines the role that sororities and fraternities play in student social life and how much interaction there is between students who are in or out of the Greek system. On some campuses, fraternities and sororities provide most of the social life; on others, Greek life is one of several social systems. Even if students don't join a sorority or fraternity, chances are that they will be able to attend Greek parties, especially if they have good friends in a house. If your daughter still wants to be a member of a sorority, there are often opportunities to join early in the sophomore year.

But what if your child wants to embrace Greek life? For example, your son calls to tell you he's decided to pledge a fraternity. You've always been anti-Greek and you're not sure you approve.

What's on Your Mind

Will my son be safe?
I've heard so many frightening stories about fraternity hazing.

What's on Your Child's Mind

Initiation was so awesome, everybody was completely out of control.
I'm in the best house here.

What's Going On

It's reasonable to be concerned about fraternity initiation activities and fraternity life. Drinking is often involved in fraternity activities, and it can get out of control. You're worried, but your son seems so happy to be included and to be a part of this select group.

What to Do

- Congratulate your son on getting into a fraternity.
- Ask your son what he likes best about the fraternity.
- Try to remember how important it was to be liked and included when you were eighteen years old.
- If you're concerned, ask your son about his fraternity brothers' attitudes on hazing and express your concerns.
- Have a frank talk about money and who will pay for fraternity fees.
- Plan to visit the house when you're on campus and meet some of his fraternity brothers.

What to Avoid

- Generalizing about fraternities and their "animal house" reputation. Your son's house may be very different.
- Recounting all the horror stories you've heard.
- Forbidding him to join.

What You Need to Know

All fraternities and sororities have strong policies prohibiting hazing and most colleges have strict rules governing Greek life on campus. Still, fraternity life can be pretty crazy and out of control. Excessive drinking is a problem, and too often fraternity parties are the sites of accidents, injuries, and illegal, underage drinking. (We deal with this issue in more detail in the upcoming section: The Big Three: Drinking, Drugs, and Sex.) Greek life can also be a very positive experience, giving students a group of close friends, a feeling of belonging, and an opportunity to learn about leadership. Most fraternities also have a charter that mandates public service and charitable work in the community.

Time Management and Working on Campus

You thought things were going along well with your daughter, Ming, until you phoned her last night.

> MING: Hi, Mom. How're you doing?
>
> MOM: Things are fine here. How are you?
>
> MING: I'm freaked out—I have so much to do and no time. I think I'm failing two of my courses.
>
> MOM: Oh, honey, that's upsetting. What's the problem?
>
> MING: I *told* you, I have no time to do any work. I get up, go to class, go to my job for three hours, go to classes all afternoon, eat dinner, and then try to study. But I'm always tired and I have an eight o'clock class in the morning. I'm so behind, I don't know if I'll ever catch up.
>
> MOM: Are you working at your job three hours every day? That seems like a lot.
>
> MING: I have to. I need the money. I really should work more hours, but I can't because of my class schedule.
>
> MOM: I thought your financial aid package included only ten hours of work a week.
>
> MING: Well, at financial aid they don't seem to know how much it costs to live here. I have extra lab fees this semester, and the books cost more than I thought they would.
>
> MOM: I wish I could send you some more money, but we're just not able to right now.
>
> MING: I know, Mom; it's okay. I just didn't think it would be so hard to keep up with everything.

MOM: You know the important thing is that you get your schoolwork done. Do you really think you're going to flunk those courses?

MING: I don't know, but my midterms were horrible. Look, I gotta study; I have tons to get done tonight. I'll talk to you later, okay?

MOM: Okay, Ming. Take care.

What's on Your Mind

I'm afraid she can't handle work and school.
I'm feeling badly that I don't have more money to help out. Should we get another loan?
She'll lose all she's worked for if she flunks out.

What's on Your Child's Mind

I'm just overwhelmed with the workload.
I don't know what I'm supposed to do. There are only so many hours in the day.
My parents have to help me or I have to work these hours at my job.

What's Going On

Your daughter may be at a critical time in the semester when midterms, finals, and papers loom on the horizon. It also may be that she *is* working too many hours and needs to cut back until she can get her studies under control. Or, she may be in a tight spot financially because she has made some unwise spending decisions.

What to Do

- Listen to her feelings of panic.
- Ask questions, such as "Could you work fewer hours just this week?"; "Can you think of any ways to solve this dilemma?"; "Could you cut back your hours for now and see how you manage for a couple of weeks during exams?"; "Can you talk to your supervisor about flexible hours for the rest of the semester?"
- Tell her how much you respect her for working and going to school at the same time; recognize that this is admirable, but also difficult to manage.

What to Avoid

- Telling her she has to quit her job or cut her hours dramatically.
- Lecturing that she has to get organized or she will flunk out and lose everything she's worked for.
- Jumping to the conclusion that she will *never* be able to work on campus and contribute to her education.

What You Need to Know

Most colleges and universities have guidelines that govern how much a student should work, particularly during the first year. The recommended commitment is usually ten to twelve hours per week. Most students have trouble managing any more than that.

Students often find the balance of work, social life, and academics difficult at first. Many students, however, actually enjoy their jobs on campus and find that work offers a welcome change from classes and studying. In fact, students can benefit from developing a relationship with an adult supervisor who is supportive and able to offer advice and nurturing. Most supervisors of college student employees recognize that studies come first and are willing to negotiate flexible hours throughout the semester.

Time management often is at the root of problems balancing work and study. Most campuses have programs to help students learn to manage competing demands. Some students thrive when they are busy; others need more downtime in order to cope with the pressures of college. Staff members in the financial aid office can review a student's package to make sure that the work commitment is not too heavy and that the student has sufficient time for academic work.

Sports/Athletics

Playing soccer has been a significant part of the life of your daughter, Erica, since third grade when she started playing in the community soccer program. She was a letter winner in high school and was actively recruited to play soccer in college. But a phone call from Erica has left you concerned.

DAD: Hello?
ERICA: Hi, Dad. How are things?
DAD: Just fine, sweetheart. How about you?

ERICA: I'm exhausted! I can't believe how tired I am all the time.

DAD: What's going on? Are you partying every night?

ERICA: No, Dad. It's just that there's no time for sleep. I have so much schoolwork and soccer practice takes three hours every day. It's so much more of a commitment than in high school, and I don't even know if I'll get to play. There are so many great players here.

DAD: Well, you probably won't get to play a lot your first year. It's understandable that the upperclasswomen have more experience and will play more often.

ERICA: But what if I can't keep up with both my classes and soccer? Pretty soon we have to start traveling to games, and that takes up even more time.

DAD: I know it's a big change, but you seemed to be able to do sports, schoolwork, and lots of other activities in high school. Maybe you're not making the best use of your time. You really have to be disciplined to play a college sport.

ERICA: Dad, it doesn't matter how disciplined I am. There are still only twenty-four hours in a day, and college is much harder than high school. I just can't believe how far behind I am already in my classes.

DAD: Well, maybe you should talk to your coach.

ERICA: That won't help. She just tells us we have to set goals and work hard. I know that!

DAD: Do you think you should quit soccer?

ERICA: But, Dad, I love playing! If only practices weren't so long every day. I get back to the dorm after practice and it's all I can do to stay awake after dinner and study.

DAD: I know it must be hard. Maybe I could talk to the coach.

ERICA: No! Promise me you won't call the coach. I can handle this myself.

DAD: Well, I just worry about you handling everything your first semester.

ERICA: I just can't wait to come home at Thanksgiving and sleep! Well, I'd better go. I have an essay to write for Spanish tomorrow that I haven't even started yet.

DAD: I hope you get it done and get some sleep, honey. Take care.

ERICA: Okay, Dad. Bye.

What's on Your Mind

Maybe she shouldn't have tried to play soccer her first year.
I worry about her handling the pressure of sports and academics.
She's not in class that much. I wonder what she does with her time.

What's on Your Child's Mind

I am really stressed out.

The coach is so unreasonable with her demands. This is nothing like playing sports in high school.

I wonder if I even want to play soccer anymore, not that I'm getting to play anyway.

I like the other girls on the team, but they are all so much better than me.

What's Going On

You are pleased that she's done so well in sports in the past but are concerned about the time commitment that college athletics require. You know it's a lot for her to handle her first year in school and you certainly don't want her to flunk out because she's playing soccer. You worry that she will get overwhelmed and give up on everything. Erica is trying to balance her social life, late hours, long team practices, and a heavy academic workload.

What to Do

- Listen to your child's fears and anxieties.
- Sympathize with her struggles, and show that you understand how hard she is working to try to stay on top of things.
- Reinforce that you have confidence in her and will love her no matter what she decides to do about playing soccer.
- Remind her of another time when she was stressed out and ask her how she handled that situation.

What to Avoid

- Lecturing her on time management.
- Telling her you think she should quit the team and concentrate on her schoolwork.
- Offering to call the coach and plead her case.

What You Need to Know

Adjusting to playing sports at the college level is a tough challenge for most new students. College teams do require a serious commitment of time and energy, and not every student will choose to continue playing because of that. It's also disheartening for a star player in high school to face the fact that she may not get to play much for the first couple of years on a college team. The competition is usually intense for the starting positions and it's discouraging to be on the bench most of the time.

It's also true that sports can be a positive and rewarding part of college life. The team provides a ready-made group of friends, easing the social adjustment for students. Coaches are usually very interested and involved in their players' development, both on and off the playing field, providing the support and encouragement that many new students need. Moreover, the commitment to a practice schedule can help students manage their time more effectively.

Many students receive the same benefits of sports in college by playing on intramural teams. This may be an option if your child wants to play but can't afford the extraordinary time and energy commitment that a varsity team requires.

Top Parent Concerns

Our extensive interaction with parents of college students reveals a number of areas of concern. Being informed, dealing with issues of safety, health, and basic security—as well as coping with worries about sex, drugs, and alcohol—emerged as the top parent concerns.

Being Informed

Your son tells you that the faculty has decided to reinstitute a foreign language requirement in his intended major. He's upset that if he has to take a foreign language, he won't be able to fit in other courses that he wanted to take.

What's on Your Mind

> I don't understand this. Can they change the requirements now—in the middle of the semester?
> How can I find out more about this?

What's on Your Child's Mind

> How can they do this to me? I'm terrible at languages.
> This will really screw up my GPA.
> I don't see why I need a foreign language anyway. I'll never use it.

What's Going On

It's common for students to get anxious when they hear about changes in the curriculum that may affect their course of study in a negative way. Often they will call you to vent their frustration before they investigate the facts of the situation. Like many other momentary "crises," this, too, will probably be over before you've stopped worrying about it. Parents can feel cut off when these issues arise; they really don't know what's going on.

What to Do

- Ask your son to check with his faculty adviser or the department office to see if this is a rumor or the truth and whether the change will affect him.

What to Avoid

- Being alarmed before you fully understand the situation.
- Telling your son you think he'll do just fine with a foreign language.

What You Need to Know

When your child starts college, the requirements for degrees remain constant until graduation. Any changes that are made to curricular requirements after he has started school will not apply to him, although they may apply to the next incoming class.

Lots of events and changes occur on campuses and many of them will affect your child in some way. Whether it is a campus demonstration about a political issue or a change in academic or student life policy that is important to your child, you will want to be informed. You may not get the information you want from your child or the university administration. Many parents feel frustrated that they receive only the tuition bills from the university and are left out of the loop when important events and changes occur.

If you want to know what is happening on campus, there are ways to find out. The college's Web site is usually the best place to start. Most Web sites contain vast amounts of information that can put your mind at ease. You may want to read the student newspaper (most colleges now have their student newspaper on the Web) or talk to alumni or other parents. Many alumni associations host informational local events and welcome parents. Most colleges and universities now have a parents' program office that can provide you with information about campus activities and they may be able to connect you with other parents living in your area. You can learn more about these programs in Chapter 7.

Safety

You are worried because your daughter often studies with friends who live across campus and walks back to her residence hall alone late at night. You've heard that rapes and assaults are becoming more common on campuses and wonder if your daughter is safe.

What's on Your Mind

Is my daughter safe walking around alone at night?
Who would be there if she was in trouble?
Does she realize how dangerous this could be?

What's on Your Child's Mind

My dad is such a worrier. He thinks I'm still ten years old.
I've never known anyone to get attacked walking across campus at night

What's Going On

Most parents list safety as a top concern when their children leave for college. Campuses, unfortunately, are not much different from the rest of the world. There was a time when campuses were more like ivory towers, and relatively immune to real world problems. No more. It is appropriate to be concerned about your child's safety and reasonable to ask your child to be careful in situations that could be dangerous.

What to Do

- Ask your daughter to have a friend accompany her or to inquire about a campus escort or bus service. She can find out what's available by calling the campus security office.
- Acknowledge that your daughter is an adult and capable of taking care of herself but remind her that everyone today has to exercise caution to be safe.

What to Avoid

- Trying to scare your daughter into taking extra precautions.
- Giving her the message that you don't trust her judgment and ability to take care of herself.

What You Need to Know

College campuses are no safer than any other environment today. In 1990, Congress passed the Jeanne Clery Disclosure of Campus Security Policy and Campus Crime Statistics Act, which required colleges to make crime statistics available to students, parents, and employees. Most colleges now provide students with extensive information and strategies for remaining safe on campus—safety training is usually an important part of new student orientation. Unfortunately, many students are so overwhelmed with the quantity of information at orientation that they forget about the many programs and services available to them. All campuses have a police presence and many have escort services, emergency phones, and continuing education on crime prevention strategies.

Awareness is the key to prevention and is the most powerful defense that a student can take to school. Many students come to college naïve and trusting and need to develop a sense of healthy suspicion. Most colleges acknowledge this fact and have taken measures (such as keeping residence halls locked twenty-four hours a day and changing locks annually) to ensure that their students are as safe as possible. If you are concerned about your child's safety, you can contact the campus security office and receive information on the crime and prevention programs that are in place.

In July 2010, new amendments to the Jeanne Clery Act took effect. These updated regulations require educational institutions to have an official written emergency plan and a summary of that plan disclosed in their annual security report. Moreover, institutions are now required to conduct at least one drill each year in order to assess the effectiveness of emergency response and evacuation systems. In the wake of the tragedy at Virginia Tech in 2007, many universities have instituted multiple emergency notification systems and test them frequently to increase their capacity to respond and notify students and staff members of imminent threats to their safety. Talk to your child about the importance of being aware of these emergency procedures and making sure his or her phone number is registered with the university in order to receive calls or texts when emergencies arise.

Health

Laura's dad has been trying to contact his daughter for a few days and is becoming increasingly alarmed that she hasn't answered or called him back. Finally, he decides to call his daughter's best friend, Julie.

JULIE: Hello?

DAD: Hi, Julie. It's Mr. McLeod. I've been trying to call Laura for a few days and wondered if you've seen her.

JULIE: Oh, hi, Mr. McLeod. Well, I got a text from Laura yesterday that said she was in the health center but I haven't talked to her. I texted her back to see if she was okay and she said she was and that she'd probably just be there overnight.

DAD: Oh, no! Do you know what's wrong? Does she have her cell phone with her?

JULIE: Well, she must have it because she texted me yesterday but maybe her battery's dead.

DAD: Julie, I really need to know what's going on with Laura. Do you have the number of the health center?

JULIE: Oh, gosh, I'm not sure what it is but I think you can get it on the Web site.

DAD: Okay, I'll try that. Listen, if you hear from Laura, would you call me back?

JULIE: Sure, Mr. McLeod, but Laura said she was okay. I'll let you know if I hear anything.

DAD: I hope so. I just can't understand why she didn't tell us she was in the hospital.

JULIE: Well, uh, I don't know. I'm sure she's going to be okay. She'll probably be back in her dorm by tonight.

DAD: Well, I'm going to find out what going on. Thanks, Julie.

JULIE: Okay, Mr. McLeod.

What's on Your Mind

Something terrible has happened to my daughter.
I've got to find out what's wrong.
Why didn't she tell me? What could it be?

What's on Your Child's Mind

Thank God I'm in the infirmary where someone will take care of me.
I'm going to get so far behind in my classes.

What's Going On

Students tend to be in their own world of classes, social life, and activities and don't always think to let their parents know right away if they are sick or injured. Their concern is with their own recovery, not their parents' worries, at least initially. College students tend to believe they are immortal and that if they are sick or get hurt, they will get better and everything will be fine. They also may be afraid to tell you if they have an embarrassing or frightening condition, such as a sexually transmitted disease. Or, the same child who wanted you to bring her chicken soup when she was sick at home over fall break may not want you to know that she is in the infirmary because she is vomiting all the time and suspects she may be pregnant.

What to Do

- Call the health center and try to talk to your child.
- Find out if she's okay before you start grilling her on what's wrong.
- Give her a chance to tell you what's wrong; if she doesn't want to talk about it, just remind her that you care about her and love her.
- See if there is any way that you can be helpful.
- Ask her for permission to talk to her doctor. If she says no, tell her you respect her right to privacy but that you're worried and need some reassurance that she's going to be okay.
- Try to keep the lines of communication open. Tell her you'd like to call her again tomorrow just to see how she's doing.

What to Avoid

- Leaping to the worst-case scenario before you know what's happening.
- Letting your panic and anger take over; yelling at your daughter for not telling you she is in the hospital
- Showing your hurt if she says she just didn't think to call you.

What You Need to Know

This is one of the worst nightmares any parent can imagine. Your child is sick or hurt in some way and you're not there. You're upset and anxious. You want to know what's going on and if she'll be okay. You're also angry that no one informed you that your child was in the hospital. It's very difficult for most parents to accept the fact that their eighteen-year-old child is a legal adult and that the hospital is bound to protect the doctor-patient confidentiality that is the right of every adult. Since the enactment of the Health Insurance Portability and Accountability Act of 1996 (HIPAA), there are federal rules that ensure privacy and confidentiality regarding a person's health care treatment and information. This means that the health center will not call you when they admit your child, unless it is a life or death situation. If the student's condition warrants a stay in the hospital, most health center staff members will ask the student if he or she has notified parents, and may even encourage him or her to do so. However, doctors and nurses are not entitled to call the parents if the child refuses, or just forgets, to make the call.

The Big Three: Drinking, Drugs, and Sex

You probably have dealt with these three issues during the high school years by talking, sharing your values, and monitoring your child's behavior. In fact, the majority of college students today have had sex and experimented with drinking and sometimes drugs before they left high school. Nevertheless, when your child goes to college, these issues seem to take on new meaning. There are new freedoms and responsibilities that come with living away from home; your child will be facing a vast array of choices in college out from under your watchful eye. Although it is true that your child will likely graduate from college with most of your core values intact, it is also true that most college students experiment with drinking, drugs, and sex.

This experimentation can cause you a fair amount of worry, even though you recognize that your ability to control your child's behavior is slipping away. It doesn't mean, however, that you have lost your influence. Most college students are too cool to admit it, but they still want your approval and often value your opinions on these issues. Most likely, you will need to initiate a continuing discussion on these issues if you want to influence your child; this can be tough because you are removed from the context of the behavior. For example, you may be concerned about what you consider to be excessive drinking because your son talks about going to fraternity parties every time you speak to him. You're not sure if he's at a party four nights a week or once a week. It's a good idea to ask about the context of the behavior if you have concerns: "Do you go to frat parties often?" And it's also a good idea to make your expectations clear: "I can understand you want to party with your friends, but I worry that your social life is going to affect your studies and your health. I hope your partying isn't getting out of control."

While it's important for you to be able to let go of control (you don't really have it anyway!) and trust your child to make reasonable, independent decisions, responsible parenting also includes making your expectations clear. This is easier said than done when your face-to-face contact with your child is minimal. It is difficult to let your child deal with consequences, especially when the consequences can be serious. Indeed, there may be times when you need to act, especially if you sense your child is in danger. We'll address those instances in Chapter 10.

For now, however, your task is to give your child the opportunity to test his or her own values and to provide support during this period of exploration and experimentation. This is the beginning of a new kind of relationship, not the end of your influence as an important role model and guide.

The following examples will help you clarify your response to these critical issues.

Drinking

It seems as if every time you talk to your son at school, he is either going out to a party or hungover from one. You begin to wonder if his drinking is out of control. All the literature from the school says that underage drinking is not allowed on campus. Your son talks about drinking as though it's the only way to unwind and handle the academic pressure.

What's on Your Mind

> I'm worried about his health and safety with all this drinking going on.
> Is it possible he could become an alcoholic?
> Why doesn't the college crack down on these parties?
> I thought liquor wasn't allowed in the residence halls.

What's on Your Child's Mind

> My dad is so clueless—he thinks we're all loser alcoholics.
> I'm having a great time, although I hate being hungover.
> Everyone drinks a lot—I actually drink less than my friends.
> I need to unwind after working so hard on exams and papers. The competition is intense and after a few beers, I feel better.

What's Going On

Although the legal drinking age is twenty-one, drinking is common on college campuses. In fact, many students have had their first drink in high school and come to college with a fake ID or find out quickly where to get one. While it's true that most colleges have rules about drinking on campus, those rules are broken with regularity. It is almost impossible for campus security officers to enforce the underage drinking laws because students are drinking in private spaces such as their dorm rooms or apartments.

What to Do

- Talk to your son about the larger issue of drinking on campus and ask questions about the social culture. Ask him what he thinks of the parties he goes to.

- Talk about responsible drinking and what that means to you, acknowledging that he is in control of how he behaves and that you trust he acts responsibly.
- Remind him of the possible consequences of breaking the law and/or drinking too much. He could get arrested and have a record that would keep him from some options later. He could consume too much and risk alcohol poisoning.
- Be aware of signs that may indicate your son is abusing alcohol. Don't be afraid to bring up the subject if you are concerned about alcohol abuse. Just start by saying, "I'm concerned about how much you are drinking. Are you?"

What to Avoid

- Moralizing and lecturing about drinking.
- Being unrealistic: "You know drinking is against the law. I want you to stop going to parties where they serve alcohol to minors."
- Encouraging the behavior by bragging about your son's ability to hold his liquor and joking about what a party animal he is.
- Supplying him with liquor when you're visiting campus; drinking a lot yourself.
- Glossing it over with "kids will be kids" remarks and denying that there may be a problem with excessive drinking.

What You Need to Know

There is great concern about the culture of alcohol use and abuse on college campuses. In 1984, Congress passed the National Minimum Drinking Age Act, which imposed a penalty of 10 percent of a state's federal highway appropriation on any state setting its drinking age lower than twenty-one. Not surprisingly, all states raised their legal drinking age to twenty-one. Although that act made it illegal for individuals under the age of twenty-one to possess or use alcohol, it did nothing to change the behavior of college students; it merely drove the drinking "underground" and created enormous problems for university administrators struggling to enforce the law. In fact, there is significant evidence to show that drinking, and binge drinking in particular, actually increased following the enactment of this legislation.

In 2008, more than 135 university presidents and chancellors signed the Amethyst Initiative, a public statement about the problem of irresponsible drinking on their campuses. Their concerns extend to the indisputable fact that, although the legal drinking age is twenty-one, this legislation has spawned a culture of dangerous, clandestine binge drinking on many campuses. These top university administrators argue that it is clear the law stipulating that twenty-one is the minimum legal age for consuming alcohol is not working. Their Initiative further posits that:

1. Alcohol education that mandates abstinence as the only legal option has not resulted in significant constructive behavioral change among their students.
2. Adults under twenty-one are deemed capable of voting, signing contracts, serving on juries, and enlisting in the military, but are told they are not mature enough to have a beer.
3. By choosing to use fake IDs, students make ethical compromises that erode respect for the law.

These college presidents and chancellors have called upon our elected officials to:

- Support an informed and dispassionate public debate over the effects of the twenty-one-year-old drinking age.
- Consider whether the 10 percent highway fund "incentive" encourages or inhibits that debate.
- Invite new ideas about the best ways to prepare young adults to make responsible decisions about alcohol.

If you are interested in learning more about the Amethyst Initiative, you can visit their Web site at www.amethystinitiative.org.

Binge drinking can have grave consequences for your child. Many serious offenses and accidents on campus are the direct result of excessive drinking. According to the National Institute on Alcohol Abuse and Alcoholism, each year 1,825 college students die from alcohol-related injuries, including motor vehicle crashes, and 599,000 are injured under the influence of alcohol.[2] Excessive drinking also figures prominently in incidents of sexual abuse, rape, and other forms of violence. Due to these realities, many universities today have modified their policies to allow officials to inform parents when a student is charged with underage drinking and enlist their support in changing drinking behavior.

What can you do if your child is charged with illegal drinking? You can talk with your child about the consequences of this behavior. You might start the conversation by offering your expectations. "I expect you to respect yourself and others. I realize that you're now a legal adult and that includes the expectation that you will make sound choices and take responsibility for them. This includes never, ever driving while drunk or being in a car with a drunk driver. Until you're twenty-one, drinking is against the law and if you break the law and are charged with underage drinking, there may be serious consequences.

"I'm also concerned about out-of-control drinking at parties and wonder if you've thought about how you'll handle those situations. Can we talk about some ways you can protect yourself and about what you can do if you witness a friend who is in danger from excessive drinking?"

(Some colleges have instituted medical amnesty policies to encourage students to bring friends for medical help rather than leaving them alone to "sleep it off" and risk the possibility of alcohol poisoning or choking death.)

If you haven't already, it's important to start talking now and continue talking about these issues. The truth is, a first-year college student is essentially a high school senior without parents around. Students are enthralled with the freedoms they have in college. The vast majority of students do well academically and stay physically and mentally healthy; however, too many students stumble into high-risk behaviors and situations, unaware of the dangers and consequences. While you may have lost daily control of your child's behavior, and while you will not be the *only* influence in your child's life, you can be an *important* influence. Don't assume that your child knows how you feel about difficult topics, such as underage drinking, smoking tobacco, drug use, and "hooking up." Keep talking, even if your child appears to be tuning you out.

Many campuses have organizations that promote responsible drinking behavior among college students. There are staff members who can answer your questions as well. If you are concerned about this issue, you can contact the college's dean of students' office or health center.

Drugs

Your daughter is home for fall break and you notice a small plastic bag that has fallen out of her shirt in the pile of dirty clothes next to the washer. It looks like marijuana.

What's on Your Mind

> My daughter is doing drugs, and that worries me.
> Should I confront her with it?
> I wonder how much she's involved in this.

What's on Your Child's Mind

> So I smoke pot with my friends once in a while. What's the big deal?
> I know my parents wouldn't like it, but they probably did it in college, too.
> Pot makes me feel relaxed; everyone I know does it.

What's Going On

Even though you may know your child experimented with drugs in high school, it's more wor-risome now because you don't have the advantage of being able to monitor your child's behavior on a daily basis and notice changes that may be due to drug use or abuse. It's easy to leap to the conclusion that your child has a serious drug problem. Depending on your values and experi-ence, you may feel it's hypocritical to insist that your child behave differently than you did when you were in college, but you also worry that drug use now seems more dangerous. You may feel very strongly that no one should ever use drugs and proud of the fact that you have never experimented with them. Or, you may feel very little concern because you have great confidence in your child's ability to handle this experimentation responsibly.

What to Do

- Tell your child that you found the marijuana.
- Without blaming her, let her know your concerns.
- Be honest if you have used drugs. Describe the context within which you experi-mented with drugs and share how you feel about it now.
- Be clear about your expectations and attitudes about drug use: "I am not so worried about a bit of experimentation with drugs, but I worry about the variety of serious drugs that might be available to you and how you would handle that," or "I am wor-ried that any experimentation with drugs will be bad for you and I feel strongly that you shouldn't be using drugs at all."
- Ask her how she feels about those expectations and attitudes. Keep the lines of non-judgmental communication open.

What to Avoid

- Reacting with anger and an ultimatum: "If you ever use drugs again, I'll make you leave school and come home where I can keep an eye on you."
- Moralizing and preaching, which rarely change behavior—instead, they almost always shut down the communication.
- Trying to make her feel guilty or ashamed. This tactic may just make your child a more defiant and committed user.

What You Need to Know

Although illegal, experimentation with drugs is common on most college campuses. This doesn't make your child's experimentation any less troubling. While students try out new lifestyles and values, they can be very dependent upon peer relationships and acceptance; most students will do what their friends do.

Because we now know that brain development is still in progress until age twenty-five and that the areas of the brain less developed in a college student are those that govern impulse control, planning, and high-level reasoning, there is increasing concern about the effect of drugs and alcohol on the developing brain. Neuroscience is providing new insights about how drugs affect the brain and how young people make critical decisions about drug use.

Findings indicate that adolescent humans show diminished sensitivity to intoxication; their higher metabolic rates allow them to consume greater amounts of alcohol than older people without feeling as intoxicated. Moreover, the tendency to seek novelty and social competitiveness in some adolescents may promote drug use in those seeking thrills and approval from peers. As psychologist Laurence Steinberg put it in his book, *Adolescence,* the emerging adult brain "has a well-developed accelerator but only a partly developed brake."

The use and abuse of drugs and alcohol in young people may be confusing to parents who know their sons and daughters to be quite capable of sophisticated mental abilities in many areas of their lives. But knowing that adolescent brains are still developing may help you understand some of your child's behavior and be able to offer calm, reasoned guidance.

You may find this discussion complicated if your son or daughter knows or suspects that you used drugs while you were in college. Whether you have been honest and open in the past about your own behavior or choose to be so now, most parents dread this conversation. But what you want to convey is wisdom, sometimes earned the hard way, and your desire to transmit that wisdom and perhaps shield your child from making the same mistakes. You can talk with your child about what we know today about the effects of drugs and alcohol on the brain that weren't known when you were young. And it doesn't hurt to admit that you made mistakes and learned from them, while bringing the conversation back to your concerns about your child's behavior.

Some parents may feel that moderate marijuana use is harmless, but that cocaine, ecstasy, heroin, and other drugs are completely unacceptable. Other parents would draw the line at any experimentation with drugs, including alcohol. Because alcohol is considered by many to be a socially acceptable drug, discussion of drinking may come up naturally; however, few students will volunteer information about other drug use. It's *your* responsibility, as a parent, to initiate discussions about drugs, including alcohol, and to continue to make your values and expectations clear to your college student.

Sexuality—Your Son

Your son has announced that he's bringing his new girlfriend home for spring break and has asked you to put away his high school girlfriend's picture and make sure his room is ready for his guest.

What's on Your Mind

> He's sleeping with his girlfriend. I'm not sure how I feel about that.
> I hope they are having safe sex.
> I don't even know this girl.

What's on Your Child's Mind

> It's going to be great to show my girlfriend my house and have her meet my friends at home.
> Mom didn't sound too thrilled about her staying in my room.
> What's her problem? I sleep with her at school.
> I hope my parents will be cool about this.

What's Going On

You must now confront the fact that your son is sleeping with his girlfriend. You may feel shocked, you may feel pleased that he is open with you, you may worry about whether he is having safe sex, and you may feel that he has a lot of nerve to expect that he can bring this girl home and share his bedroom with her.

What to Do

- Be honest with yourself about your feelings.
- Talk with him. Don't be afraid to tell him that you're uncomfortable with this arrangement if that's the way you feel.
- Acknowledge that your son can disagree with you if you don't condone premarital sex, but let him know that your feelings need to be respected when he's in your home.
- Take this opportunity to start a dialogue exploring values about sexuality. Share your thoughts about responsible sexual behavior with your child. For example, you may feel premarital sex within a mutually respectful relationship is okay, but that a series of one-night stands or multiple "hook ups" with casual acquaintances is not okay.

- Find out if your son has talked about the proposed sleeping arrangements with his girlfriend. She may not be comfortable sleeping with him in your home.
- Make sure he has information about practicing safe sex and understands the consequences of unprotected sex, even if you had the same discussion when he was younger.

What to Avoid

- Judging his behavior.
- Judging his girlfriend's behavior or character before you've met her.
- Giving him a lecture on the dangers or immorality of premarital sex.

What You Need to Know

In addition to exploring new freedoms, lifestyles, surroundings, and activities, students are also discovering new friendships and creating new intimate relationships. This can take the form of seeing a number of people, having one steady partner, or engaging in casual sex. This experimentation can also mean forming intimate relationships with partners who come from different backgrounds, lifestyles, and value systems.

Sexuality—Your Daughter

It's winter break and you overhear your daughter and some of her old high school friends regaling each other with stories of guys they have "hooked up" with during fall semester at college.

What's on Your Mind

I know she's on the pill, but I still worry about her safety and this casual attitude toward sex.
How many guys has she slept with?
Is she out of control? Should I say something to her?
I'm worried that she'll get hurt, emotionally or physically.
And what, exactly, does "hooking up" mean?

What's on Your Child's Mind

I'm sure glad I'm on the pill. At least I don't have to worry about getting pregnant.
Everybody "hooks up" in college.

> I wonder what my parents would think if they knew how many guys I've had sex with this semester.

What's Going On

You find this behavior shocking but you're not sure what you can or should do about it. Although you're relieved that your daughter is on the pill, you are very concerned that she is at risk of contracting a sexually transmitted disease of some kind. You also wonder how she can feel good about sleeping around and how she's handling this emotionally.

What to Do

- Keep in mind that she may just be trying to impress her high school friends with her sophistication.
- Tell her that you overheard the discussion and tell her you want to talk about it.
- Let her know that you respect her right to privacy, but that you have concerns if she's having sex with many different guys.
- Share your values and attitudes regarding sex, and ask her what she thinks of your point of view.
- Tell her if you feel uncomfortable with her behavior, but reinforce that you love her and care about her.
- Be prepared to honor her feelings if she tells you that her sex life is none of your business. You can still share your expectations without discussing her sexual behavior.

What to Avoid

- Jumping to the conclusion that she's having sex with a different guy every night.
- Preaching and moralizing about "easy" girls and their ruined reputations.
- Warning or threatening her about the consequences of her behavior.
- Shaming her in the hope that she'll stop "hooking up."

What You Need to Know

"Hooking up," "friends with benefits," "booty calls," "fuck buddies"—these are all terms that characterize the current social culture on many college campuses. These terms can be more than a little disconcerting to parents. There is no doubt that the sexual climate on campus is dramatically different from what it was when you were eighteen to twenty-two years of age, and it may be difficult to figure out what's really going on.

There was a major shift in American college dating culture that occurred following the sexual revolution of the 1960s. By the mid-1980s, the practice of "formal dating" had been replaced by "informal group partying" and "hanging out" with groups of friends. College bars and parties became the places that facilitated contact between men and women. There was a dramatic decrease in what was considered "dating" for previous generations of students.

In recent years, "hooking up" has taken the place of the traditional practice of dating as a way for (heterosexual) students to get together. While the definition of hooking up is often a puzzle to parents, scholars, who have studied this cultural shift through extensive research with college students, found that students described hooking up as a situation in which two people are hanging out or run into each other at an event (often a party), and they end up doing something intimate and sexual, which can range from passionate kissing to petting to oral sex to sexual intercourse.

A key component in hooking up is that neither party has the expectation that this encounter will result in a relationship. Hooking up is a distinctive "sex without commitment" interaction that is widespread on college campuses and, of course, this activity has a profound effect on campus culture and the individuals involved. Although some students reported that they hooked up with "randoms" (people they had not met before), most often the hook-up partner was at least a friend or classmate.

Another component of hooking up is that it usually occurs after a good bit of drinking. Recent research indicates that the median number of drinks men consumed before their last hook up was six, whereas women had consumed four. This consumption level is the definition of binge drinking.

While these descriptions may leave you puzzled and worried, they reinforce the importance of talking with your son or daughter about drinking and sexual encounters. You would not be alone if you find this social culture disturbing, particularly in light of the epidemic of sexually transmitted diseases.

Many new college students see only the two extreme ends of the range of choices: not having sex at all or having casual sex with lots of partners. You need to be clear with your child about what kind of sexual conduct you feel is responsible and healthy. Parents, while often not aware of the intimate details of their child's sexual experiences, can play an important role in modeling trusting and respectful intimate relationships and talking about sexual values and expectations. Undoubtedly, you will have to initiate these discussions, while taking care to respect your child's privacy.

Even now, there is a lingering double standard for young men and women when it comes to sex. Particularly in the first year of college, some young men and women engage in unhealthy sexual activities, especially when alcohol and drugs are involved. But young women are more likely to find themselves in exploitive and dangerous situations. The aftermath of these experiences can leave them feeling anxious and guilty. Moreover, the physical and emotional consequences of this behavior can be much more serious for young women than for young men.

There have been recent movements (one of which is called the Love and Fidelity Network) that appear to be challenging this trend. Not surprisingly, these initiatives to step away from hook-up culture are most often championed by college women. Although deciding to quit hooking up is clearly a minority position, these budding organizations, dedicated to helping college students begin a discussion about a lifestyle that does not include casual sexual activity with anonymous or uncommitted partners, are likely to gain favor with many students.

"Hooking up" appears to be a college-specific lifestyle. Traditional dating practices seem to reemerge as students graduate, take jobs, and begin to pursue relationships that they hope will result in a long-term commitment. While this is an encouraging sign of appropriate maturation, the college years still present significant challenges for students and parents alike.

Your Adjustment Issues

Although you may be most concerned about how your child is adjusting to college life, it's good to keep in mind that this is a transition period for you as well. Many parents feel like check-writing spectators as their children cope with the changes that are part of college life. You may have been involved in each phase of your child's development and education to date and now you are faced with parenting from afar with little direct interaction with your child.

You are also adjusting to the unique culture of the college or university. Whether your child chose a large state university, a small private college, a prestigious Ivy League institution, or a nearby community college, your role in your child's education will be very different from now on. You may feel that you don't know much about the college, and you will probably not get to know other parents as you did in elementary, middle, and high school. In Chapter 7, we discuss the overall college experience in greater detail.

You won't know much about the kids your child is hanging out with, and they may come from different backgrounds. You're cut off from your child's daily experiences for the first time and that means your role as parent is changing dramatically. In dealing with many of these adjustment issues, you may want to refer again to the first chapter in which we explored the changing nature of your relationship with your college child.

Chapter 5

Is Your Child Confident, Confused, or Coasting?

The Search for Identity and Autonomy

When Dan came home for semester break last week, I hardly recognized him! He had grown his hair and looked like he had rolled out of a dirty laundry bag. I could live with his appearance, but then he started spouting off about how the Republicans were responsible for all of the country's problems and that he no longer wanted to study economics and support the "conservative agenda." I snapped! I started yelling, "Who do you think you are?" He was rejecting everything we stood for, everything we'd worked for, and everything we'd taught him.

This chapter will help you understand the puzzling things that your college student may do while on the quest for identity and autonomy. Just remember two things:

1. It is necessary for your child to be on this quest; in fact, it would be troubling if he or she weren't!
2. It is also natural if his or her behavior drives you crazy and you begin to wonder, "Where did I go wrong in raising this child?"

Identity

"Who am I?" is a question your child will ask often during the college years. For example, "Who am I as a distinct person?"; "Who am I in relation to others?"; "Who will I be in the future?" Grappling with these questions is an essential part of becoming an independent adult. Most parents have no trouble with these questions—they have trouble with the behavior and lifestyle experimentation that accompanies them.

The search for identity is a lifelong process, but late adolescence and the college years are a particularly intense period, because for the first time, your child has the physical, intellectual, and social maturity that makes this quest possible. Drawing on our years of experience working with college students, and our background in adolescent development, we will show why this search is a natural process in the transition from child to adult. Many facets of your child's life will reflect this search for identity, as illustrated in the examples that follow.

Appearance

You eagerly looked forward to your son's arrival home for Thanksgiving break. But when he walked in the door, you were alarmed to see his shaved head and the Celtic knot tattoo on his forearm. You can't imagine what your relatives are going to think when they arrive for Thanksgiving dinner.

What's on Your Mind

> Why is he doing this?
> What will people think of me as a parent?
> Where will this lead?

What's on Your Child's Mind

> What's the big deal?
> Why is my mom so hyper about a tattoo?
> My family is so boring.

What's Going On

Parents who are excited about having their child come home for a holiday may be shocked to see dramatic changes in their child's appearance. Parents assume those changes are profound and lasting; they probably aren't. While the student will maintain a no-big-deal attitude toward these changes, they are symbolic of the need to differentiate from parents and to begin to create a distinct and separate identity.

What to Do

- Keep in mind the important priorities. Will this matter a year or five years from now? Decide what really matters and pick your battles; tell your son if this bothers you, but listen to his ideas as well.
- Remember this is a healthy process for your child. It doesn't have to do with the quality of your parenting.
- Remember this, too, shall pass.

What to Avoid

- Fighting the small fights over issues that don't matter much to you. How important are the shaved head and tattoo?
- Judging and criticizing: "I can't believe you did that to your hair. It looks ridiculous."
- Generalizing beyond the issue at hand: "Is this the beginning of a slide into crazy behavior?"

What You Need to Know

Most experts on human development point to late adolescence as a particularly important time in an individual's identity formation. Erik Erikson, one of the most well-known human development experts, argued that, ideally, adolescents need a period of moratorium. This moratorium (a kind of accountability "time out") gives teenagers the opportunity, removed from the burdens and responsibilities of adulthood, to explore their identities and to learn critical lessons about who they are in the world. College presents the ideal setting for late adolescents/emerging adults to "try on" new identities.

As the parent of a college student experimenting with a new identity, you need to decide which battles to wage. Most students will experiment a bit with new looks and personal appearance. Remember the late 1960s and early 1970s, when families engaged in raging battles about hair length and rock music? A lot of damage was done over relatively trivial issues in those days. Today we are faced with tattoos, body piercing, and even stranger tastes in music and entertainment.

These aspects of popular culture are important to adolescents. For example, take a walk in the mall and notice how you can categorize young people. You can tell the jocks from the nerds, the Goths from the popular crowd, simply by the way they dress. When your son or daughter became a teenager, you probably noticed how they all looked alike and spent a lot of time talking to friends about what kind of music and what musical groups they liked. Music, appearance, and other somewhat superficial aspects of popular culture define social groups for adolescents, much as neighborhood, profession, church affiliation, and political and community involvement define social groups for adults. For adolescents, these social groups provide a temporary group identity while they search for their own individual identity.

Friends

Your daughter, Alexis, calls to tell you that she wants to go home with her roommate for fall break.

> ALEXIS: Hi, Mom. What's up?
>
> MOM: Oh, hi, hon. Not much new here. What's up with you?
>
> ALEXIS: I just wanted to tell you that Claire invited me to visit her family in New York City over fall break. Isn't that cool? Can I go?
>
> MOM: Well, I don't know. I was really looking forward to seeing you for the long weekend. Don't you want to come home?
>
> ALEXIS: Well, yeah, but I've never been to New York and it would be so fun to see the city.
>
> MOM: Where do Claire's parents live?
>
> ALEXIS: Some place in Brooklyn, I think. Anyway, we could ride the subway into the city and she's promised to show me all the sights.
>
> MOM: But, we don't know anything about her family. Does she live in a safe place?
>
> ALEXIS: Mom! She's my roommate, remember? I know I'll have a good time. Her older brother is going to take us to some really cool clubs.
>
> MOM: What kind of clubs?
>
> ALEXIS: You know, dance clubs and stuff.
>
> MOM: I don't know, Alexis, I feel a little nervous about you being in the city all alone.
>
> ALEXIS: I won't be alone. Her whole family will be there. I think her dad's a cop. How much safer could I be?
>
> MOM: Well, I guess it's okay.
>
> ALEXIS: Thanks. This is going to be so much fun. I can't wait. Talk to you later.

What's on Your Mind

> Why doesn't she want to come home? I miss her.
> She sees her roommate all the time, why can't she spend some time with her own family?
> Will she be safe in New York City?

What's on Your Child's Mind

> My roommate's family is so much cooler than mine.
> I'm dying to go to New York City.
> What's the big deal? It's just a long weekend.

What's Going On

Part of trying on new identities in college is interacting with people from different backgrounds and regions. This doesn't mean that your daughter is rejecting you. She's excited about exploring a whole new city and culture and meeting her roommate's family.

What to Do

- Try to give your child permission to experiment and learn about other ways of living.
- Remember that she is not rejecting you and your family; she is merely trying to create her own identity separate from you.
- Remind her that she needs to be more aware of her personal safety in the city and ask her how she thinks she can do that.

What to Avoid

- Being overly disappointed that she won't be home for break.
- Saying no, just for the sake of saying no.
- Trying to make her afraid of this adventure.

What You Need to Know

Friends are very important to college students. When your child was young, being a friend meant being a playmate, able to share and interact in play. When your child reached adolescence, however, the nature of friendships changed. Your teenager needed to develop a complex set of skills in order to have close friendships—these included the ability to share intimate feelings, provide emotional support to friends, and trust friends to be open and honest in return. These skills help adolescents form intimate attachments and build self-esteem. By the time students have enrolled in college, many would prefer to spend more time with peers than parents. This doesn't mean that you are no longer important in their lives. It means that they are exploring who they are in other relationships, a necessary step in eventually forming the intimate attachments central to independent adulthood.

Opposites Attract

In her recent calls home, your daughter has been gushing on and on about her new boyfriend. You met him when you were on campus for parents' weekend and are concerned about her interest in him. He's so different from anyone your daughter dated in high school and you wonder how she could be so infatuated with someone from such a different background. You hate to admit it, but you're worried that she's falling in love with this young man who was raised in the projects in a big city.

What's on Your Mind

> This young man just isn't right for her.
> We didn't send her to college to fall in love with someone with such a different background.
> She seems to spend all of her time with him.

What's on Your Child's Mind

> I'm really in love.
> He's so special and much more mature than other boys.
> I don't think my parents like him. They're so conservative and narrow-minded.

What's Going On

This behavior is typical of many college students who have grown up in relatively sheltered environments with few opportunities to meet different types of people. Having a relationship with someone from a totally different background may help students understand other life experiences and begin to explore their own values more deeply.

What to Do

- Try to understand why she finds him so attractive.
- Ask her what characteristics he has that appeal to her.

- Let her know your feelings without assaulting his background. You could say, "I know that his motivation to put himself through college attracts you and that is impressive, but I worry about your falling in love with someone from such a different background. Do you think that's a problem?"
- Listen to her response and let her know that you trust her to make good decisions.

What to Avoid

- Telling her that you think he is wrong for her and that you wish she'd stop seeing him.
- Warning that couples from such different backgrounds have many problems to deal with later.
- Jumping to the conclusion that this will be her lifelong mate.

What You Need to Know

Some experts believe that intimate relationships can come only after an individual has established a stable identity. However, other researchers have found that some individuals, particularly girls, tend to discover who they are through forming intimate relationships and emotional bonds. Boys may be more likely to discover who they are before they form intimate relationships. Either way, relationships help adolescents explore their identity.

There is evidence suggesting that students today are less likely to be looking for a life partner, through dating and commitment to one person, during the college years. We discuss this phenomenon in greater detail in Chapters 4 and 10

Career Choices and Majors

When Sam went to college, everyone marveled at his maturity. You were proud of your son's goal to become a research scientist and his determination to tackle a demanding course of study. You are surprised when, during spring break at home, he sits down at the kitchen table and tells you the following:

SAM: Mom, I've been thinking lately about changing my major.
MOM: You have? I thought you always wanted to be an environmental scientist.
SAM: I know. I really liked science in high school, but it's so different in college.
MOM: How?

SAM: It just seems so dry. And if I major in chemistry I'll be taking almost all science courses from now on.

MOM: But you used to love your science courses.

SAM: I did, but before I always got to take English, history, and art, too. I'm taking this art course right now that I really love. I think I want to major in art history.

MOM: But what would you do with a major in art history?

SAM: Well, some of the kids in my class are talking about being teachers or going into advertising or publishing. That sounds kind of cool.

MOM: Oh, Sam, I don't know what to say. Do you really think you want to be a teacher or work in advertising?

SAM: I don't know for sure, but I'm volunteering at the art museum on campus and it's really fun. I got to lead a tour with local elementary school kids. I think I might like teaching.

MOM: This is kind of hard to believe. You always seemed so sure that science was your interest.

SAM: I know, Mom, but I'm not sure anymore. Are you upset with me?

MOM: No, I'm just surprised and confused.

What's on Your Mind

Sam has always wanted to be an environmental scientist. What happened?

I'm worried about how vague his plans seem now.

We're sacrificing a lot to keep him in school and now he's not taking advantage of this great science program.

What's on Your Child's Mind

I'm so confused and worried about my future.

I really don't like science anymore, but art history is really interesting.

My parents seem so disappointed in me.

What's Going On

Sam, like many other college students, is discovering that what he always thought he wanted to do doesn't fit his interests anymore. This discovery often happens in the sophomore year when it becomes necessary for most students to declare a major course of study. Parents who have sent a focused and confident child off to college may wonder what has happened and feel concerned about his future prospects. In fact, it is common for this questioning to occur more than once during the college years.

What to Do

- Open up the discussion and listen to your child's interests, concerns, and fears.
- Give him permission to be confused and to explore.
- Let him know if you're worried and be specific about why. For example, "I am concerned about your dropping your science major and what that may mean for your future job prospects. Tell me more about how you feel about your decision."
- Reinforce that this is his decision. Remind him that you love him regardless of his major and future career choices.

What to Avoid

- Trying to convince him to change his mind and continue with science.
- Using "you" messages: "But you always wanted to be a scientist. What's happened to you?"
- Blaming him for being so confused and indecisive.

Confident, Confused, or Coasting

In our work with students, we have found that they tend to fall into one of three types—confident, confused, or coasting—when it comes to exploring who they are and making decisions about their lives. A confident student has solid goals in mind and sticks to them; a confused student actively tries out alternatives and questions everything; a coasting student goes with the flow, seemingly unconcerned about taking action and making decisions. Parents have difficulty with the shifting that goes on between these three states during the college years. Few students stick to one type throughout college; in fact, most move in and out of these states frequently as they face new situations. Although this behavior can frustrate parents, going through these states is a critical exercise in identity formation for your child.

A student can be confident in one arena (certain of which fraternity to pledge) and confused in another (unable to choose a major). He or she may coast for a semester (not worried about his major), be confused for a semester (exploring two or three different majors), and be confident a year later (finally choosing a major).

Let's look at Sam's situation from the previous dialogue and see how he fits these types. He began college confident that he would be a scientist. A year later, he was confused and began exploring alternatives, but he still was not ready to make a commitment. After his conversation with Mom, Sam may return to school and coast for a while. In time, he may become confused again, as he actively examines alternatives. After investigating options, he may be able to make a commitment and become confident again. This pattern is common as college students make decisions and explore who they are.

An Identity Formation Model

Our experience in working with college students follows a model of identity formation developed by James Marcia, a developmental psychologist.[1] Marcia's model offers another way of understanding your child's behavior as he or she struggles with achieving a unique identity. The chart shows Marcia's Four Statuses of Identity—identity achievement, identity moratorium, identity foreclosure, and identity diffusion. According to Marcia, the degree to which an adolescent either explores or commits to a course of action results in that child being (at that moment) identity diffused, identity foreclosed, in identity moratorium, or identity achieved.

FOUR STATUSES OF IDENTITY

		Exploration	
		High	Low
Commitment	High	Identity Achieved	Identity Foreclosed
	Low	Identity Moratorium	Identity Diffused

Let's look again at Sam's situation and try to understand his behavior using this model. When Sam was in high school, he was confident that he would be a scientist—he was low on exploring alternatives and high on his commitment to science and, therefore, identity foreclosed. He committed to study science in college without exploring alternatives. During college, he actively began to pursue other courses of study. When he spoke to his mom he had entered a moratorium stage—exploring other options and low on a commitment to science. Simply put, he had become confused. Over time, Sam may develop a firm commitment to an art history major and to a career in advertising. He will have explored art history courses and careers in advertising, and will finally decide to be an art history major. At this point, Marcia would say he has achieved his vocational identity—he has sufficiently explored options and then made a commitment. Sam, however, could have decided that he really doesn't want to think about this big decision anymore. At this stage, according to Marcia, he would be identity diffused (coasting)—he has ceased exploring alternatives and yet isn't making a firm commitment to a course of study, either.

While we have characterized students as simply "confident," Marcia maintains that there are two distinct categories of confident—identity foreclosed or identity achieved. A student who enrolls in college with a premed focus, for example, without having explored other vocational interests, is confident and identity foreclosed. He has decided to be a doctor based on little or no exploration. Ultimately, he may end up being a doctor and happy with his choice, but problems can arise when a student hasn't explored other paths. If an identity-foreclosed student begins to question his commitment to medicine, it can upset his sense of himself and confuse his parents. In order to truly be confident and identity achieved, however, it may be necessary for him to experience other phases of Marcia's model. This could take the form of coasting for a while, being confused about alternatives, or choosing to go back to being confident in the identity-foreclosed manner and forging ahead with his decision to study medicine. Or, he may explore other majors and decide, finally, to make a commitment to medicine—at that point he would be confident and identity achieved, having explored various options.

It's good to keep in mind that throughout their life spans, people usually move back and forth many times between these states. In fact, one of the ironies of this stage of adolescent development is that it can be quite similar to adults in midlife. Parents may be asking similar identity questions during the time their children are in college. Although careers and vocations do not necessarily define a person's identity, they can signal change in identity formation throughout life.

Values/Lifestyle

Your son seems thrilled with his new friends at college, all of whom come from wealthy families and have lots of money for expensive vacations, clothes, alcohol, and, you're afraid, recreational drugs. He's been asked to a friend's vacation home in Florida over spring break and wants some extra money to buy some new clothes for the trip.

What's on Your Mind

> He sure is infatuated with all of that money.
> We can't afford to support his adventures with this crowd.
> I'm also concerned about the drinking and whether drugs are involved.

What's on Your Child's Mind

> I am so psyched about going to Florida for spring break.
> These guys are so much fun.
> I wish my parents had more money.

What's Going On

Your son is exploring how he fits into the peer culture of college. This is a vital part of his ability to form a unique identity. During this period, his peers will have a definite impact on his desires and expectations. This can be intimidating for parents, but these experiences help adolescents formulate their own value system by observing other families' values.

What to Do

- Let your son know that you're pleased he has this opportunity for a nice vacation.
- Ask him what he likes most about his new friends.
- Be honest about what you can afford to do to support this adventure. If you can't afford to give him extra money for clothes, tell him.
- Suggest that he could earn some extra money by taking a temporary job.

What to Avoid

- Reminding him that you're not made of money.
- Questioning the values of his friends and their families.
- Saying no because you're not sure about his new friends.

What You Need to Know

As we've said before, the vast majority of college students eventually adopt most of their parents' values. Not all of them do, however. For example, liberal, socially conscious parents who believe in egalitarian values may have difficulty accepting that their child wants to be an investment banker and have tons of money to live what he or she considers "the good life." Just as you no longer can choose the environment in which your child lives and makes friends, you no longer can control his or her values and lifestyle choices. However, if your parenting style shows respect for his or her individuality, you will have a better chance to sustain an intimate and satisfying relationship, as he or she finds a comfortable niche and moves into the adult world.

Values/Religion

Your family has always had a strong religious commitment. Most of your activities have revolved around the church, and you feel that religion is an important part of life and central to your family's value system. The following phone call with your son, John, has you wondering what is going on with him.

> DAD: Hi, John. How're you doing?
>
> JOHN: Pretty good, Dad. I got an A on my philosophy paper.
>
> DAD: That's great. What did you write about?
>
> JOHN: Well, you're not going to like this, but we've been reading and talking about world religions and I'm seriously rethinking whether Jesus was all that everyone thinks. I mean, who knows how his ideas were interpreted over the years?
>
> DAD: You're right, I don't like your attitude. Don't you remember anything you learned in church?
>
> JOHN: Yeah, but I'm not sure I really believe it anymore. I mean, if Jesus is the only son of God, where does that leave Buddha?
>
> DAD: But you're not a Buddhist!
>
> JOHN: Well, I know you won't be happy with this, either, but I'm not going to church anymore. It just doesn't seem all that relevant here, and I like to sleep in on Sunday morning.
>
> DAD: You're not going to church?
>
> JOHN: Well, no, I haven't been going lately.
>
> DAD: I can't believe you're throwing away years of being involved in the church because you want to sleep in on Sunday.
>
> JOHN: Dad, chill. It's not like I'm a heathen or something. I just don't see why this is so important to you. I mean, I know it's important to you, but it's just not that important to me right now.

What's on Your Mind

I'm really upset that John is rejecting his religious training.
Religion has always been so important to our family.
I wonder what they're teaching him up there? To reject Christianity?

What's on Your Child's Mind

My dad is so rigid about religion.
I wish he'd get off my back about it.
I wonder what I really do believe.

What's Going On

During college, students typically question many of the values with which they've been raised. A family with a strong religious tradition may feel shocked to find that their child is rejecting all of that training; even more upsetting may be their child's questioning of basic religious beliefs that the family holds sacred.

What to Do

- Engage your child in a discussion about religion. Use this as an opportunity to talk openly about different religious belief systems.
- Share your beliefs, but recognize your child's right to choose whether he practices your religion.
- Ask what he is learning about himself and explain how you came to believe in your Christian values.
- Remember that the values you have instilled in your child are powerful and lasting, even though he is questioning them at this point.

What to Avoid

- Trying to make your child feel guilty for not going to church.
- Berating his philosophy professor for filling his mind with crazy notions.
- Cutting off the discussion and refusing to listen to his ideas.

What You Need to Know

Scholars have found that most students have a dualistic way of approaching intellectual and ethical problems when they enter college. Dualistic means having a narrow understanding of right and wrong and good versus bad. When tackling intellectual and ethical dilemmas, students who think dualistically tend to believe in an absolute right and wrong, and that authority figures always know the right answer. Throughout the college years, most students move from being dualistic to relativistic in their thinking. They reject dualism in favor of thinking critically about multiple perspectives and trying to determine the most suitable answer to a particular question.

John came to school believing in the Christian values he had learned through church and family. He believed that Christianity was right and other religions were wrong. But when he enrolled in his first philosophy class he began to question the absolute "rightness" of "Jesus as the only son of God," and began to explore the truths expressed in other religious ideologies. He began to see that religious questions may have multiple right answers and that the authority he once accepted without question had only one of the possible right answers. At this point, he may conclude that all religions have equal value and believe that "everyone is entitled to his or her own opinion."

In this dialogue, Dad assumes that John has rejected his Christian values, while John is simply thinking that there is not one absolute right or wrong answer; that is, Buddhism's ideology is just as valid as Christianity's. Parents may interpret this type of thinking as intellectual curiosity, confusion, rebellion, or just plain wishy-washiness. But to John's dad, it signaled that John had taken the first step on a slippery slope to rejecting his Christian heritage and values. However, the chances are good that John, after this period of relativistic thinking in which he explores other ideologies and value systems, will return to a belief in Christianity and have a stronger belief for having questioned it. Before he went to college, John was committed to the family's values; now he is exploring *his* personal religious beliefs. It's possible that he'll eventually make a personal commitment to Christianity; it's also possible that he'll make a commitment to a different religious belief.

Many parents feel alarmed when they realize they have sent a child with cherished values and ideals to college, only to find that their child is questioning and, at least temporarily, rejecting them. As students explore their role and identity in the world, they may also question ideas that are a part of their value system. This intellectual and ethical questioning is an important part of John's identity development. While you can't dictate your child's personal beliefs, you can have an influence on his or her thinking through continuing to discuss these topics openly.

Values/Politics

As a card-carrying liberal Democrat, you were disturbed when your daughter, Caroline, called to tell you she was going to a Right to Life rally over the weekend.

MOM: Hello?

CAROLINE: Hi, Mom. How are you?

MOM: Good, honey. What's up?

CAROLINE: Not too much, other than that I've just decided to attend the Right to Life March on Washington this weekend.

MOM: You are? Did you say, "Right to Life"?

CAROLINE: Yes, I've decided that I'm against abortion and I'm going to do something about it.

MOM: Caroline, no one is *for* abortion. No one would want to have to make that choice, but don't you think women should be able to decide? After all, these are our bodies.

CAROLINE: Mom, that's just such a liberal cop-out. Abortion is killing and that's wrong. How can you be against the death penalty and pro-abortion?

MOM: I'm not pro-abortion. I just told you, I'm pro-choice. And I support Planned Parenthood to help ensure that abortion doesn't have to be the only choice.

CAROLINE: I'm happy that Planned Parenthood is working to increase contraceptive use, but I think it's wrong that they kill babies. So many families want babies and can't have them. And besides, how can you condone killing defenseless babies? It's just wrong.

MOM: Oh, Caroline, it's such a complex issue. Maybe we should talk about it when we have more time.

CAROLINE: It doesn't seem too complicated to me—you either kill babies or you don't. I'll tell you, I'm really beginning to change my mind about a lot of issues. So many of my friends here are in the Young Republicans Club on campus. I went to a meeting last week and I've decided to join. For example, do you know how much we're spending on welfare each year? It's unbelievable, we give all this money to people who just don't feel like getting up and going to work. If we don't stop this now, my generation will have nothing.

MOM: You're joining the Young Republicans? I can't believe it.

What's on Your Mind

What is the matter with her?

Doesn't she realize how hard women have fought for the right to choose?

I can't believe I have a Republican daughter. No one in our family is a Republican.

What's on Your Child's Mind

> I've been brainwashed by my liberal parents.
> I don't believe all the Republican ideas, but I'm not a liberal, either.
> My parents are so "sixties." They don't know what's really going on now.

What's Going On

Politics, like religion, is an expression of personal values and attitudes. Students usually question these basic values during college when confronted with different points of view. Peers, and the general political climate on campus, will undoubtedly influence this exploration of political and social values.

What to Do

- Engage your child in an open discussion of her political beliefs.
- Ask her what is appealing about the Republican point of view.
- Challenge her to think through her opinions on social issues: "I'm curious about why you feel abortion rights should be limited. I'd like to know what you're thinking about this issue."

What to Avoid

- Insisting that she rethink her political views.
- Dismissing her opinions: "You're just not thinking about this in the right way."
- Telling her you're disappointed that she's rejecting everything you've tried to teach her.

What You Need to Know

Caroline, like John in the previous example, may have come to college committed to the political principles with which she was raised. Opening up to new people and ideas in college, she is now questioning some pretty fundamental political and social policy values. She has moved from dualistic thinking ("Democrats are right, Republicans are wrong") to relativism. She questions her Democratic beliefs and begins to see that some of the Republican beliefs she's been exposed to at college are valid and true as well. It's easy for parents to overreact to these intellectual and ethical changes and try to persuade their children to return to an earlier point of view. It may be helpful for parents to remember their own young adulthood and recall in-stances in which they may have moved from dualistic to relativistic thinking before making a commitment to their current values.

Parents who became more liberal than their own parents when they were in college may be surprised when their children are attracted to conservative political views. Your children's values may become more liberal or more conservative than yours, often depending on the be-liefs of friends, the current social culture, and the political climate of the school he or she at-tends. Showing a genuine interest in your child's new ideas and continuing to discuss your own values with your child will help ensure that you maintain a strong relationship.

Special Identity Issues for College Women

During the college years, young women begin to face choices about the future and are often confused about balancing relationships and careers.

Although our culture has come a long way in supporting young women, there are still special questions and challenges for daughters in college, especially those who are pursuing the so-called STEM fields (science, technology, engineering, and math) that have traditionally been dominated by men.

Confused and Unsure

When your daughter, Audrey, was home for midyear break, the following conversation took place.

MOM: What are you planning to do over the summer, honey?

AUDREY: I'm not sure. One of my professors at school told me that I should apply for an internship at Arnold, Jamison, and Cutter, the big accounting firm

MOM: Really? That sounds interesting.

AUDREY: Yeah, but it's really competitive and I probably won't get it. If I did, it would be really intense working with all those math geniuses all summer.

MOM: But, Audrey, you're hoping to become a CPA some day. Wouldn't this be good ex-perience?

AUDREY: I guess so. My professor says that Arnold, Jamison usually hires the people that have done summer internships with them.

MOM: Wow, you might even get a job offer before you graduate from school!

AUDREY: Mom, don't get so excited. I probably don't have a chance at this internship anyway, and I'm not so sure I really want to be away from home and from all my friends for the summer.

MOM: But, Audrey, it sounds like such a great opportunity. Your professor wouldn't have suggested that if she didn't think you were qualified.

AUDREY: Okay, okay. I'll apply for it but I'm not sure I want to do it.

What's on Your Mind

What's wrong with Audrey?
She actually seems scared to apply for this internship.
Why is she dragging her heels on this?

What's on Your Child's Mind

I don't know what to do this summer. Everyone's pressuring me to take this internship.
I don't want to be away from my friends all summer.
I bet I don't know enough about accounting to get this internship.

What's Going On

It's great that Audrey's professor (not surprisingly, a woman herself) has taken an interest in Audrey and is encouraging her to compete to achieve her career goals. We've found that college women, especially those in nontraditional fields for women, need mentoring by important people in their lives, including parents, friends, relatives, teachers, and professors. Daughters need parents and other adults to support their emotional, intellectual, and career development during the college years. Even the brightest and most motivated college women can find themselves losing confidence in themselves and confused about their goals when they see very few women in fields that interest them.

What to Do

- Ask your daughter what has caused her confusion.
- Try to sympathize with the difficult choices she's facing.
- Reinforce how proud you are of her achievements and how much you admire her hard work.

What to Avoid

- Blaming her for her lack of decisiveness and focus.
- Asking her why her friends are more important than this great career opportunity.
- Reminding her of how lucky she is to have so many choices.

What You Need to Know

Several decades ago, Carol Gilligan, and other psychologists who studied girls' development, found that self-confident young girls often became confused when they reached the teen years, and that confusion continued to plague college women as well.[2] More recently, Susan Harter and her colleagues have found that not all adolescent girls lose confidence; those who do are girls with a highly feminine gender-role orientation.[3] This research also revealed that both girls and boys lose confidence when the people who matter to them do not take their views seriously.

Androgynous girls (those who describe themselves as having both typically masculine and feminine characteristics; for example, assertive and gentle) and all adolescents who feel supported by the significant people in their lives remain confident in expressing their views and pursuing their goals throughout high school and college. It is evident that parents can have a great deal of influence by taking their daughters' opinions seriously, especially those daughters who are interested in nontraditional fields of study.

A Chilly Climate for Women

Your daughter has always been an outstanding science student and won numerous awards and scholarships when she graduated from high school. She's now in her sophomore year at the university and she has become disillusioned about going on for a graduate degree in science. Her faculty adviser has told her it can be really tough for women in science when they get to graduate school. She's wondering if she should reconsider her major in physics and her plans to get a PhD.

What's on Your Mind

What has happened to my daughter?
She went there feeling so confident in what she wanted to do.
Why didn't her faculty adviser encourage her?
Is it still so tough for women in science today?

What's on Your Child's Mind

I'm so confused.
Do I really want to commit six or seven years to study science and get a PhD?
My faculty adviser doesn't seem to think I can do it.
What if I *do* want to have a family someday, too?

What's Going On

It's understandable that your daughter is taking her adviser's comment to heart. She's not sure if she can get into graduate school or if she really wants to make that long-term commitment. She may not know any women who have become professors in physics and it's hard for her to see herself as an accomplished scientist if she hasn't seen or known a woman who has taken this path.

What to Do

- Encourage her to seek out women faculty members in science and ask them for advice.
- Remind her that she can switch academic advisers if her current one is not actively supporting her plans.
- Let her know that you have confidence in her ability to make choices about her major and her future course of study.

What to Avoid

- Reinforcing her image as a star science student and discounting her current dilemma.
- Pushing her into going to graduate school or readily accepting her fears.
- Encouraging her to make a quick decision.

What You Need to Know

Although there has been some progress, many colleges and universities have very few, if any, women in the physical sciences to act as mentors or role models for young women. This inadequacy is being addressed by many national science organizations that recognize the vital importance of role models in encouraging young women to pursue careers in the sciences and mathematics. But it may take many more years before women are represented in significant numbers in the scientific community and are able to change the social culture of organizations that have been long-time male enclaves.

Having It All

The following phone call from your daughter, Sara, who is in her junior year at college, has you troubled.

SARA: Hi, Dad.

DAD: Hi, Sara. How are you?

SARA: Pretty good.

DAD: Just pretty good? You don't sound too happy.

SARA: I'm just worried because I'm not sure I want to go to law school anymore.

DAD: What? You just took the LSAT; I thought you were on your way.

SARA: Yeah, I took it, but now I'm not sure where to apply or even if I want to go.

DAD: What's going on? Tell me about it.

SARA: There are so many things I don't know. Where I should go, if I want to go through three more years of school right now, and, of course, the Jake issue.

DAD: What do you mean, "the Jake issue"?

SARA: Well, he's applying to law schools, too, and I really want to be with him. Even if I apply to the same schools he's applying to, we may not get into the same one. Then what will I do?

DAD: Is this about Jake or about law school?

SARA: No, I really want to go . . . well, I think I do, but I also really want to be with Jake.

DAD: Honey, it sounds like you need to decide what *you* want to do. I know Jake is important to you, but, after all, it's just for law school. You can still have Jake in your life if you're not at the same school.

SARA: But, Dad, it would be so hard. I don't know. I'm just so torn.

DAD: But, Sara, you can't plan your whole life around Jake.

SARA: But I love him and I want to be with him. Maybe I'll just put off law school for a few years.

DAD: Is that what you really want to do?

SARA: I don't know! Why do you keep pushing me on this?

DAD: Sorry, honey, I was just trying to help.

SARA: I know. I'm sorry.

What's on Your Mind

I thought Sara was set on going to law school. What happened?
This can't be just about Jake. I hope not.
I wonder how I can help her.

What's on Your Child's Mind

What am I going to do about law school? I have to make a decision soon.
I don't want to follow Jake around but I don't want to be separated, either.
Why is this so hard?

What's Going On

Even though many college graduates today put off marriage and family until their late twenties or early thirties, young women may still be confused about competing roles and demands when making career and graduate school decisions.

What to Do

- Empathize with your daughter's confusion and indecision.
- Ask her if she has discussed this dilemma with her boyfriend.
- Remind her that she is a capable, smart young woman who has worked hard for the opportunity she has now.
- Let her know that you appreciate how torn she is in making this decision.

What to Avoid

- Telling her she can't throw away law school for her boyfriend.
- Reminding her that this relationship may not last anyway.
- Trying to talk her into going to law school regardless of her feelings.

What You Need to Know

Many young women place a high value on relationships and emotional bonds; their search for an answer to the "Who am I?" question is often intimately connected to significant others. This poses a formidable dilemma for young women when looking at their future prospects. More-over, many college women have not had the benefit of the mentoring from faculty that young men receive in formulating career plans. Fathers, in particular, can have a significant impact on how their daughters approach vocational decisions. But fathers can also find it disturbing that their daughters are so focused on personal relationships, seemingly at the expense of their career advancement.

Because intimate attachments and relationships can be so central to many young women's identity development, keep these factors in mind when trying to understand your child's decision-making process. There are no easy or generally applicable solutions, but parents can be sensitive to this dilemma and try to help their daughters sort through conflicting expectations and desires.

Identity Issues for Ethnic and Racial Minority Students

Although we are rapidly becoming a nation of a majority of minorities, young people who are not members of the dominant white culture still face special identity issues during the college years. The scenarios below will help you understand and respond to these challenges.

Exploring Racial Identity

Your son, Eric, is home for fall break and the following conversation takes place:

MOM: Eric, what's this with the dreadlocks?
ERIC: All the brothers at school have dreads, Mom. My college friends are so cool; they're so much more mature than my high school friends were.
MOM: How so?
ERIC: Well, you know, in high school all my friends wanted to be so "white" and do every-thing the white kids did. Now, at college, I hang with the black kids. I haven't even met many white kids there.
MOM: Really?
ERIC: Yeah, my friends at school really understand what's happening. One of them actu-ally got harassed by campus security for being on the quad late at night. He was just walking home and this security guy gave him a hard time. When he told us about it,

we were really steamed. We decided to go to the dean, tell him what happened, and ask him to do something about it.

MOM: Did you get in trouble with the dean?

ERIC: No, Mom, but somebody has to stand up and let people know they can't push us around.

MOM: Well, I just don't want you getting into trouble up there. You need to tend to your studies.

ERIC: I am, Mom, but I'm just sick of our crowd always being suspect. It's not right and you know it, too.

MOM: You can't fight all those battles yourself you know.

ERIC: Maybe not, but I'm going to stick up for my black brothers anyway. They're my friends.

What's on Your Mind

Eric seems so angry.
I wonder what's going on with him at school.
He's never been an activist before.

What's on Your Child's Mind

I'm really angry that black students get harassed.
This never happened in high school.
It's really great to have black friends. They really understand me.

What's Going On

Ethnic and racial identity can take on a new dimension when students get to college. Students who have been raised in middle-class African-American families often suddenly realize that they have not really interacted with other members of their racial group, and that their high school was dominated by white values and attitudes.

What to Do

- Support your child in exploring his racial identity.
- Ask him what it is that makes him feel comfortable with his new friends.
- Let him know that you are proud of his identification with his African-American heritage.

- Tell him about situations in which you have experienced discrimination and what you did about it.
- Reinforce that his academic work should be his highest priority, without dismissing his concerns about racial issues.

What to Avoid

- Reminding him that he lives in a white culture and that he needs to conform.
- Telling him he must keep a low profile and stay out of trouble.

What You Need to Know

The search for identity can be complex for ethnic and racial minorities. Members of nondominant groups often find that their racial identity comes to the forefront when they get to college, according to William Cross, who has studied identity development in African-American students. His findings, although limited to African-Americans, can also be helpful in understanding other minorities' experiences in searching for identity in the dominant culture. Cross found a predictable progression in their ethnic identity development.[4]

If we look at Eric we can see this progression. In high school, Eric tried to fit into the dominant culture. The incident in college with his friend and the security guard jolted him out of his acceptance of the dominant culture when he encountered racism on a personal level. He began to reject the dominant culture and immerse himself in his culture of origin. When Eric came home he had even changed his appearance to more closely identify with his minority group. His friends, for the first time, were mainly African-American. He began to feel pride in his cultural heritage.

Cross would predict that Eric would eventually recognize that there are some good things about the dominant culture, as well as his own minority culture. He would be able to pick and choose which aspects of each culture fit his emerging sense of self and adopt some aspects of each one. He may eventually become committed to helping others deal with the racial identity issues he has experienced. For example, he may become a Big Brother to an African-American youngster and help that youngster feel proud of his minority culture, while helping him succeed within the values of the dominant culture.

While not every college student goes through this process of racial or ethnic identity development, Cross's observations can help parents understand their child's experience as a racial minority in what is still a dominantly white culture in most colleges. Moreover, research indicates that minority students who explore their racial identity have higher self-esteem than those who don't.

Finding Comfort in a Shared Background

Your daughter, Maria, seemed pretty unhappy when you had the following conversation with her this evening:

MARIA: Hi, Mama.

MOM: Hi, Maria. How are you?

MARIA: I miss you guys so much. How is everyone?

MOM: Just fine. Pablo and Grandpapa are out fishing, and Papa has just come home from work. Grandmama is helping me fix dinner. Wish you were here.

MARIA: I miss you all so much. I can't wait to come home for Christmas.

MOM: Aren't you happy there?

MARIA: I'm okay, but everyone here is so different from me. My history professor asked me today what it feels like to be a Latina at the university. I was so embarrassed. I didn't know what to say.

MOM: What did you say?

MARIA: I just told him that I don't have any friends who aren't Latino. It's hard, though, because the whole class is different from me. There are blacks and Asians, but I'm the only Latino in the whole class. And I don't like to speak up anyway.

MOM: Do you know anyone who isn't Latino?

MARIA: Not really. I just feel so much more comfortable with my Latino friends. We're having a party on Saturday night at the student union.

MOM: That sounds like fun, but do you think it's a good idea to be friends with Latinos only?

What's on Your Mind

Maria sounds so homesick.
I hope she can be happy there.
I'm worried about her fitting in.

What's on Your Child's Mind

I feel so out of place here; I really miss my family.
I don't know what I'd do without my Latino friends.
We're so different from everyone else here.

What's Going On

There are so many other adjustments to be made in college that minority students are often drawn to the security of spending time with others who are like them. All students, minority and majority alike, find comfort in relationships with students who share common experiences and backgrounds, especially during the initial transition to college.

What to Do

- Sympathize with your daughter's feelings of isolation and homesickness.
- Let her know that you understand that these feelings are difficult.
- Recognize that this is an important part of the process of exploring her identity in the dominant culture.

What to Avoid

- Asking her if she wants to come home and go to school nearby where there are many other Latinos. (She may do this anyway, but it needs to be her decision.)
- Telling her she'd better get to know some white students or she'll never make it in the "real world."
- Reminding her that you knew she'd feel different at that college and that she'd better learn to speak up in class.

What You Need to Know

Some students have always lived in a minority community and have had little contact with other cultures. For students like this, college may be the first time they have had to live immersed in the dominant culture. In this environment, many minority students are asked to "speak for their entire ethnic group" in class, or become the "token" minority in their residence hall or in college activities. It is not surprising that students, such as Maria, feel more comfortable with other students who share their ethnic background. It's a secure and comfortable place where they can relax and be themselves.

Interracial Dating

Last night you received a phone call from your son, David, and he asked if he could bring his girlfriend home for spring break.

DAVID: Hi, Mom. How are you and Dad and the girls?

MOM: We're fine. How are you? How are your studies going?

DAVID: Oh, I'm fine and I'm doing pretty well in school. I wanted to talk to you about spring break.

MOM: Okay.

DAVID: Well, I was wondering if I could bring Kristen home with me for break? Her parents live in Chicago and it's too far for her to go home.

MOM: Who is this Kristen? Is she Chinese?

DAVID: No, Mom. I think she's part Swedish or something. I'm not sure. But she's really nice. I know you'll like her. She's a premed student, too.

MOM: Aren't there any nice Chinese girls there? I know there must be.

DAVID: Mom! Why do you always ask me that? We're American now and so is Kristen.

MOM: But, David, I don't know how your father will feel about this.

DAVID: I know Dad will like Kristen. She's really smart. In fact, her grandfather is Japanese but he's lived in California since World War II. Her parents were here for fall weekend and they're nice, too.

MOM: Well, I'll talk to your father and we'll see.

DAVID: Okay. And, Mom, if you and Dad say Kristen can come home with me, can we speak English while she's there? You should practice speaking English more anyway.

MOM: We won't say anything. Would that make you happy?

DAVID: Mom, you know what I mean. I like Chinese, but Kristen only knows a few words. She'd feel weird if we spoke Chinese all the time.

MOM: If only you would meet a nice Chinese girl, this wouldn't be a problem. She'd fit in here. What are we going to tell your sisters?

DAVID: I'm sure they'll like Kristen, too. Why are you making such a big deal about this? It's only for a week. It's not like I'm marrying her!

MOM: I'll talk to your father and call you back.

DAVID: Thanks, Mom. Say, "Hi," to everyone.

What's on Your Mind

David is going against his Chinese heritage and everything we've taught him.
I don't understand why he can't find a nice Chinese girl.
What kind of family does this Kristen come from? We'll have nothing in common.

What's on Your Child's Mind

My parents are so old-fashioned.
They're Americans now; why can't they behave like Americans?
I hope they let me bring Kristen home. I really like her.

What's Going On

David wants to be a typical American college student and feels a little embarrassed that he isn't like everyone else. He can live a completely different life on campus. He accepts the dominant culture and likes the white friends he has made. His parents can no longer control who he meets and are worried that his new friend represents a rejection of his Chinese heritage.

What to Do

- Try to accept your child's freedom to choose new friends, even though you'd prefer they were all Chinese.
- Make it clear to him that you are proud of your Chinese culture.
- Ask him to tell you more about his girlfriend and her family.
- Do your part to help his girlfriend feel welcome by speaking English when she's around.

What to Avoid

- Refusing to allow him to bring a new friend home. You are the one who will ultimately lose if you remain inflexible.
- Telling him that you'll never accept it if he marries a non-Chinese girl.
- Trying to make him feel guilty for rejecting his heritage.
- Refusing to speak English to his girlfriend.

What You Need to Know

David is like many second-generation children who have adopted the dominant culture's values as their own. He feels a strong desire to be fully American and may work very hard to "fit in" and be accepted by members of the dominant culture. David may reject his minority culture for years or he may have an experience that leads him to reexamine the role his ethnic culture plays in his identity. For example, he may join a Chinese students group in protesting the treatment of Chinese dissidents and become fascinated with Chinese culture. He may even want to travel to China to study and learn more about his heritage. It's important to remember, though, that he must work through his ethnic identity on his own. Parents can't force a child to embrace his heritage before he's ready, but they can make this process more comfortable for everyone if they support him throughout his development, even during times when they disagree with him and feel rejected.

Identity Issues for Lesbian, Gay, Bisexual, and Transgender Students

Campus communities vary in their tolerance and acceptance of lesbian, gay bisexual, and transgender students. If your child has come out before choosing a college, he or she probably assessed the college's climate before enrolling and may have an easier adjustment. However, if your child comes out during college you will need to be especially aware of and sensitive to the identity issues that will arise.

Coming Out—Your Son

When your son, Jacob, arrived home for holiday break, he said he had something important to discuss with you.

> JACOB: Mom, Dad . . . I have something to tell you. I'm gay and actually I've known I was gay for quite a long time.
> MOM: Oh, Jacob, no. How can you be gay? No one in our family is gay.
> DAD: What made you come up with this crazy notion? You've always been a regular guy, a good athlete and everything.

JACOB: I know this is a surprise to you guys, but I wanted to be honest with you. I've never been attracted to girls and I've been hanging out a lot with a guy I recently met at school.

MOM (crying): How can you do this to us? Haven't we always been good parents?

DAD: Look what you've done to your mother. No son of mine is gay!

JACOB: Mom, Dad . . . I'm sorry if you're upset, but I hoped you'd understand.

DAD: Look, let's calm down. I know what we can do. Our minister talked about a group that helps homosexuals recover. I'll call him right now. We'll straighten out this mess.

JACOB: Dad, you don't get it. I'm gay and I don't need to be cured. It's not a disease.

DAD: Well, I think it is and it's a sin as well. We're going to do something about this *now*!

JACOB: Well, you go right ahead, but I'm going back to school *now*!

What's on Mom's Mind

What's happened to Jacob? He's always been such a good boy.
I can't believe this is happening to us. We've always tried to be good parents.
What are his grandparents going to think? We can't tell them—or our friends.

What's on Dad's Mind

Jacob's been taken in by some weirdo group up there at the university.
He can't do this to us.
I'm going to get him in that program and fix this before anyone finds out.

What's on Your Child's Mind

I really wanted to be honest with my parents.
I hoped they would understand.
I guess they're going to disown me now.
I feel so lost and ashamed after talking to them.

What's Going On

Many parents are shocked and hurt when a son announces that he is gay. This admission can go against deeply held values and religious beliefs, and parents can find it difficult to set aside their fears and listen to their child.

Coming Out—Your Son: The Replay

Let's replay this dialogue with Jacob and his parents, and see how it could have gone. We recognize that the conversation below is an ideal one and that very few parents could make such a rapid adjustment to this surprising news.

JACOB: Mom, Dad . . . I have something important to tell you. I'm gay and actually I've known I was gay for quite a long time.

MOM: Oh, Jacob! I guess I am shocked. How do you know?

JACOB: Well, as I said, I think I've known since seventh grade that I wasn't attracted to girls. I just didn't know what to do. I was afraid to tell anyone. When I got to college, I decided to be honest with myself. I went to a meeting of the LGBT Coalition on campus and I met so many great people. They were so nice and I started to feel much better about myself.

DAD: I'm really sorry that you've been troubled about this for so long. It must have taken a lot of courage for you to tell us.

JACOB: I was worried that you'd be upset, but I wanted you to know. It's important to me.

MOM: Of course it is, Jacob. I'm so glad that you found some support at school.

JACOB: Yeah, there's a big group up there. We do things together and it's fun, but there's still a lot of homophobia on campus.

DAD: That's not surprising. I'm glad you told us, but I worry about how hard your life is going to be. It won't be easy.

JACOB: I know, Dad, but I can't change who I am.

MOM: I worry about your health.

JACOB: I do, too, Mom. And I promise you I'm not going to take any chances. I would never have unsafe sex with anyone.

MOM: That's good. I guess we're going to need some time to think about this news.

DAD: You know, son, we'll always be your parents and, no matter what, we'll always love you.

JACOB: Thanks guys.

What's on Mom's Mind

I always wondered why Jacob didn't go out with girls. Now I know.
I'm worried about what lies ahead for Jacob.
How am I going to tell the relatives? I hope they'll accept Jacob's homosexuality.

What's on Dad's Mind

This is a huge shock, but I'm glad that Jacob felt he could tell us.

I wonder what this means about my fathering. Is it nature or nurture?

This is hard to accept and understand, but we have to. He's going to have a difficult enough time without us giving him grief.

What's on Your Child's Mind

I'm relieved that I finally told Mom and Dad.

They seemed pretty cool about it. I hope they're not too worried.

I guess I'm lucky. Some of my friends' parents really freaked out when they came out.

What's Going On

Although Jacob's parents were shocked by his news, they were able to focus on his feelings and respond with love and compassion. This represents a model scenario, but one that may not reflect the time, care, and concern necessary to absorb the impact that this revelation can have on families. It may take years for parents to come to terms with having a gay child; this interaction does not take place once and get settled for good.

It's normal for parents initially to wonder what they did wrong and to question their parenting. Parents often see their children as a second chance at life and they want their kids to be richer, smarter, happier, and wiser; coming out can mean lost hopes and the necessity to change expectations. Many parents feel a measure of grief when a child comes out. Jacob's parents set their feelings aside to let him know that they accepted his sexual orientation and that they would always love him. They have begun a dialogue that is respectful of Jacob, and have shared their concerns with caring, not judgment. Because of this attitude, Jacob can continue to share his life and choices with them openly as he explores his gay identity.

What to Do

- Try to focus on your child and the importance, to him, of coming out.
- Recognize how difficult this is for him.
- Let him know what your concerns are in a reasoned and calm way.

What to Avoid

- Making this your problem.
- Letting him know how disappointed you are.
- Blaming yourself or your parenting for his choice.
- Keeping this a secret from friends and family.

What You Need to Know

There is a great variation in the age at which individuals identify themselves as homosexual. Most gay men realize they are gay in high school or earlier; others may not fully know this about themselves until they get to college. Coming out to parents is a critical event, one during which parents need to separate how they feel about their child's sexual orientation from how they feel about their child. Acceptance is the most important gift a parent can give a lesbian, gay, bisexual, or transgender child.

Coming Out—Your Daughter

Your daughter Rebecca, is home for fall break and has brought a girlfriend with her. At breakfast on Saturday morning, you have the following conversation with her.

MOM: Hi, honey. How did you sleep?

REBECCA: Fine, Mom. What's for breakfast?

MOM: You can have cereal or eggs, or I could make waffles.

REBECCA: Waffles. I love your waffles!

MOM: What about Lauren? Is she coming down for breakfast?

REBECCA: I doubt it. She's definitely not a morning person. We probably won't see her 'til noon.

MOM: Lauren seems like a nice girl but I was wondering, does she always dress like that?

REBECCA: What do you mean, "like that"?

MOM: Well, she just looked so mannish with those boots and all. I mean, she's not very feminine is she?

REBECCA: Mom, she's a lesbian!

MOM: Honey, you don't have to yell at me. I was just asking.

REBECCA: Well, aren't you going to ask about me? After all, I slept with her last night.

MOM: I know she slept in your room last night. I made the beds.

REBECCA (loudly): No, we didn't just have a "sleepover," Mom. I mean we're sleeping together, we're in love.

MOM: Why are you shouting at me?

REBECCA: Because I want you to listen to me. I'm attracted to women, okay?

MOM: You can't be! You've had lots of boyfriends.

REBECCA: I'm not saying I don't like guys. I'm saying right now I'm in love with Lauren.

MOM: Rebecca, I don't understand this. Are you trying to pick a fight?

REBECCA: No, Mom, I'm just trying to tell you I'm a lesbian or I may be bisexual. I'm not sure.

MOM: Honey, I've heard lots of kids go through phases like this. It's okay. I know you'll find a nice young man someday and settle down.

REBECCA: Mom, you are so clueless! Don't you hear what I'm saying?

MOM: Yes, I do, and I don't like you raising your voice like that.

What's on Your Mind

Rebecca can't be a lesbian. I don't even know what that means really.
She's always had boyfriends.
This is a just a phase. She'll get over it.
Why is she so confrontational with me?

What's on Your Child's Mind

I can't believe I finally told my mother and she won't listen.
This is important to me and she's treating me like I'm ten years old.
I wish I hadn't said anything.

What's Going On

When Rebecca tried to tell her mother about her relationship with Lauren, her mother dismissed her announcement. They began shouting at each other, neither one really listening to the other. Rebecca's mother started the interaction by commenting on Lauren's looks, which made Rebecca feel defensive, and the conversation went downhill from there. This is probably not how Rebecca envisioned coming out to her mother.

What to Do

- Listen to your child. Respond to what your child is saying.
- Ask her what she means if you don't understand.
- Recognize that she is going to make her own choices and that it is difficult for her to be open with you.
- Be willing to accept her girlfriend, just as you would be willing to accept her boyfriend.

What to Avoid

- Brushing off your child's announcement. Scolding her for being confrontational.
- Telling your child that this is just a phase that she'll get over.
- Letting your fears impede your ability to listen.

What You Need to Know

Today, young women, as well as young men, are coming out when they are in high school or college. Parents often believe that their daughters are involved in this one unusual relationship and that they'll "grow out of it" in time. Many young people switch between bisexual and gay/lesbian orientations at different points in their identity development. If a child identifies as bisexual, parents should not assume that this is just a phase or confusion. Bisexuality exists and it's not necessarily a 50/50 situation. Interviews with college women revealed a wide range of behavior. Some bisexual women reported that only 20 percent of their attractions were for women and others reported that 80 percent of their attractions were for women.

Whether young people identify as gay, lesbian, or bisexual can depend on their current relationship. For many lesbian and bisexual women, the primary concern is not "labeling" themselves but the importance of the relationship they currently have. More women than men come out in the context of a specific relationship. This doesn't necessarily mean that the child is confused about her sexual identity. In fact, most gay men and lesbian women have agonized for years about their sexual orientation before coming out to their parents. Parents need to realize the struggle involved when their kids come out—usually it is not a passing phase or an adolescent rebellion. This revelation requires that both parents and children exercise patience, while recognizing that it may take time for them to feel comfortable with this reality. Parents need to stand by and support their children as they mature into their identity as a homosexual, lesbian, bisexual, or transgender man or woman.

Fortunately, most campuses today have support systems in place for lesbian, gay, bisexual, and transgender students. (There is more about on-campus services for LGBT students in Chapter 7.) PFLAG (Parents, Families, and Friends of Lesbians and Gays) is an organization devoted to helping parents learn about homosexuality and support each other in coming to terms with being the parent of a lesbian, gay, bisexual, or transgender son or daughter. This organization has chapters all over the country and it may be something you want to explore.

Autonomy

A natural outgrowth of achieving an individual identity is a desire for autonomy or independence from parents and family. This doesn't mean disconnection or detachment. In fact, the healthiest adolescents remain connected to family as they become increasingly self-directed and independent. But one of the disturbing parts of a child's search for autonomy is that it often begins with a rejection of parents in favor of friends.

Parents' Weekend

When you called your daughter to talk about your trip to campus for parents' weekend, she seemed excited to see you. However, when you arrived at her dorm room at noon, she had left a note on the door saying she had to study for a midterm and would see you at dinner. You were surprised and slightly hurt. When you returned at six o'clock in the evening to meet your daughter, you had an awkward dinner together. You eagerly grilled her about college life, and she responded with one-word answers. The only time she seemed to engage in the conversation was to remind you that she had to get back to the dorm to get ready for a party. The weekend went downhill from there—you hovered and felt unwelcome; your daughter spent a lot of time sleeping, in the library, and with her friends. The only shared activities were having dinner and going to the mall to buy things for her room.

What's on Your Mind

> Why did I even bother to come for parents' weekend?
> I feel hurt and rejected by my child.
> All she wants from me is money.
> I want to be a part of her life.

What's on Your Child's Mind

Why did my parents have to come this weekend? I have so much to do.
What am I supposed to do with them when they're here? They don't fit in.
I wish I could just be with my friends.

What's Going On

Parents' weekend is often a disappointing time for parents. Your child may not yet be comfortable enough at college to welcome you into the social mix. The independence your child is beginning to feel may not be strong enough to "test" by including parents in this new reality. Your child is taking the first steps toward autonomy and needs to shift dependence on you to dependence on friends as a step toward independence. This shift usually begins in middle or high school, but because you were a part of your child's everyday life, it probably didn't seem so dramatic. Eventually, she will see how she can maintain a relationship with you while still being independent and self-directed. It will help if you can step back and see the big picture regarding your child's development.

What to Do

- Prepare yourself before you go to parents' weekend.
- Ask your child if he or she really wants you to come—midterm exams or papers may loom ahead.
- Make your needs and expectations clear and find out what your child's needs and expectations are before you make travel plans.
- Ask your child to arrange a dinner with some of her friends' parents—at least the other parents will talk to you.
- Plan some activities for yourself. Don't expect your child to be an attentive host all weekend.

What to Avoid

- Feeling rejected and angry.
- Arriving with expectations that are hard for your child to fulfill, such as spending lots of time with you.
- Expecting your child to be thrilled to see you and be able to entertain you all weekend.

What You Need to Know

First, it's helpful to remember your child as a two-year-old. You can probably recall your child shouting "No!" and running away from you. Seconds later, that same child would clutch your legs and want to be picked up. The two-year-old needs to push away and separate from parents; at the same time, he or she is completely dependent. Two-year-olds and adolescents have a lot in common—they both tend to ricochet between the security needs of being a child and the individuality needs of learning to be a separate person. While it is frustrating and confusing to deal with these extremes, it's comforting to know that this push-pull process of trying to separate from parents is absolutely necessary and typical behavior—in a two-year-old and in an adolescent.

The tumultuous twos were followed by the relatively placid childhood years when your child idolized you, followed by the preadolescent and teen years when your child began to break away from you in favor of peer relationships. All of these stages happened while you were there, playing the traditional role of parent—monitoring, supporting, directing, caring, and being involved in your child's daily life. Now your child is away from home for most of the year and, truthfully, you may not have much daily influence on your child's behavior. You can't know what is going on all the time and you may not want to know all the details!

How can you maintain a good relationship while your child is on this roller-coaster quest for identity and autonomy during the college years? How can you still be a positive influence as your child takes on the privileges and responsibilities of fully independent adulthood? We suggest that you review Chapter 1 for pointers on laying the groundwork for a new kind of relationship with your child.

Big Trouble

You called your son, Peter, yesterday and the following conversation took place:

> PETER: Hello?
>
> MOM: Hi, Pete. How are you?
>
> PETER: All right, I guess. I've been meaning to call you.
>
> MOM: Why? Is something wrong?
>
> PETER: Well, I'm sort of in a bit of trouble.
>
> MOM: What kind of trouble?
>
> PETER: A couple of weeks ago at a fraternity party, I was in a fight with a real jerk from another house who crashed the party. He started hassling me and I just lost it. I

punched him and he was so drunk he fell down and broke his arm. Now I'm in deep trouble with the dean of students.

MOM: Oh, Peter. That's awful. What's going to happen? Is the other boy all right?

PETER: I don't know what's going to happen yet. Yeah, the other guy has a cast but he'll be all right I guess.

MOM: Well, what's going on now?

PETER: The dean of students has decided to bring me in front of the student judicial board and let them decide the punishment. I'll have to present my case. I have witnesses that the other guy was hassling me, but I don't know what they'll do to me.

MOM: That sounds really serious.

PETER: I know. I could get kicked out of school. I just can't believe this is happening. It's a nightmare.

MOM: Why didn't you call and tell us?

PETER: I just thought I could handle this myself. Now, I'm not so sure. I guess the dean wants to talk to you and Dad. Could you call him?

MOM: Yes, of course. But, Peter, what can we do to help you?

PETER: Nothing really, Mom. I have to argue my case and hope it comes out okay.

MOM: Do you need an attorney?

PETER: No, it's just the school judicial board. I don't think they have lawyers.

MOM: Do you have anyone who can advise you on preparing your case?

PETER: I don't know. I can ask the dean.

MOM: I hope you can get some help.

PETER: I'm really sorry to worry you and really sorry this happened.

MOM: I guess we all make mistakes and have to learn from them the hard way. What have you learned from this so far?

PETER: Not to let your emotions get control of you, especially after you've had a few drinks. And how scary it is to really hurt someone. I mean, what if he had hit his head and died? This mistake has really made me think.

MOM: That's good, Peter. It's important that you learn something from this and that you let the dean and others on campus know what you've learned.

PETER: Do you think I should tell them that? Isn't that kind of like admitting I did something wrong?

MOM: Yes, it is. But, you know, and they know, that you did something wrong. They need to know that you learned something from this incident that will help you grow into a more mature person when faced with these situations in the future. Do you see what I mean?

PETER: Yeah, I guess so.

MOM: It's called being an adult and taking responsibility for your actions, Sometimes we learn the most from the most painful situations. I'm sorry you have to learn this hard lesson. Remember that we love you and think you are a good person in spite of what you did.

PETER: Thanks, Mom. I'll call you tomorrow after I meet with the dean again. Maybe we can work something out so I can stay in school. I hope so.

MOM: So do I, honey. You know you can call on us if you need help and I'll wait to hear from you tomorrow. Take care of yourself.

PETER: Okay. Bye, Mom.

What's on Your Mind

I can't believe Peter is in so much trouble and we didn't even know it.

These frat parties seem really out of control.

I hope Peter doesn't get kicked out of school. That would be hard on all of us.

I'm worried about him and feel so helpless.

What's on Your Child's Mind

Boy, I really blew it this time.

I'm glad my parents still love me even though I screwed up.

I sure hope I don't get kicked out. What would I do?

This is so unfair. I'm not the only one who gets in fights.

What's Going On

Peter is trying very hard to be independent and to handle the consequences of his behavior. He didn't automatically call on his parents to straighten things out for him. While it's not easy for his parents, Peter is showing healthy signs of achieving autonomy and taking responsibility for his actions.

What to Do

- Accept the fact that this is your child's dilemma to resolve, not yours.
- Be supportive and make suggestions as he handles this problem without trying to "fix it" for him.
- Listen to his fears and anxieties and let him know that you sympathize.
- Remind him that you are willing to help if you can and that you love him.

What to Avoid

- Scolding your son. He doesn't need reminding that he screwed up.
- Protecting him from the natural consequences of his behavior. The college will see to it that he's held accountable.
- Calling the dean and trying to plead your son's case for him. When you call, it's appropriate to let the dean know that you are aware of the situation and that, while you support your son, you understand the gravity of the infraction and can appreciate the college's point of view as well.

What You Need to Know

Adolescents who have become autonomous can relinquish their dependence on their parents and take responsibility for their actions. However, students who have achieved a sense of themselves as separate and responsible people still need parents as trusted advisers. Although students may wish their parents could bail them out of difficult situations, it is important that they learn how to manage these predicaments on their own. In this instance, Peter's mom reacted appropriately, exhibiting what we would call an authoritative style of parenting—valuing her son's developing autonomy and independence while still providing a loving and supportive connection.

    The development of identity and autonomy is a complex and interactive phenomenon. You have had significant influence on your child's development from the beginning and your child's unique personality has, no doubt, affected the parenting style you adopted. This is a two-way street and it's important to keep in mind that, particularly when your child is a late adolescent, his behavior is not necessarily a direct response to your parenting style. But it is still true that the way you parent, especially during the college years, can continue to have an impact on your child's ability to develop his or her own identity and autonomy.

How Parenting Styles Relate to the Search for Identity and Autonomy

Researchers have developed the following scheme for classifying parenting styles.[5] They have identified two aspects of a parent's behavior toward a child as critical: parental responsiveness and parental demandingness. In the following chart you can see that authoritative parents are high on responsiveness and demandingness.

PARENTING STYLES

Demandingness

	High	Low
High (Responsiveness)	Authoritative	Indulgent
Low	Authoritarian	Indifferent

Authoritative parents are warm but firm, setting high expectations that are consistent with the child's developing abilities and needs. They value their child's developing autonomy and self-direction and provide a solid and loving base of support for their child's exploration. When disciplining their children they explain their rules and decisions. Authoritative parents are more likely to have healthy, supportive, and satisfying relationships with their children.

Authoritarian parents value obedience and believe that children should accept their authority. They tend to discourage independence and do not want their children to question the standards they set. There is little give and take in these relationships.

Indulgent parents take little interest in shaping their child's behavior. They impose few demands and allow their child a great deal of freedom. They tend to believe that their child will continue to rely on them for help and that any imposition of expectations would be an infringement on their child's freedom.

Indifferent parents spend as little time as possible interacting with their children and know very little about their children's activities, friends, and school performance. Indifferent parents structure their lives around their own needs and interests, rarely engaging their child in discussion or considering their child's opinions when making decisions. In extreme cases, indifferent parents may be considered neglectful parents.

In summary, researchers have found that adolescents raised by authoritative parents are more responsible, confident, socially competent, self-reliant, adaptive, creative, curious, and successful in school. Adolescents raised in authoritarian homes, in contrast, are more dependent, passive, anxious about social comparison, and less socially skilled, self-assured, and intellectually curious. In addition, they tend to have poor communication skills and difficulty initiating activity. Adolescents raised in indulgent households are often more irresponsible and conforming to their peers, less mature, and less able to assume positions of leadership. They often have difficulty abiding by rules and regulations and exercising self-control and, hence, are less socially adept. Adolescents raised by indifferent parents are often impulsive and more likely to be involved in delinquent behavior and in precocious experiments with sex, drugs, and alcohol.[6]

Authoritative parenting provides a healthy balance between restrictiveness and autonomy. This style allows you to have continued influence in your college student's life, while being supportive, warm, and loving as they experience the challenging process of developing identity and autonomy. Of course, your child's temperament—whether your child is compliant or defiant—will have an effect on your parenting style as well. But whatever your child's temperament, the combination of responding to his or her needs while expecting mature and responsible behavior will serve you well.

It is a major task for college students to forge an individual identity and to achieve autonomy from parents. This process starts in early adolescence and may extend well into young adulthood. During the college years, however, students live in a kind of "bubble of safety" in which they can safely explore and experiment with the key question: "Who am I?" Being out from under parental supervision and control and not having the day-to-day responsibilities of taking care of themselves (i.e., earning a living and paying bills), they are free to "try on" a number of identities to see if they fit. This is not frivolous "acting out," it is a necessary step along the path to maturity.

While it may be disturbing to witness your child ricochet from one lifestyle, major, value system, or fashion statement to another, it is reassuring to know that, while you may not have as much influence on their tastes, friends, and fashions, the vast majority of young adults do not stray far from the basic values that are important to their parents. Parents who understand and expect this behavior can relax a bit and enjoy watching this process unfold during the college years.

It's also useful to know that this process of developing identity can be significantly different for individual students. The amount and extent of experimentation a college student engages in depends largely upon his or her social class, family background, temperament, ethnicity, race, and/or gender. Some students, due primarily to family circumstances, do not have the freedom to engage in this sort of experimentation.

Understanding that your child is working hard at adjusting to college life, developing a unique identity, and striving to be an independent adult will help you to see the big picture in all kinds of situations throughout your son's or daughter's college years.

Chapter 6

Just When You Get Used to the Empty Nest, They're Back!

Coping with Continuing Changes in the Family

We were all looking forward to having Lauren come home for fall break, but the weekend was a nightmare. None of us had anticipated how different she would be. She was rude and ignored us most of the time. The truth is, we could hardly wait for her to get on the bus back to school so that we could return to our normal family life again.

Your Family System

The family system is like a mobile. Just as a mobile must find a new balance when a piece is removed, the family, too, needs to readjust when a child goes off to college and creates an imbalance in the family system.

Let's say you are a family with a mother, father, and two children. When one of your children enters college, several changes take place. You may notice a change in your relationship with your spouse; you will probably have more time to spend together, due to a decrease in child-related responsibilities and activities. You may refocus your attention on your remaining child, who essentially becomes an only child overnight. Your son or daughter still at home may feel at a loss without a brother or sister around and may not welcome your undivided attention. The balance in a family system is altered if any member leaves the fold, but the adjustments can be particularly unsettling when a child goes to college, because that child will breeze in and out of the family home often during breaks and vacations. You may feel more like you're running a respite home for a stressed-out student rather than welcoming your child back into the family unit.

Whether you live in a family with a mother, father, and children, or in a single-parent, blended, or in other ways nontraditional family, your family will change dramatically, especially when your first or last child goes off to college. This chapter will help you understand your family as a dynamic system that can support the growth and development of all of its members.

The Empty Nest

A few weeks after Courtney left for college, her parents had the following conversation:

MARTHA: Boy, it sure seems quiet around here without Courtney and her gang of friends coming in and out all the time. I can't wait 'til she comes home for fall break.

DAN: I know. It's funny, but I even miss her arguing about her curfew, running up to her room, and slamming the door.

MARTHA: Yeah, I can't believe I complained about driving to all of her soccer games and having dinner on the table at a certain time to fit her schedule.

DAN: I guess we have a lot more freedom now. We can eat whenever we want and we could even go away for the weekend on the spur of the moment. Maybe we should drive up north this weekend and look at the fall color. What do you think? I could get us a reservation somewhere. We could sleep late and go for walks in the woods.

MARTHA: I guess we could. Just the two of us, huh?

DAN: Hey, it could be fun. Just the two of us on a romantic weekend alone. Let's do it!

MARTHA: Okay, but we'd better call Courtney and let her know we're going away.

DAN: Yeah, I'm sure she's going to miss the homecoming activities worrying about where we are! Seriously, hon, I doubt if she cares much about what we're doing, but let her know if you want to.

MARTHA: Okay, but what will we do for a whole weekend up north?

DAN: We'll just enjoy each other's company. Remember when we used to spend whole weekends just talking and hanging out together, before we had the kids?

MARTHA: Sort of.

DAN: You don't sound too excited about getting away. What's the matter?

MARTHA: I don't know. I guess I still feel pretty sad about Courtney leaving home. It didn't seem so dramatic when Matt left for college. That seems like ages ago. Doesn't it feel strange to have our kids gone?

DAN: Yeah, but it could be worse. They could both still be hanging around here! Come on, hon, lighten up. We've been good parents, now we get to be a couple again.

What's on Martha's Mind

I miss being a mom. Who am I now?

It's strange spending so much time alone with Dan.

Our family will never be the same again. That makes me sad, even though I know it's for the best.

What's on Dan's mind

I miss the kids, too, but Martha seems really heartbroken that they're gone.

I wonder if she still loves me as much as she did before we had the kids.

Why can't she enjoy just being with me?

What's Going On

Martha and Dan feel that odd combination of emptiness and freedom now that their last child has gone off to college. They are not sure how to relate to each other without the buffer of children and the involvement that childrearing required for so many years of their married life.

What to Do

- Talk to your spouse about your feelings.
- Give yourself time to come to terms with the changes occurring in your family and in your relationship. These adjustments don't feel comfortable overnight.
- Consider getting some marriage counseling if you feel that your relationship needs work.

What to Avoid

- Ignoring the major change that the empty nest presents.
- Expecting your spouse to be cheerful about this loss.
- Criticizing your spouse for not having the same reaction to this change that you have.

What You Need to Know

When your last child leaves home for college, it is not unusual to feel confused and conflicted about your relationship with your spouse. You may have put your marriage on hold during the all-consuming years of child-rearing, and it may now be obvious that your marriage has been neglected. Suddenly, the focus in your relationship with your spouse is shifting from primarily parenting together to the satisfaction and enjoyment you feel in each other's company. More than ever, your reasons for being together stem from what you have to offer one another as life partners and less from what you shared as parents. If there are problems in your marriage, they will probably surface now.

Even though your child will reappear from time to time during the college years, and your older adult children undoubtedly will have a presence in your life, the old family structure has changed forever. In fact, many couples find this a liberating and rewarding change; they welcome the opportunity to rediscover who they are as a couple and as individuals. Letting go of your parenting role doesn't happen overnight, but it can bring long-term satisfaction in reconnecting with your spouse or partner.

The Lone Sibling

You're a little disturbed by the following conversation you had with your younger son, Aaron, a few weeks after his older brother left for college.

> MOM: Aaron, what's the matter with you? You spend all of your time in your room lately.
> AARON: It just seems so quiet around here without Chad.
> MOM: I thought you couldn't wait 'til he left and you had first dibs on the car!
> AARON: Yeah, he was a pain most of the time, but it really feels weird with him gone.
> MOM: Well, he'll still come home for vacations.
> AARON: But that's a long time from now. You and Dad don't seem to miss him too much. I guess you get to bug me full time now.
> MOM: Of course we miss him. What do you mean we're bugging you full time?
> AARON: It just seems so weird without Chad here. I can't wait 'til I can go to college, too. It's so boring here! Could we call Chad and see what's going on?

What's on Your Mind

> What's wrong with Aaron?
> I thought he'd be happy with all of the attention.
> Maybe he misses Chad more than he wants to admit.

What's on Your Child's Mind

It seems so strange here without Chad. I thought I'd really like it when he left. It's no fun here. Mom and Dad are either breathing down my neck or ignoring me. I wonder what Chad will be like when he comes home. I bet he's forgotten I exist.

What's Going On

It's easy for parents to overlook the impact this change can have on younger children. Aaron may not like to admit it, but he's feeling the loss of his big brother. It will take time for the family to readjust to Chad's absence and realign their relationships as a family group. Everything Chad is doing seems exotic and interesting, while Aaron is just the same old Aaron, hanging around the house and having to deal with his parents on his own.

What to Do

- Encourage Aaron to talk about his feelings about Chad's departure.
- Let him know that it's natural to feel ambivalent about being left home alone.
- Ask Aaron if he'd like to talk to Chad about planning a weekend visit to him at school.
- Be honest about your feelings of loss, but reinforce how important Aaron is, too.

What to Avoid

- Reminding Aaron of how anxious he was to get rid of his older brother and have the house to himself.
- Ignoring his feelings of loss, even though he doesn't express them directly.
- Telling him not to worry, that Chad will be home soon for break.

What You Need to Know

It's easy for parents to dwell on their own feelings of loss and overlook the feelings that their other children may have. Parents need to engage younger siblings in discussions about how they feel when an older child leaves. Even though your children might have had a contentious relationship, that doesn't mean that the younger child will accept this change easily. In many families, the younger child genuinely misses the older child's companionship. The older child may have played the role of mediator between the younger child and the parents and now the younger sibling must deal with the parents directly without much experience in doing so. Moreover, the older child may have been a caregiver to the younger one, almost a surrogate parent, as well as a pal. These are big changes.

It's usually not a coincidence if younger children act out when an older child leaves for college. The family is thrown into imbalance and the younger child may question his identity within the family group. He may believe that you expect him to fill the vacuum left by the absent brother and this can make him feel angry and isolated. The child left behind needs to be reassured that he is still a unique and valuable member of the family.

The Boomerang Effect

Your daughter is a freshman at college. When she comes home for fall break, the whole family is eager to reconnect with her and listen to her stories of college life. She, however, has a different agenda. She arrives home late Friday night and immediately phones her old high school friends. She dumps her dirty laundry in the basement and announces that she's going out. You don't see her again until she drags herself out of bed at one o'clock the next day and calls her college roommate. The rest of the break you hardly see her—she's either sleeping, holed up in her room, hanging out with friends, or talking on the phone.

What's on Your Mind

> I was really looking forward to seeing her and hearing about college.
> She acts like this is a bed-and-breakfast, not her family home.
> Why doesn't she want to spend any time with us?

What's on Your Child's Mind

> Boy, it's nice to be home. I love my room.
> It's so great to get some sleep, eat good food, and not worry about classes.
> It's fun to see my old high school friends.

What's Going On

Your daughter has been away from home long enough to feel like a free agent in the world. It doesn't occur to her that she has some responsibility to interact with the family. She's on break and enjoying the comforts of home, oblivious to the family's needs. Her family is excited about being together again but has some unrealistic expectations for the weekend.

What to Do

- Talk to her about what she wants to do during her break before she comes home.
- Discuss your expectations with her. If you don't want to stay up worrying about her coming in at 3:00 A.M., let her know that.
- Have a family meeting to discuss important issues: who gets to drive the car and when, expectations about meals and get-togethers with extended family members, chores you expect your child to resume, and whether curfews are still in force.
- You will need to renegotiate her hours and family responsibilities while she's home from school. Remember that she's been able to set her own hours at school. Don't assume that she'll easily revert to the curfew you set during high school.
- Prepare yourself and other family members. You will be welcoming home a child with her own set of expectations.

What to Avoid

- Planning family activities before discussing them with her.
- Feeling rejected because she doesn't spend much time with the family.
- Being a doormat—cooking all of her favorite foods and putting your life on hold while you wait for her to interact with the family.

What You Need to Know

Family members need to prepare themselves for an adjustment every time a college student comes home and every time he or she leaves again. Most students get used to having complete autonomy at school and they may have trouble returning to rules and siblings during weekend and vacation visits. Parents who have grown accustomed to the relative peace and quiet may be dismayed by the sudden influx of friends, loud music playing at all hours, and the erratic schedules that college students keep. And those same parents may find the loneliness and adjustment hard when their child returns to school. Imagine how it would be if any member of the family went away for significant periods of time, only to return for a few days and then leave again.

It's appropriate and necessary to set new guidelines with your college student about her behavior during breaks. Don't assume that she will fall right back into the family routine. Before vacations, talk to your child about your expectations. For example, if you had a curfew during high school, talk about whether it still applies. It's okay to ask your child to make some adjustments when he or she comes home. While your child has no family responsibilities at school, it's different when she comes home and is part of the household again. It's not helpful to say, "You're living under my roof now, you'll do what I say." You might say, "I understand that you have lots of freedom to set your own schedule at school and that's okay; however, when you're home with the rest of the family, we expect you to respect our schedules, too. Can we compromise on your hours and activities?"

You may expect the same high school child to return home from college; however, your child will want to be seen as different and independent from the family. This family change requires that you talk about your needs and be clear about your expectations. You have a right to expect that your son or daughter treat you and other family members with respect when he or she returns home. You also need to prepare yourself for the inevitable range of feelings you'll have as your son or daughter moves between college and home many times during each year.

Single Parent

Anna, a single mother, is surprised by the behavior of daughter, Leah, in the following phone call:

MOM: Hi, Leah. How are you doing?

LEAH: Oh, hi, Mom, I'm glad you called. I've been wondering how your new job is going. What's it like?

MOM: It's good. I think it's going to be a good change for me.

LEAH: That's great.

MOM: There's another change in my life, too.

LEAH: Really? What?

MOM: Well, I met this really nice man last week and we've already gone out a couple of times. We had the best time last night. He took me out for dinner and a movie.

LEAH: You're dating someone?

MOM: Pretty amazing, huh?

LEAH: So, do you like him? Are you going to go out with him again?

MOM: I hope so.

LEAH: Mom, you sound like a teenager. What are you doing?

MOM: I'm just having a good time.

LEAH: Well, I guess that's cool. So, are you still coming down for parents' weekend or do you have a hot date?

MOM: Leah, *really*, of course I'm coming. I can't wait to see you!

What's on Your Mind

Leah seems almost annoyed at me for going out on a date.
What's her problem?
I have a right to have some fun, too.

What's on Your Child's Mind

I can't believe my mom's dating. This is so weird.
I wonder who this guy is.
It's always been just my mom and me. What will happen now?

What's Going On

Anna and Leah have had a close relationship since Anna divorced her father when Leah was three years old. Anna has focused on being a good parent and has put her own needs on hold while raising Leah. Now that Leah is in college, Anna feels that it's time for her to move on with her life. This is not a comforting thought to Leah who has counted on her mother being there for her always.

What to Do

- Recognize that your daughter may feel threatened by this new relationship.
- Let her know that she will always be very important to you.
- Remind yourself that her reaction is probably temporary, but that she may continue to be uncomfortable with the idea of a new person in your life.

What to Avoid

- Putting your life on hold for your child
- Expecting her to accept this new relationship without some questions and concerns.

What You Need to Know

A single parent with an only child can be the tightest family unit. A dramatic change occurs in a single parent/only child family when the child goes off to college; this can result in a particularly wrenching separation. If the single parent begins to have a life separate from the child, the child may feel abandoned; conversely, when the child leaves home, the parent many feel abandoned. In either case, one or both may try hard to keep the same family balance. Moreover, the child may feel guilty that she has left her mother to go to college or the parent may feel guilty if she goes out and creates a life for herself. The changes in this type of relationship can be fraught with emotional turmoil.

First Generation to Go to College

When your son left for the university in another state, the whole family went to the bus station to see him off. All the grandparents, aunts, uncles, cousins, brothers, and sisters waved good-bye to the first family member ever to go to college. When he got on the bus, you felt excited but also worried and sad. Although he received a full scholarship, his departure created a financial hardship for your family. Not only had he provided a steady part of the family income for years through his after-school job, he had also taken care of his younger brothers and sisters while you worked.

What's on Your Family's Mind

> We're so proud.
> When will we see him again?
> I wonder how he'll be treated; will there be other kids like him?
> Now his younger sister will have to get a job and help out more.

What's on Your Child's Mind

> I'm going to miss all of them so much. They have always been there for me.
> What will it feel like to be alone at college?
> I feel excited but also sad.

What's Going On

This new college student is a pioneer in his family. The first child in a family to go to college will deal with many unknowns. His parents don't understand nor are they able to prepare him for the college experience. They may feel intimidated about interacting with the university. While his family knows that education is the key to upward mobility, they also value the close family ties that exist and wonder if he will ever really return to the family again. Moreover, his departure creates added burdens for the rest of the family.

What to Do

- Take pride in your child's accomplishments.
- Encourage him to express his feelings, even though they may be upsetting to you.
- Keep in touch regularly.
- Try to support him in any way you can because this will be an enormous change and challenge.

What to Avoid

- Making him feel responsible for your feelings of sadness.
- Pressuring him to do well at school to make the family proud of him.
- Insisting that he get a job at school and send money home to help out.

What You Need to Know

Individuals who are the first in their family to go to college face many obstacles and challenges. Although their families may place great emphasis on continuing education, first-generation college students do not have the benefit of parents who are knowledgeable about the college experience and able to guide them through the process. Many first-generation students also face the added burden of being a racial or ethnic minority and/or coming from a family of lower socioeconomic status. Even though first-generation students may have been stars in their high schools, they often find the adjustment to college-level work formidable. In addition, they can feel great pressure to succeed and excel. First-generation students may carry the hopes and expectations of a large family group, as well as those of a neighborhood, church, and sometimes an entire community. These pressures are intense, especially when a student has academic or social difficulties. Many first-generation college students feel the loss of the extended family's support just when they need it the most, and this can add to their feelings of isolation.

There is anecdotal evidence, however, that these students, if they successfully complete their college degrees, have a level of personal motivation and independence that serves them well postgraduation. Having to navigate an unfamiliar environment and being forced to draw on personal determination, without the "benefit" of hovering parents, can actually go a long way toward preparing these students for adulthood. While hard-won, this capacity to persist in the face of struggles can be ultimately very beneficial. This is not to ignore the very real challenges that often derail a college career.

Many colleges today recognize the obstacles that first-generation students face and have programs in place to address these special circumstances.

Other Family Changes

In addition to changes you can anticipate when a child goes to college, there may also be unexpected changes in the family and in your child during these years. Even though your child is living away from home most of the year, it's important to acknowledge the impact the following situations can have.

A Family Move

You're a bit surprised by the reaction of your daughter, Margaret, when you told her that the family would be transferred to a new city in a few months.

MOM: Hi, Margaret. I've got great news.

MARGARET: Really, what?

MOM: I just found out that I'm getting a big promotion at work. I'm going to be head of a whole new division of the company starting next May.

MARGARET: Wow, Mom, that's awesome!

MOM: Yeah, I'm really excited. It's going to be lots of work but this is such a great opportunity for me.

MARGARET: So, I bet Dad and Billy are really proud of you, huh? Were they surprised?

MOM: Well, I've been working for this for a long time, but I don't think any of us thought it would happen this year.

MARGARET: That's cool, Mom. I'm happy for you.

MOM: There's just one drawback.

MARGARET: Yeah?

MOM: The new job is in Seattle, and it means we'll have to move.

MARGARET: What? Move to Seattle? When?

MOM: Well, I'll probably go out to Seattle in the beginning of May, but Dad and Billy will stay here at least through June so that Billy can finish eighth grade here. Dad also has to find a new job in Seattle, which may take a few months. We hope we'll all be living there by the time school starts for Billy in the fall.

MARGARET: But, what about me? What's going to happen to me?

MOM: Well, it probably makes sense for you to look for a summer job in Seattle and then you'll be going back to school in the fall.

MARGARET: What about our house?

MOM: We're getting ready to put it on the market. It may take a few months for it to sell. There's so much to do. My head is spinning.

MARGARET: I can't believe you're selling my bedroom without even asking me!

MOM: Margaret, relax. You'll have a bedroom in our new house.

MARGARET: But what about my friends at home? I'll never see them again. Why do you have to take a new job now?

MOM: I don't have to. I want to. This is a great opportunity for me; I can't turn it down. I know that all of you will have to move and adjust to a new place, but we'll be doing it together. I think you'll love Seattle—it's such a beautiful city and there are so many things to do there.

MARGARET: Maybe I'll just stay here for the summer if I don't have a home anymore.

MOM: Don't be silly, Margaret, you'll always have a home. You're away at school most of the time anyway and it won't be long before you're out on your own. Dad and Billy are going to have to adjust to a new place, too; it's not just about you. Can't you be happy for me?

MARGARET: No!

What's on Your Mind

Why is Margaret so upset?
She's hardly home anymore anyway.
She only cares about herself.

What's on Your Child's Mind

I can't believe Mom is doing this to me.
They obviously don't care about me!
I don't know anyone in Seattle. It will be terrible there with no friends.

What's Going On

College students can be pretty self-centered. They want everything at home to stay the same while they explore their world away from the family. For some students, this is not a big deal; for others, it's really upsetting.

What to Do

- Try to give your child as much advance notice of a move as possible.
- Recognize that this may be a major unwelcome adjustment, even though your child is away from home for most of the year.
- Listen to your child and empathize with her feelings.
- Understand that leaving hometown friends and a house they grew up in is a big deal to most college students.
- Be flexible about your child's summer plans. Offer choices.

What to Avoid

- Springing the news on her.
- Expecting her to be happy for you.
- Criticizing her for being so selfish.
- Demanding that she spend the summer in the new city.

What You Need to Know

College students are going through so many developmental changes that they may resist any shift at home with great vigor. Fear usually underlies the reaction; it's important for parents to be aware of that and help their child adjust to the change. Students who are in the process of transferring their sense of identity from the family to friends may find it hard to return home for breaks and vacations when they don't have any friends in the new city.

It may be a good time to consider alternatives to having your child come home for every break if you are relocating the family to a new city. She may welcome the opportunity to stay with old friends in her original hometown, and you won't have to deal with a moping, angry child. You might also suggest that she bring a friend from school to your new home for break. This adjustment is a tough one for everyone, but it can be especially hard for a student who has relied on home as a safe haven during a time of great change in his or her life at school.

Divorce

Ned and Jan have known for a long time that their relationship wasn't satisfying or close anymore. They have talked about divorce or a trial separation on many occasions when their children were teenagers but they couldn't face the disruption that such a decision would cause. Now they are alone. Their last child has gone to college and the deficiencies in their relationship are starkly apparent. They decide that it's time to move forward with a separation agreement. And now they must tell their children, the youngest of whom is in his first year of college.

What's on Your Mind

I just want to get this over with so I can get on with my life.
We've waited a long time to make this decision.
Now that the kids have their own lives, this shouldn't affect them too much.

What's on Your Child's Mind

I can't believe my parents are doing this to me. How long have they been lying to me?
What's going to happen to me?
Will I still have a home?

What's Going On

Ned and Jan are typical of thousands of couples every year who decide to separate once their last child leaves home. They believe that this change won't be so devastating for their children because they are now away from home and less dependent on them on a daily basis.

What to Do

- Realize that this may come as a big shock to your child, even though he may have been aware of your marital difficulties for many years.
- Choose an appropriate time to tell your child. Don't do it over the phone and don't burden him with this news during a stressful period at college, such as final exam time.
- Be honest and frank with your child without blaming one another for this situation.
- Reinforce that you love him and that you'll always be his parent regardless of changes in your relationship.
- Make specific arrangements for how you will handle your child's support and share those plans with your college student.

What to Avoid

- Keeping this change a secret until you have divorced and surprising him with it.
- Putting your child in the middle of any difficult negotiations, such as who will pay for college from now on.
- Expecting your child to behave rationally and counting on him to accept this decision more readily now that he's away from home.

What You Need to Know

Many parents think that if they hold their relationship together until the last child goes to college, the effect won't be as damaging. In fact, a divorce during the college years can have a devastating effect on college-aged children. As a child searches for identity and autonomy during the college years, his or her need for a stable family becomes paramount.

While it may seem to parents that their child is grown up, independent, and not in need of their daily attention during the college years, he or she still needs to be able to count on a secure base at home. This decision can rock a child's foundation profoundly and have an effect on the child's ability to form his or her own intimate attachments and to trust in relationships. Parents planning to separate or divorce while their child is in college need to be especially aware of the consequences and try to understand their child's reaction. The more parents discuss this decision with their child, and listen and empathize with their child's feelings, the better it will be for the whole family over time.

Some parents have a pattern of placing their child in the middle of their relationship; this creates a triangle that can have negative long-term effects on the child. A triangle occurs in the family system when two people are unable to solve a problem and they draw a third person into the controversy. Parents need to ensure that they don't place their child in this situation. It happens most frequently in families when the parents don't have the capacity or skills to work on their relationship.

If a child often mediates disagreements between the parents, that child may feel that the divorce is his fault and try to fix things between the mother and father. Parents need to make it clear to their child that this change has to do with their marital relationship, not with the child's behavior.

The most important thing you can do for your child is clearly explain your decisions and accept responsibility for them. Communicate to your child that this is a difficult situation but one that you can manage without his or her help. Treat your spouse with respect, even though you may be angry and hurt. Help your child to believe that you, as parents, are united in your love and caring for him. At all costs, avoid the pitfall of asking your child to take sides; handle the divorce negotiations without involving your child. Reassure your child that you are still a family that cares and provides for one another. Make sure that what you *do* speaks as loudly as what you say.

Death of Grandparent

Stephanie, a junior in college, received the following phone call from her mom:

STEPHANIE: Hello?

MOM: Hi, sweetie. How are you?

STEPHANIE: I'm okay, How's Grammy?

MOM: Well, I've got some bad news for you, honey. Grammy died this morning.

STEPHANIE (starting to cry): Oh, Mom, no. What happened? I thought she was getting better.

MOM: She did seem a little better when we saw her on Sunday, but she was still very sick you know.

STEPHANIE (now sobbing): But you told me she was *better*! I can't believe she's gone and I never got to say good-bye. Why didn't you call me? I could have come home. I can't believe I've lost my grammy. I'll pack my bag right now and get the next bus home.

MOM: Stephanie, I know you're upset. We all are, but there's no need for you to rush home. The funeral isn't until next Saturday and you have work to do at school. There's nothing for you to do here right now, honey.

STEPHANIE: I don't care. I'm coming home right now. I wouldn't be able to concentrate on anything here anyway.

MOM: But, Stephanie, you have classes and exams coming up. I think you should stay at school through the week and come home Friday night. That's plenty of time to be here for the funeral.

STEPHANIE (still crying): Mom, I just want to come home. I want to see Grammy right now.

MOM: Honey, she's . . . well, her body's at the funeral home. It won't matter to Grammy when you get here

STEPHANIE: I just wanted to say good-bye. Now I'll never be able to see her again. I can't believe Grammy is gone.

What's on Your Mind

I knew Stephanie would be upset but I figured she knew Grammy wouldn't be with us much longer.

Stephanie seems so sad and angry.

She'll have the whole weekend here. Why is she insisting on coming home tonight?

What's on Your Child's Mind

I can't stop crying.

I loved Grammy so much.

She was the only one in the family who really understood me. What am I going to do
without her?

What's Going On

When students are in college, they want everything to stay the same at home. The death of an
important person in a student's life can be a traumatic experience. Even if Stephanie was at home,
she might not have been right there when her grandmother died; but being away at school, she
feels left out and angry that she couldn't say good-bye. Stephanie's mother doesn't seem to understand the depth of Stephanie's feelings, urging her to be rational and sensible while Stephanie is
shocked and upset.

What to Do

- Listen to your child's feelings of loss and grief and let her have those feelings.
- Ask her what she would like to do.
- Respect your child's feelings and encourage her to do what feels right for her.
- Ask her if she has a friend she can talk to at school.

What to Avoid

- Trying to manage your child's feelings and reactions to this loss.
- Insisting that she be mature and get on with her life.
- Imposing your expectations on her behavior.

What You Need to Know

Students often lose a favorite grandparent while in college, and this loss can be devastating,
especially if the relationship was a close one. With life expectancy what it is today, your child
might well believe that she'll have grandparents in her life for many years after graduating from

Just When You Get Used to the Empty Nest, They're Back!   **181**

college. Most college-aged children have had little experience with death and the death of a beloved grandparent can be a great shock, even if that grandparent is old and sick.

Grandparents can play a unique role in the lives of children, offering unconditional love and support. It's not unusual for a child to be as close to a grandparent as she is to her parents. In fact, many grandparents take an active role in their grandchildren's lives, providing for them emotionally and financially from infancy through the college years and beyond. Parents need to be especially sensitive to what this loss means to their children and make sure that they have opportunities to express their grief. It's important, too, that their child has a support system at school to help her through this difficult time.

Religious Changes

Your son has fallen in love with a young woman at college who is Jewish. He is taking classes on Judaism and has announced that if he eventually marries his girlfriend, he has agreed to have a Jewish wedding, keep a kosher household, and raise their children in the Jewish faith. You are puzzled about how this could have happened; your family has always been Christian.

What's on Your Mind

> How can he dismiss his Christian heritage?
> Why can't his girlfriend convert to Christianity?
> If he marries her, our family will never be the same.

What's on Your Child's Mind

> I really love my girlfriend and respect her Jewish faith.
> Religion is very important to my girlfriend.
> I think I can happily adopt Judaism.

What's Going On

As college students begin to form their own values and to make lifestyle choices, parents may find departures from the family traditions hard to accept. While this may bother parents and other family members, they need to respect their child's choice. You may worry about the consequences of your son's or daughter's decisions, but you need to be open to understanding these choices and resist the temptation to try to change your child's mind. Having a son or daughter reject deeply held values, such as religion, can be a difficult issue for parents. Parents need to give themselves time to adjust to these changes and allow themselves to feel the loss and sadness that this represents.

What to Do

- Ask your son to help you understand his choices.
- Make an effort to learn about Judaism.
- Let your son know that you respect his right to make choices even if they differ from the family's traditions.
- Remind yourself that this is not a rejection of you as much as it is an expression of your child's emerging adult identity.

What to Avoid

- Threatening to disown him if he converts to Judaism.
- Trying to break up the relationship.
- Making disparaging remarks about Jews or Judaism.
- Sharing your worries about how the family will respond.

What You Need to Know

Parents need to remember that they don't have to agree with their child's choices in order to respect their child's right to make those choices. Studies of identity development have shown that religious commitments are shaken and questioned during the college years; religious exploration is often the result of the college student's quest for autonomy regarding values and lifestyle choices. It is generally understood that late adolescence is a time when individuals begin to form a system of personal religious beliefs rather than relying solely on the teachings of their parents. As they seek their own religious beliefs, some young people explore other ideologies and eventually return to their family's religion; others make a commitment to another religion or belief system. In both situations, however, adolescents are engaged in a fundamental task of developing individual identity and autonomy—that is, making their own decisions based on their unique, evolving value system.

This may indeed represent a significant change in the way your family celebrates holidays in the future, as well as more fundamental changes such as eventual childrearing practices. Your challenge is to accept the change (even if you don't agree with it), support your child, and keep your eye on the ultimate goal of continuing to have a good relationship with your son or daughter.

Lifestyle Changes

Your daughter has become a vegan and is living in a vegetarian coop at school. She's told you that being a vegan means that she doesn't eat any animal or dairy products. You're wondering how to accommodate her new diet when she's home for summer vacation.

What's on Your Mind

> What exactly is a vegan?
> Is this a healthy diet?
> Does this mean preparing special meals for her?

What's on Your Child's Mind

> I feel so much healthier now.
> I'm never going to eat animals again.
> How am I going to survive while I'm home over the summer?

What's Going On

Your daughter's interest in being a vegan may have begun within her new circle of friends at college. College students, for better or worse, tend to be influenced by their peer group when it comes to lifestyle choices. Or, it may be a totally independent choice based on health and environmental concerns. Whether this is a temporary or lifetime commitment, give her the respect that comes with taking this choice seriously.

What to Do

- Find out more about what it means to be a vegan.
- Ask your daughter about this change in her diet.
- Expect your daughter to take care of her special dietary needs when she is home but think about cooking with her occasionally.

What to Avoid

- Jumping to the conclusion that this is some sort of unhealthy fad diet.
- Insisting that your daughter eat the same food as the family when she's home on breaks.
- Ridiculing or criticizing her weird lifestyle and choices.
- Trivializing this choice, assuming that it's just a "phase" she'll outgrow in time.

What You Need to Know

Vegetarianism and veganism, practiced intelligently, are healthy food regimens and shouldn't alarm you. In fact, it is generally accepted that eliminating animal products is a responsible and healthy dietary choice. The key with vegetarian or vegan diets is to ensure that the individual is getting adequate protein, vitamins, and minerals to promote healthy growth and development.

Food can be a major source of contention between parents and adolescents. If you have maintained an open dialogue with your child about health-enhancing behaviors and choices, it should not come as a surprise when your child makes the decision to become a vegan. A child who makes a healthy diet choice needs encouragement and support. Rather than viewing this choice as a rejection of *your* lifestyle, learn more about alternative diets and congratulate your child for making healthy decisions.

It's not easy to keep up with the explorations and changing habits that characterize late adolescence. While the changes may occur quickly and seem whimsical to you, that doesn't mean they are superficial or transitory to your child. Learn about these lifestyle choices, even if you are not interested in adopting them yourself. It can provide an opportunity for you to begin to interact with your child on a more adult level.

Families That Resist Change

Roles and relationships in some families become fixed over time. If parents are not able to accommodate the changes in their children during the college years, they force their children to make a choice between remaining part of a rigid family system or continuing to grow and develop as individuals.

The Inflexible Family

You are upset and surprised when your daughter, Debbie, calls to tell you that she's coming home from school.

DEBBIE: Hi, Dad. How's Mom?

DAD: She's pretty good, considering how much she misses her little girl. What's up with you?

DEBBIE: I've got some bad news, Dad. I've been asked to take a leave from college. My grades are so bad that they want me to take a semester off and take courses somewhere else to prove that I can handle the work here.

DAD: Oh, Debbie, what happened?

DEBBIE: I don't really know. I just can't seem to focus on my schoolwork. I think about you guys all the time. I know Mom's been really depressed since I left for college. Do you think she's all right, Dad?

DAD: I think so. It's been hard on her to have you gone. But, Deb, you were such a good student in high school. I'm surprised you're having trouble in college.

DEBBIE: I know, but it's really hard here. I miss you and Mom.

DAD: We miss you, too, honey. So, are you coming home?

DEBBIE: Yeah, I guess so. Can you pick me up this weekend? I really don't want to stay here any longer than I have to.

DAD: Okay, I guess you can still get into some courses here at the community college. Do you want me to check it out to see if it's not too late?

DEBBIE: I don't know. Maybe I'll just come home and decide what to do later.

DAD: But, Debbie, what will you do here?

DEBBIE: Well, I thought I could talk to Mr. Miller about getting my old job back for a while.

DAD: Is that what you really want to do?

DEBBIE: I don't *know*, Dad. I'm so confused right now. I just want to come home

DAD: Well, okay, I'll call you later about picking you up on Saturday. I'll tell your mother. She's not home right now, but I know she'll want to talk to you later.

What's on Your Mind

What's happened to Debbie? She seemed so excited about going to college.
Wait until her mother hears about this. She's going to be really upset.
I worry about her coming home, but she sounds pretty miserable.

What's on Your Child's Mind

I really miss home.
I'm not sure I can handle college right now.
It's hard to be here. I think about home all the time.

What's Going On

Debbie is an only child and she has always been close to her parents. In fact, her parents have taken so much responsibility for her daily life that she finds being away from home extremely difficult. She's confused about what it means to be on her own at college and has spent most of her time missing home and communicating with her parents every day. She's also been her mother's friend and support for so many years that she feels responsible for her mother's happiness and for keeping the family in balance. We know of children who actually quit or flunk out of college so that they can go home, reclaim their place in the family, and preserve those relationships as they've always been.

What to Do

- Try to understand how unhappy your child is about flunking out.
- Ask her what she thinks is going on and empathize with her feelings of homesickness.
- Think about getting some help for her. She may benefit from talking to a counselor who specializes in family systems.
- Discuss with her what she plans to do while at home.
- Let her know what your expectations are if she comes back to live at home.

What to Avoid

- Taking on responsibility for your child's difficulty; making it your problem to solve.
- Blaming her for not working hard enough to get passing grades.
- Expecting her to understand how embarrassing and difficult this is for you.
- Encouraging your child to feel responsible for your happiness.

What You Need to Know

Debbie and her parents are stuck in a family structure that no longer works when she goes to college. Instead of recognizing her departure for college as a normal change in the family, her family was unable to find a new balance when a piece of the mobile was removed. Debbie felt the need to return home to restore that former balance. Her parents might support that return because they, too, were unable to adjust to the new family structure. This disruption to the family can cause a student to inexplicably drop out or flunk out of college.

Salvador Minuchin, a family therapist and pioneer in the field of family systems theory, describes three ways that families interact with each other: disengaged, clear about boundaries, or enmeshed.[1] When family members are disengaged, they become extremely autonomous and lack feelings of loyalty and belonging. This type of environment makes it difficult for individuals to find support from other family members when they need it. A college student may feel cut off from parents and unable to count on support unless the need is extreme. The family that establishes clear boundaries among its members has the healthiest interaction of the three. It allows for appropriate dependence when children are young, encourages independence when children begin to mature into adulthood, and values the interdependence that results when children are fully functioning adults.

Debbie's family is an example of an enmeshed family system. In order to belong in a highly enmeshed family, the members must relinquish a measure of independence and autonomy. The family responds to the slightest problem immediately, often with excessive speed and intensity. Family members, lacking clear boundaries, take on everyone else's problems as their own. Because of this enmeshment, Debbie can't break away from her parents, and may even feel an inappropriate responsibility for their happiness and well-being. Hence, she sabotages any situation in which she has to act autonomously and independently from her family—she fails out of school so that she can return home and restore the family balance.

Debbie's parents, perhaps unwittingly and with the best intentions, have done her a great disservice by encouraging her enmeshment with them. Debbie's parents probably raised her with an authoritarian or indulgent parenting style, as discussed in the last chapter, thus limiting her ability to be independent or secure in herself without constant parental support and reinforcement. Debbie has been asked to serve her parents' needs at the expense of her own development. With help, however, Debbie's family can address the issues of enmeshment and help her move on to find her own identity and establish interdependence with her parents in a healthy, affirming way.

In healthy families, changes in roles and relationships will occur during the college years. As your child moves from dependence, to independence, and on to interdependence, the family system will change and flex, much as a mobile responds to the natural movement of wind and air around it. Think of your family as a beautiful work of art in progress.

Chapter 7

Understanding the College Experience

Resources for Students and Parents

When we attended orientation, college faculty and staff members talked about all of the academic programs and services available to our daughter and about how different college is from high school. They even have a parents' program. I wonder how this compares to being in the PTA. This is going to be a learning experience for us as well as our daughter!

As you move toward a new relationship with your child, you will also have a different type of relationship with your child's school. This chapter will help you understand the unique academic structure of higher education and how you can access the many programs and services available to you and your child. It will also help you balance your need for involvement and information with your child's need to master the academic and social challenges of college.

The Academic Experience

Faculty Advising

Your son is in his first semester at a large state university. He calls to complain that he can never find his faculty adviser and that he needs his adviser's approval by tomorrow so that he can enter his next semester's courses on the computer.

What's on Your Mind

> Why isn't his adviser there when he needs her?
> Does this adviser care about my son's education?

What's on Your Child's Mind

My adviser is never in.
I should have signed up for her office hours but I didn't get around to it.
What am I going to do now?

What's Going On

Faculty members expect students to be able to manage a demanding academic workload and to take the initiative in formulating and carrying through on a course of study; however, adjusting to the academic expectations of college is a challenge for most students and, at times, it may be confusing for you as well.

Students often wait until the last minute to have their courses approved by an adviser. At large institutions where faculty members have a long list of advisees, this may pose a problem. While students complain that their adviser is "never there," sometimes the reality is that the student hasn't made a reasonable effort to see the adviser. In fact, faculty members often complain that they hold office hours and no one schedules an appointment or shows up.

What to Do

- Recognize that this is not your problem to solve.
- Listen to your son's frustration and offer some ideas: for example, he could ask the department office staff or registrar to assist him in getting his courses approved in time. Most universities have backup systems in case a faculty adviser is not available when deadlines are imminent.
- Ask him to think of ways that he can avoid this situation in the future.
- Remind him that he can request a change of adviser if the relationship isn't working for him.

What to Avoid

- Taking on the problem for your son.
- Calling the university and demanding that his adviser do her job.

What You Need to Know

The relationship between adviser and advisee at a university or college is best described as a professional collaboration in which the student and the academic adviser accept joint responsibility for the success of the relationship. This is new territory for most students—dealing with a professor is fundamentally different from interacting with a high school teacher.

High school teachers usually check completed homework, remind students of incomplete work, approach students if they believe assistance is needed, provide students with the information they missed when absent, are available for conversations before and after class, lead students through the material in the class textbook, and remind students of upcoming assignments and due dates. College faculty members, however, will probably do none of the above. They will assume that students are going to take responsibility for their learning. That means they expect students to take the initiative in managing their class work and seeking assistance. Most students have never experienced this sort of relationship without parental involvement and guidance.

Particularly at large universities, students need to be assertive about meeting with their adviser; scheduling time with an inaccessible one can intimidate some students. Parents can reassure their children that advising is part of a faculty member's job and a service that they are entitled to when they need it. At the same time, parents need to recognize that their children bear responsibility for this relationship as well. College students need to take the initiative in scheduling appointments, preparing for advising meetings, and changing advisers if the relationship is not satisfactory.

Students have a right to expect their academic adviser to be knowledgeable about the curriculum, willing to make referrals when necessary, helpful when selecting courses and formulating a plan of study, and able to engage students in thinking about their undergraduate education in the context of long-range goals.

The older son of Helen, one of the coauthors of this book, attended a large research university, received minimal help from his academic advisers and felt intimidated by his interactions with one adviser, who was a Pulitzer Prize–winning novelist. My younger son, who attended a small private college, was invited to have dinner at his adviser's home during the first week he was on campus and, therefore, felt much more comfortable about calling on his adviser for guidance during his first semester in college.

In reality, academic advising can vary a great deal, depending on the commitment of both faculty member and student to making the relationship a productive one. A student at a large university may have to be more assertive to receive advice and guidance. At a small college, this relationship may be easier to establish and more personal. In either case, however, a college student is entitled to adequate advice and counsel from a faculty adviser. It's generally the student's responsibility to make that relationship work or to seek another adviser if it doesn't. Your role is to act as a consultant to your child, not as an intermediary; resist the temptation to get in touch with a faculty adviser on your child's behalf.

Professors Versus Teaching Assistants

Your daughter is in her second semester at the university and she still hasn't had any contact with a "real" professor. One of her classes is actually taught by a graduate student who is a teaching assistant. Your daughter is having trouble in chemistry class and she maintains that the teaching assistant can't speak English well enough to explain concepts to the class.

What's on Your Mind

I'm paying an enormous tuition bill and my child isn't even being taught by a professor.
No one told us that this would happen.
What do I do about this?

What's on Your Child's Mind

I can't understand half of what the TA is talking about in my chemistry lab.
Who should I go to for help?
The classes are so big here. I feel like just a number.

What's Going On

Particularly at large research universities, teaching assistants play a significant role in teaching first- and second-year undergraduate classes. While some graduate student teaching assistants make excellent teachers, this is not always the case. In many undergraduate classes, a professor will provide the weekly lectures and rely on graduate assistants to teach discussion or lab sections and assist in grading papers and examinations. Your concern should be the quality of the teaching, whether that job is performed by a professor or graduate teaching assistant.

What to Do

- Suggest that she make an appointment with her professor to explain the situation.
- If she doesn't receive any help from the professor, recommend that she talk to her academic adviser, or the director of undergraduate studies in her department.
- Ask her if she can seek additional help through a tutoring or learning skills center on campus.

- Remember that this is your child's dilemma, not yours. Your role is to listen to her frustrations and offer advice about how she might find some help.

What to Avoid

- Assuming that her TA really can't speak English adequately. Although this may be true, it may be that the concepts are just difficult to learn and your daughter would need extra help regardless of the teacher's language ability.
- Calling the department and demanding that an English-speaking faculty member teach your daughter's class.

What You Need to Know

The Carnegie Foundation for the Advancement of Teaching found that large research universities too frequently offer undergraduates minimal academic guidance and support. Moreover, students at these universities are often taught by untrained teaching assistants, not the famous professors touted in catalogs or recruiting materials.

The quality of undergraduate education generates serious debate on many campuses; the focus of this debate has been directed primarily at universities that emphasize faculty research above teaching. Although research universities comprise only 3 percent of the nation's institutions of higher education, each year they graduate about one-third of all college seniors; hence, it is not surprising that the quality of undergraduate education is a serious concern for many parents.

In order to have contact with faculty in large research universities, students need to take the initiative. They can make appointments with faculty during their office hours, enroll in small seminars, or do an independent study with a faculty member. Students can often obtain course credit for assisting a faculty member with research. But students must seek out these opportunities and be persistent. Usually faculty members take an interest in the students who exhibit serious commitment to their studies and excel in their courses.

Academic Difficulty

Your daughter, Linda, called home last night and you're disturbed by her predicament.

LINDA: Hi, Mom.
MOM: Hi, Linda. How are you doing?

LINDA: Not so well. I think I'm going to flunk my anthropology course.

MOM: What's happening?

LINDA: I just can't seem to figure out what my professor wants. I failed the midterm and I got a D on my paper. I got it back today and I don't know what to do. I thought it was okay; I worked really hard on it.

MOM: Have you talked to your professor?

LINDA: No. I wouldn't know what to say.

MOM: Well, what are you going to do about this?

LINDA: I told you, I don't know what to do!

MOM: But, Linda, you can't fail the course. Do you want me to call your professor?

LINDA: No!

MOM: But you obviously need extra help. Why can't you ask for it?

LINDA: I just can't, Mom. You don't understand.

MOM: I *do* understand. You're supposed to be learning and passing your courses. What about your other courses? Are you doing okay in them?

LINDA: Yeah, I'm doing okay, but I'm definitely not going to make the dean's list here.

What's on Your Mind

What's happening with Linda?

Is there something that I can do to help?

I don't understand why she won't talk to her professor.

What's on Your Child's Mind

I can't believe I'm going to flunk anthropology.

I just can't figure out what my professor wants.

I've never failed anything before. What's wrong with me?

What's Going On

While it may be unreasonable to expect that your daughter will achieve high grades her first year in college, it also alarms you and your daughter that she may flunk a course. Many students find the competition and quantity of work required in college courses a surprise. It takes time to adjust to increased academic demands and students often feel overwhelmed by the challenge.

What to Do

- Listen to your daughter's feelings about her failing grades.
- Empathize with her anxiety about the workload at college.
- Reassure her that you know she is capable of handling college-level work.
- Continue to encourage her to talk to the professor of the course she is failing.
- Suggest that she seek help through a writing workshop, learning skills center, or by engaging a tutor.

What to Avoid

- Taking on her dilemma as your own.
- Overreacting and calling her professor to find out what's going on.
- Threatening to take her out of school if she can't get good grades.

What You Need to Know

It's not unusual for a student to receive his or her first failing grade in college. Even the brightest high school student will find the adjustment to college life and academics a challenge. This doesn't mean that she won't be able to do the work and get her degree. It may mean that she will have to learn new study skills and habits to cope with the rigors of college-level work.

There are services on campus to help students who are overwhelmed by their workload. Most colleges and universities have learning skills centers, writing workshops, and tutors available to help students through academic difficulties. It is important, however, that the student take the initiative to get help. A good first step is to encourage your child to seek information and advice from the professor of any course in which he or she is struggling. Your role as a consultant is to offer advice and counsel, not to take over, decide what should be done, or call the professor yourself.

If your child continues to perform poorly in college, she will probably be placed on academic probation and you may be notified of this decision by the college. In this case, you may need to be more actively involved; not in solving your child's problem, but in making sure that he or she gets the assistance needed to achieve passing grades. Your role could be to contact a member of the advising staff (with her knowledge and consent) to find out what services are available to her and help her devise a plan to take advantage of the academic support services on campus. Your skills as a consultant will be useful in helping your child receive the help he or she needs, especially if your child is shy, overwhelmed, or temporarily incapable of seeing the forest for the trees.

Grade Reporting and Transcripts

You just had a frustrating call to the registrar at your child's college. Your daughter is out of the country on a semester abroad program and has asked you to fill out the forms for her financial aid and scholarship package for the following academic year, as the deadlines will pass before she returns. You called to get a copy of her transcript and were told that you could not have it without your daughter's written authorization.

What's on Your Mind

> Why can't I have her transcript? I pay her tuition.
> What am I going to do now?
> By the time I get a note from my daughter, the deadlines will have passed.

What's Going On

Most colleges and universities will not release grade information over the phone to a so-called third party. Students who are over eighteen years old have the legal right to privacy regarding their academic and financial records. Most parents are unaware of this regulation and are angry when they can't have ready access to their child's records.

What to Do

- Explain clearly to the registrar's office that you need the transcript in order to complete scholarship and/or financial aid forms for your daughter who is out of the country. Most registrars' offices will be happy to mail the official transcript directly to the scholarship or financial aid granting agency.
- Have your daughter file a release form with the registrar so that you don't have to deal with this again.
- If you want to see a grade report every semester, make that clear to your child and ask her to share it with you.

What to Avoid

- Simply asking for your daughter's transcript without giving the reason for the request.
- Threatening to withhold tuition payment until you can get the information that you need.

What You Need to Know

As your child adjusts to the academic challenges of college, you, too, will adjust to a new set of procedures for reporting grades. When your child was in primary and secondary school, you were probably used to seeing report cards.

The Family Educational Rights and Privacy Act (FERPA) was passed in 1974. It guarantees an emancipated student (one who has become financially independent) the right to privacy of his or her educational and financial records. A third party (parents or others) cannot have access to that student's grade reports, transcripts, or financial records without the student's written permission. Under this act (also referred to as the Buckley Amendment), institutions are authorized to protect the privacy rights of all students who are eighteen years of age and older, whether or not they are emancipated. However, most institutions will honor the disclosure of grades and financial records to parents who claim their child as a dependent for tax purposes or who can prove with documentation that they provide more than 50 percent of that student's financial support.

Most grade reporting now occurs online and students have a password to access their grades. As technology continues to play a larger role in organizing and reporting information, students have instant access to all of their academic and financial records. At most institutions, it is possible for you to log on to your child's records, but only if your child gives you the password.

Some parents are angry when they don't automatically receive grade reports from the institution. They need to keep in mind, however, that this privacy protection can work to their child's benefit. For example, if the institution provides information on a student to any third party, a stranger can have access to her course schedule, grades, financial data, and maybe even an unlisted address. Several tragedies have resulted from the disclosure of this kind of information. For example, an estranged boyfriend might have access to a former girlfriend's class schedule and confront her after class.

Parents who are engaged in a struggle about grades need to have a frank discussion with their child. This controversy usually is symptomatic of a deeper communication problem. Your child may have any number of reasons for being reluctant to share grades with you, but if you provide most or all of your child's support in college, you do have a right to know how he or she is doing in school.

Academic Integrity

Your son turned in a research paper that one of his fraternity brothers wrote last year. The professor figured it out and has brought your son up on academic integrity charges before a review board.

What's on Your Mind

I can't believe he did this.
I'm so ashamed and embarrassed. Where did I go wrong as a parent?

What's on Your Child's Mind

I guess I really blew it; I just didn't have time to finish that paper.
A lot of my friends do this when they get in a pinch.
I'm really scared that I'll get kicked out of school.

What's Going On

Colleges and universities take the issue of academic integrity very seriously and often impose stiff consequences if they find a student has plagiarized work without attribution, stolen other people's work, or cheated on an examination or paper. Schools have an academic integrity code that they expect students to adhere to and have judicial boards to address violations of this code. These violations can, and should be, very sobering experiences for students.

What to Do

- Above all, try to keep in mind that this is *his* problem even though it will surely affect your life as well.
- Try to empathize with his fears and ignore his "excuses."
- Ask him how he plans to deal with this crisis and how he will keep you informed.
- Focus on what he is learning from this violation.
- Tell him that you are disappointed in his behavior but that you still love him.

What to Avoid

- Yelling at him for being dishonest. It will only make him defensive.
- Threatening to disown him, take him out of school, or remove your support.
- Focusing on how embarrassed and ashamed you are.
- Offering to call the school and try to "fix" the situation.

What You Need to Know

Unfortunately, cheating on exams and plagiarizing papers has become an increasingly serious phenomenon on most campuses. A recent study revealed that 75 percent of all high school students cheat and it's often the brightest and those who have the most to lose that cheat. The pressure to succeed weighs heavily on students today and, while not an excuse, this constant imperative to get good grades, take honors and advanced placement (AP) classes, and get into a good school can explain why some students are so desperate to do well. By the time many students get to college, they are often experienced cheaters and justify their behavior as vital in order to get ahead.

What can parents do to address and counteract this epidemic of dishonest behavior? Talk to your student about the importance of personal integrity in all aspects of his or her life, make your expectations clear, discuss the consequences that may result, and refuse to condone and participate in dishonest behavior yourself. That means refusing to rewrite or edit a paper for your student even if they insist that they will fail without your help. Better they learn the lesson of failure than learn that dishonesty is acceptable and that they are incapable of doing their own work. Parents do their children a great disservice if they place a higher value on success than on personal integrity. Sadly, there are many examples in the world that reinforce this "get ahead at any price" behavior. You can refuse to be that kind of "role model."

All colleges have academic integrity policies and some have an honor code that students are asked to sign when they first arrive on campus. These policies and codes address the critically important issue of academic integrity and include specific rules about plagiarism, cheating, lying, and stealing. The use of the Internet has complicated these issues, as many students (and parents) are unclear about the copyright rules governing information on the Web. Encourage your child to read the academic integrity information provided by the college and to abide by those rules.

While there are many tools today, thanks to technology, which can assist faculty members and teachers in detecting cheating and plagiarism, most faculty members can recognize dishonesty simply because they are experts in their fields and intimately familiar with the material covered in their classes. Unfortunately, there are a number of organizations that sell term papers and writing help through the Web. This is a disturbing development that undercuts the very notion of learning and honesty among college students. Moreover, research has found that many of these so-called services are themselves guilty of blatant plagiarism. You can make it clear to your child that buying a term paper is unacceptable.

If your child is struggling with writing projects or other classroom work, there are resources on campus to help with those challenges. Campus writing workshops and tutoring centers are available to help your son or daughter; these on-campus resources are staffed by knowledgeable people who understand and operate within the guidelines of the college's academic integrity policies.

Reinforce with your child that there is no excuse for cheating or plagiarism and that you expect him or her to behave with honesty and integrity in all areas of campus life.

Googling a Paper

When your daughter is home on fall break, she announces that she's going to spend the afternoon working on a research paper. When you ask her if she's going to the library to do the research, she replies, "No, Mom, I don't need to go to the library, I'll just Google it."

What's on Your Mind

How can she do research without going to the library?
I can't believe she only needs Google to do a term paper.
I wonder if this is okay with her professor.

What's on Your Child's Mind

My mom is so old-fashioned.
She thinks you need to go to the library to do research.
I can get all the information I need on Google.

What's Going On

Research means a Google search for many college students. Students believe that everything they would possibly need to know exists on the Web and they are quick to go online for all of their information needs, from writing a paper to connecting with their friends and family. As Google continues to add to its vast database of information, students may never feel the need to visit a library on campus.

Today's college students have embraced this extraordinary search engine with enthusiasm; most students use Google to access information that former generations of students had to glean from hours combing through dusty stacks in libraries. At the stroke of a keypad or the click of a mouse, today's students have instant access to a flood of information without ever leaving their room, let alone trekking over to a library.

What to Do

- Ask your child how she goes about researching a topic on Google.
- Let her show you the process she uses.
- Talk to her about making contact with a reference librarian just to make sure she has the best information available to write a good paper.

What to Avoid

- Assuming that her grasp of the material will be superficial without an in-depth library research effort.
- Insisting that books will always be better than the Web.
- Telling her that she must go to the library to do research.

What You Need to Know

Google was incorporated in 1998 with the mission to create a search engine that would make the vast resources of the Internet accessible and navigable. In just over ten years, Google has become a ubiquitous noun and verb; every day billions of people "Google" and are instantly connected to a world of information that was previously unimaginable in its scope. Although there are a number of search engines, Google took this powerful tool for filtering and disseminating information to a level and complexity that is literally mind-boggling.

This fairly new technology has dramatically changed libraries and the work of college librarians. The limited number of librarians who interact with students now do so as technology guides presiding over a largely self-service information environment; most students don't even know what a reference librarian does and how helpful that expertise can be. A librarian's skill in being able to direct students to high-quality, but perhaps obscure, information is largely lost, due to this preoccupation with the Web.

A recent study by an international consortium of libraries examined students' perceptions of libraries and information resources. The study concluded, in part, that although libraries have vast electronic resources, the majority of students are not making use of them, believing that search engines deliver better quality and quantity of information than library-assisted searches. Students tend to use the wired physical library as a place to study with their laptop, socialize with friends, get away from the residence hall environment and make use of specialized digital equipment, such as cameras, scanners, and editing equipment.

Parents and students generally do not know that libraries are not just book storehouses but gateways to very expensive, high-quality online research tools and databases that can help students find far better resources and actually save time. Most college libraries offer orientation sessions for students to help them learn to navigate the most sophisticated and respected research venues. Your student will probably be introduced to library resources by a professional librarian in one of his or her introductory courses, such as English 101. Encourage your student to take advantage of these superior academic resources.

Nicholas Carr, author of *The Shallows: What the Internet Is Doing to Our Brains,* offers a cautionary note on the use of standard search engines for intellectual inquiry. "Intellectual technologies promote the speedy, superficial skimming of information and discourage any deep, prolonged engagement with a single argument, idea, or narrative. There is nothing wrong with browsing and scanning—the ability to skim text is every bit as valuable as the ability to read deeply. What *is* different and troubling is that skimming has become our dominant mode of reading. We are evolving from being cultivators of personal knowledge to being hunters and gatherers in the electronic data forest."[1]

The main goal of an electronic search engine is to get users in and out quickly, as advertising profit is directly related to the velocity of users' information intake. The more sites users click on, the greater the opportunity for search engines to feed users advertising and collect data on users to sell to advertisers. One of the genius initiatives on the part of Google's creators (and the reason the company was able to make money) was to tie users' Web behaviors to targeted advertising and marketing opportunities.

This may make little difference to a student who just wants to find information for a research paper, but John Palfrey and Urs Gasser, authors of *Born Digital: Understanding the First Generation of Digital Natives,* argue that "faced with way too much information and lack of life experience to filter out lower quality information, they (digital natives) are likely to sort for the information they already agree with, narrowing their frame of vision rather than expanding it." Hence, they may resort to "tailoring their information input to their own preferences, never confronting information that challenges their viewpoint or forces them to think critically."[2] Google's structure conspires in limiting the scope of inquiry by ranking Web pages according to their popularity, not necessarily their veracity; hence, the number of clicks on a certain site gives it front-page status, determining the order in which Web sites are listed in response to a key word search. Few individuals explore sites beyond the first page that pops up after a Google search, and few students have the perseverance or desire to dig deeper. They have been trained, through media usage, to be efficient and speedy, as they are deluged with vast amounts of information.

Among the top "hits" that appear when doing an electronic search is Wikipedia, The Free Encyclopedia, which was created in 2001. Wikipedia (a combination of the Hawaiian word *wiki,* which means "quick" and "encyclopedia") is a source of information written largely by anonymous Internet users; that means anyone with information can post it. With over 78 million monthly visitors, Wikipedia is one of the largest reference Web sites, with 91,000 active contributors working on more than 16 million articles in over 270 languages. To its credit, Wikipedia acknowledges that "you should not use Wikipedia by itself for primary research" because not everything is accurate, comprehensive, or unbiased. But many users believe Wikipedia has advantages over other reference works because it offers fast, up-to-the-minute coverage of many topics, including hyperlinks that are not available in traditional paper reference sources. In many ways, Wikipedia typifies both the good and bad features of electronic information sources—good because it's open, nondiscriminatory, fast, and immediate; bad because it's open, nondiscriminatory, fast, and immediate.

The Web is accessible, egalitarian, and participatory—all admirable qualities, which greatly help individuals and organizations. And there is little doubt that the speed of accessing vast amounts of information can improve productivity and breadth of knowledge. The challenge is the potential danger of sacrificing depth by increasing breadth.

Often professors will tell students not to use Google to do research for an academic paper. That does not mean that professors are discouraging the use of electronic resources. Remember the old card catalog? The same information that was formerly in a card catalog is now available electronically, often on a library Web site that students can access on their computer in their room. In addition, many databases and electronic versions of academic journals are available on library Web sites. Often professors will suggest that students use a particular database that is relevant to the academic field of the course. Encourage your child to speak to a reference librarian about a specific research assignment. The librarian can often direct them to databases and electronic resources that are much better for academic research than standard search engines.

When academic journals are available online, it becomes easy for students to cut and paste sentences or paragraphs from these sources into their papers. Students should always put any words or phrases that they take from another source in quotes and provide the source of that information in a citation. Electronic resources have made plagiarism easy for students, but it has also made it easy for professors to find the original source of the information. Typing a suspicious sentence into Google Scholar will often reveal its source. Students should be as careful about academic integrity when using electronic sources as they would be with printed material.

Life Outside of the Classroom

Most college graduates would agree with the person who said, "I learned a great deal in college, but only about 10 percent of that learning took place in the classroom." Colleges are learning-living laboratories in which students receive an education both inside and outside of the formal classroom setting. Some of the most valuable and lasting learning experiences occur as students learn to live with others and discover who they are as responsible adults in the college community.

Social Adjustment

You are worried about your son's social adjustment to college and decide to call the department office. They connect you with the faculty member who is director of undergraduate studies.

PROFESSOR: Hello?

DAD: Oh, hello, Professor James. My name is Mike Farrell and I'm calling about my son, Tim, who is a second-year transfer student in your department. I'm concerned about him.

PROFESSOR: Is he having difficulty in his classes?

DAD: No, classes seem to be going fine, but he seems so lonely and isolated. He hasn't really met any new friends, and I guess he's spending all of his time studying alone in his room. He calls home almost every day and complains about being bored.

PROFESSOR: So, he isn't finding the course work challenging?

DAD: No, I think the courses are going fine, but he doesn't seem to have any social life. He spends too much time alone. I'm concerned that he's becoming depressed.

PROFESSOR: Ah, I see. Are you worried that he might be depressed enough to harm himself in some way?

DAD: I don't think so. I just think he needs to meet some other kids and have some fun once in a while.

PROFESSOR: Well, you see, I'm a professor here and I don't have much to do with student life outside of the classroom. I think we have a counselor on staff in the college who might be able to help if your son would go and talk to her. Would you like me to transfer you to Ms. Taylor in our counseling center?

DAD: Well, maybe Ms. Taylor could call him and ask him to come in. I could give you his phone number to give to Ms. Taylor. I don't want him to know I called about him. Maybe she could just say that she was interested in seeing how the transfer students were doing.

PROFESSOR: Why don't I transfer you to Ms. Taylor and you can ask her about that?

DAD: Well, okay.

What's on the Professor's Mind

Why is this father calling me?
I don't know how to deal with students' psychological problems.
I'm a teacher, not a counselor.

What's on Your Mind

I'm really getting worried. He seems so unhappy.
Can't someone at the college help him?
I don't think he's in serious trouble, but I don't really know.
I don't want him to know that I called and how worried I am.

What's Going On

Students who have a difficult social adjustment to college often complain to their parents who feel at a loss to know how to help them. This is especially true of transfer students who come into a new situation where it seems that everyone else has already found a group of friends. Social life is an important component of the learning environment at college and parents should be concerned if their child feels isolated and lonely most of the time.

What to Do

- Take your child's unhappiness seriously. Let him know that you empathize with his feelings of isolation.
- Reassure him that you have seen him make friends in the past and that you know he can do it again.
- Ask him if he needs some help finding out about what services are available on campus to help students make the adjustment to a new place.
- Suggest that he talk to someone in the college counseling office.
- Tell him that you'd like to be in touch with him more often just to see how he's doing.

What to Avoid

- Jumping to the conclusion that he's chosen the wrong school and will never be happy there.

- Calling the college yourself to get some help before talking to your son about it.
- Making an appointment for him with the counseling center and insisting that he go talk with someone.

What You Need to Know

It's difficult, if not impossible, for a parent to assess from afar how unhappy their child is at school. A student may call on a parent when he needs to make a "stress dump," and this can be upsetting to the parent. The student may feel much better, having just unloaded his or her anxieties onto his parent, but the parent now feels rotten.

In these situations, it's important for the parent to be able to talk openly with the child. Don't be afraid to ask your child if he or she feels too depressed to cope at all. If this is the case, you need to act to get some help. We discuss these kinds of crisis situations in Chapter 10. This usually isn't the case, however. Tim's situation is a fairly common one. It's tough to be a transfer student in a new place. He may not have realized how difficult it would be to make new friends, so he begins to spend too much time alone instead of taking steps to meet new people. He could be shy in new situations or he could be overwhelmed with all of the adjustments he has to make.

It would have been helpful for his father to know that faculty members are typically not useful in situations like this. He may not have known where to turn for help and assumed that the college or department office would be able to assist him. While this may have been true in a small college, where faculty members tend to have more interaction with students and take an active interest in student life outside of the classroom, this is usually not true in a large college or university. But all institutions have a dean of students. The dean of students' office is a good place to begin if you want to find out about services for your child. Someone in that office will be able to help or make a referral.

In this case, maybe the student will gradually begin to make friends and handle this situation for himself. He may not be seriously depressed and in need of counseling; he may simply need to share his frustrations with his father and get it off his chest. It's crucial that the parent listen and empathize with the child rather than overreact and come up with a quick fix for the situation. It's especially damaging to the parent-child relationship if the parent goes behind the child's back and forces a solution. This urge to do something to make you feel better will backfire and certainly break the trust you have established with your child. In fact, most college counselors will not agree to engage in subterfuge in getting a student to come in for counseling. They may, however, be willing to counsel you on the worries *you* have about your child's situation. Difficult as it may be, your role is to listen, sympathize, encourage, and support your child in finding a solution to his or her dilemma.

Psychological Services

Your daughter has suffered from a mild, but persistent, form of depression since she was sixteen years old. She's now at college, and during an argument when she was home over fall break, she blurted out that she was seeing a shrink at school. You asked her to tell you about it and she yelled, "It's none of your business," and stormed off to her room. You're worried that she's getting worse and decide to call the counseling office and find out what's going on with her. You're angry and frustrated to find that no one will talk to you about your daughter's therapy.

What's on Your Mind

> I've always been involved in her therapy before.
> Why won't they tell me anything?
> I have a right to know. I'm her mother.

What's on Your Child's Mind

> My mom is so nosy. Believe me, she doesn't want to know what I'm talking to my
>   counselor about!
> When is she going to start treating me like an adult?

What's Going On

It's natural for a parent to want to know what's going on when a child is depressed and seeking psychological counseling. The mother may have been involved in a family counseling situation with that child when she was in high school and now she feels left out and worried. However, her daughter is taking personal responsibility for her mental and physical health and doesn't feel she has to share anything with her parents if she doesn't want to.

What to Do

- Let her know that you are proud of her for seeking help.
- Express your concern that she may be getting worse and that you are not sure if she is getting the help that she needs.
- Ask her if she wants to share what is going on with you.

- Respect her right to privacy if she doesn't want to talk about it.
- Be grateful that you have a child who is mature enough to take care of herself.

What to Avoid

- Insisting that she tell you what's going on.
- Threatening that you're going to find out even if she won't talk to you.
- Telling her you're going to withhold financial or emotional support if she doesn't talk to you.
- Reminding her that she's still your daughter and you have a right to know.

What You Need to Know

If your child is eighteen years of age or older, she is entitled to the right of patient confidentiality if she seeks medical or psychological treatment. This means that you will not have access to her records and that doctors and psychologists will not talk to you about your child's condition without her permission. This can be frustrating to a parent who has been able to talk to doctors or therapists in the past.

Most health-care professionals working at colleges will encourage a student to talk with her parents, particularly if they feel it will help the student. They are mandated by law, however, to keep their interactions and prescribed treatments for any patient confidential. This assurance of confidentiality is often crucial to a student's willingness to seek and receive treatment, and it will not be broken unless the health-care provider feels that the student is in an extremely dangerous situation. Even then, the provider will first attempt to get the student to deal directly with his or her parents before breaking the confidentiality rule.

It's difficult to respect your child's status as a legal adult when you know, as a parent, she is not yet truly independent and not always capable of making mature and responsible decisions. Now, more than ever, you need to be patient and honor your child's right to privacy. Your child may need to exercise extreme autonomy from you for a while and you need to work on respecting that.

Residence Hall Staff

You've been trying to make contact with your son for over a week. The last time you talked to him, he was feeling pretty sad about the breakup with his girlfriend. You're beginning to worry and wonder who you could call. You don't know any of his friends' last names or phone numbers.

What's on Your Mind

I wonder if he's all right.
We usually talk to him during the week.
The last time we spoke he sounded really unhappy.
I wonder if anyone would notice if he's in trouble.

What's on Your Child's Mind

I'm really bummed out.
Will I ever have another girlfriend who I like as much?
I'm so lonely without her.

What's Going On

It's easy for parents to forget that social life and relationships are important to college students. The breakup of a close relationship can leave a student feeling lonely and isolated from the social scene. Many students want to withdraw from everything. The last thing on their minds is to worry about how their parents feel. Their own pain is the only thing that's real for them.

What to Do

- Try to respect your son's need to withdraw and lick his wounds for a while.
- Call your son's residence hall director and ask if anyone has seen your son lately and if they noticed anything different in his behavior.
- Ask the residence hall director to check on him and ask him to call home.

What to Avoid

- Jumping to the conclusion that your son is in serious trouble. He's probably just trying to cope and doesn't need to have any further demands placed on him.
- Blaming him for not calling when you finally reach him.
- Deciding immediately that you have to get to campus and find out what's going on.

What You Need to Know

Residence hall staff members are a wonderful resource for parents who are worried and need to check in with someone. Resident directors are usually professionals hired by the college to manage the problems, large and small, that confront students living in residence halls. Some schools have directors and resident advisers, as well, who are usually graduate students or third- or fourth-year undergraduates. They live in the residence hall and are trained to deal with situations that arise when large groups of students share living quarters. They know all of the students in their hall, and may even see them on a daily basis; they are usually aware of changes in behavior and are there to intervene if necessary.

Residence hall staff members mediate roommate disputes, check on students in trouble, and notice if a student is withdrawn or appears depressed. At least one staff member is on call at all hours of the day and night, available to help students deal with the problems and difficulties they face, either personally or academically. Moreover, residence hall staff members tend to be people who students can relate to because they are not that much older and have recently gone through the college experience themselves. They are the most likely to notice if your child seems to be in trouble, and they can be a great resource for parents who are concerned about, but removed from, their child's daily life. Ordinarily, however, you should not call on residence hall staff members without your child's knowledge and permission unless you are convinced that your child is in serious danger.

Legal Trouble

Your daughter, a sophomore in college, was caught with a fake ID buying beer for her friends at a local convenience store. She's been arrested and has to appear in local court and deal with sanctions from the college as well. You're upset and angry with her, but you want to help.

What's on Your Mind

> How could she be so stupid?
> Where did she get a fake ID?
> Now she'll have a "record" and she may even be expelled.
> What can I do to help her out of this mess?

What's on Your Child's Mind

> Why did I have to get caught?
> I should have let someone else buy the beer.
> What's going to happen to me?

What's Going On

Falsified IDs are common on most college campuses and many students each year get caught buying liquor or beer using fake IDs. Because the legal drinking age is twenty-one, it is illegal for students to be in possession of or purchase alcohol during most of their college years. If this is her first offense, she will probably not be treated too harshly by the local authorities, but she will have to appear in court and will also be punished in some way by the college.

What to Do

- Ask her if she's thought about what she's going to do.
- Listen to her fears and let her know that, while you are unhappy with her behavior, you still love and support her in coping with her predicament.
- If you are willing, help her find legal counsel if she wants it.
- Let her know that you expect her to behave more responsibly in the future and that she is likely to have to deal with tough consequences if she breaks the law.

What to Avoid

- Letting your anger and embarrassment take over.
- Telling her that you'll get her an attorney and deal with the authorities at school.
- Agreeing with her that everyone has a fake ID and that you think it's unfair that she happened to get caught when everyone breaks the law about alcohol at college.

What You Need to Know

While it's true that most college students break the law by drinking alcohol sometime during their college years, having a falsified driver's license or other form of identification is a serious offense and should not be taken lightly. The repercussions can be especially harsh if an individual is caught purchasing alcohol with a fake ID.

The consequences and punishments for this behavior can vary widely, but the college has no other choice than to respond to students who break the law. Underage drinking is a major issue on most campuses and a great deal of energy and resources are spent trying to control students' drinking. (See more on this issue in Chapter 4.) In large part those efforts fail, and drinking remains a major social activity carried out with varying degrees of secrecy and ingenuity on the part of students. Falsifying a legal document, such as a driver's license, however, escalates the offense and the local police department may well be involved when this occurs.

Parents may need to act if there is an arrest and their child needs support and help in getting legal counsel. No parent wants to deal with this situation, but it is, unfortunately, quite common on college campuses today. Parents do have the right to insist that their children refrain from breaking the law and be ready to accept the consequences if they do.

Additional Programs and Services on Campus

While all colleges and universities are committed to providing the best possible programs and facilities to carry out their mission of educating young people, many have been profoundly affected by the current economic environment and have had to reduce costs and curtail services. In some cases, institutions have had to lay off staff members and drastically reduce budgets for programs and services. This is a reality that is hard for parents to accept, especially in the face of ever-increasing tuition costs, but it is a reality, nonetheless, and one that will probably exist for several years to come. The college or university environment at the start of the twenty-first century is a significantly different one from what it was twenty or thirty years ago. Expectations that are based on your own college experience may need to be examined and altered to fit what is possible in an era of declining resources.

Even parents who have attended college themselves often find the structure and organization of higher education today a bit confusing. And not all colleges and universities are organized in exactly the same way. We hope this description of offices, programs, and services will help you make sense of the college's unique way of doing business and ensure that you know where to go to receive the assistance you need when you have questions and concerns.

Dean's Office

The dean's office is the central location for all academic matters of the college or university. If your child is at a large university within which there are several colleges or schools, each of those units will have a dean's office dealing with the administrative issues relevant to the academic business of the college. The dean's office usually coordinates academic advising and oversees the hiring and promotion of teaching and research faculty members. You may want to contact this office if you are concerned about your child's academic advising situation or to ask questions about curricular offerings, course requirements, or other academic issues.

Dean of Students' Office

The dean of students' office oversees and is responsible for all aspects of college life outside of the classroom. This office is usually in charge of new student orientation, parents weekend, student activities, fraternities and sororities, and student government, and may also run special programs, such as time-management and self-defense workshops, among others. They may also coordinate public service and volunteer activities for student involvement in the campus and/or local community. The dean of students' office is the appropriate place for parents to get information and referrals on all aspects of student life. For example, parents might call this office for information on rules and policies governing the Greek system.

Bursar's Office

A strange name for a rather ordinary function—keeping track of student accounts and sending bills for tuition and room and board payments. Although ordinary, the processes are not necessarily simple or easy to understand. One parent complained that even though he was a certified public accountant, he couldn't understand the bursar's bill.

Depending on how the office is organized at your child's college, all kinds of charges may appear on this bill: some include tuition, room and board, campus store purchases, parking fees, dry cleaning and laundry, computer lab charges, and even pizza ordered from campus dining services. Most colleges have a student ID card that doubles as a charge card at locations around campus. Make it clear to your son or daughter what charges you are willing to support. It may take persistence to get answers to your questions, but you should feel free to contact the bursar's office if you have questions about your child's bill.

Financial Aid

You may be quite familiar with the financial aid office even before your child begins college. What you need to know is that your child's financial aid is calculated on a yearly (and sometimes on a term-by-term) basis. If there are changes in family circumstances, such as a parent losing a job, the financial aid office should be willing to readjust your child's aid package to reflect your change in financial status. Financial aid offices have counselors to assist you and your child in unraveling the arcane financial award systems. Encourage your child to make an appointment with a financial aid counselor if there are questions or problems regarding the financial aid package. College Parents of America is a membership organization dedicated to advocating on behalf of college parents. Their Web site, at collegeparents.org, offers valuable information on college costs and follows legislative initiatives that affect higher education.

Campus Security and Police

Even the smallest colleges employ security guards and often have a resident police presence. On most campuses, there are special campus police officers who have all of the jurisdictional rights of a regular community police force and are charged with enhancing safety and security on campus. They are authorized to enforce local, state, and federal laws.

Most college police personnel are individuals who have shown a particular interest in and sensitivity to working in a college environment. They are usually considered a part of the student services team and work around the clock to ensure that the campus environment is a safe one. They must comply with all of the federal- and state-mandated reporting and emergency advisory requirements.

You and your child are entitled to the information on campus crime that colleges and universities are required by law to compile and make available to the campus community. Many campus police and security operations offer free escort service and all of them provide emergency help twenty-four hours a day.

Student Employment Office

If your child is eligible for federal work study funds, he or she can be employed on campus as a part of the financial aid package. Most colleges do not assign students a job; students are responsible for seeking out available opportunities and deciding where they want to work. Studies have found that students who work on campus find this a very positive experience if the work hours are kept to a manageable number each week. Having to work for ten to twelve hours each week can actually help a student structure his or her time and learn useful time-management skills.

Campus jobs can provide a valuable connection to the campus community and many students develop close relationships with their supervisors, thus benefiting from additional mentoring and adult support. Some students who do not qualify for the federal work-study program also take jobs on campus and reap the benefits of these connections.

Learning Skills Centers and Writing Workshops

It's not unusual for even the brightest high school student to find the adjustment to college-level work a challenge. Most colleges and universities recognize that they need to provide additional support to students who need to develop more effective study skills and who may need help in writing college papers. Many offer supplemental instruction in introductory-level science, mathematics, and economics courses, as well as tutoring and workshops in critical reading and thinking. Urge your child to take advantage of these helpful services which are usually provided free of charge.

Career Services

All colleges and universities have a career services or career development office that provides a range of services to help students make the transition from college to a first job or to graduate or professional school. Career offices employ trained counselors who can help your child identity his or her career goals, develop job-search skills, and explore postgraduate educational options. Many offer recruiting programs for students interested in summer jobs, internships, and/or permanent jobs after graduation. They may also offer a credentials service that records, stores, and transmits confidential letters of recommendation for students. More information about career services programs is offered in Chapters 9 and 12.

Campus Crisis Services

In addition to health and psychological services, many campuses operate telephone crisis lines that are available around the clock to students who are dealing with difficult issues. Whether staffed by trained volunteers or mental health professionals, hotlines and crisis centers offer immediate help and a supportive environment for students struggling with thoughts of suicide, depression, sexual abuse, sexual orientation, substance abuse, stress, grief, family and relationship problems, and disordered eating. Most college towns also have a crisis hotline service available to students as well as to community members.

Equal Opportunity Office

All students have the right to study in a safe environment that is respectful of their race, ethnicity, gender, sexual orientation, age, veterans status, or learning or physical disability. The equal opportunity office on most campuses is equipped to counsel, advise, and assist students who have experienced bias, prejudice, sexual harassment, or any other form of discrimination in their course of study or in their extracurricular life on campus.

Computer Support Services

Due to the widespread use of computers and computer technologies on campuses today, all colleges and universities have computer support staff members who are available to assist students with learning new programs and applications and trouble shooting problems.

Campus Religious Organizations

Whether it's through the college or the local community, students will have access to religious services and counseling. Most schools employ chaplains and religious advisers who offer special services and support for students. Many also have nondenominational chapels that offer a variety of services.

Minority Students' Programs

If your child is a member of a racial or ethnic minority group, he or she can get support from the college's minority students program. These programs exist on most college campuses today and provide an important connection for students, as well as special programs and services to address their unique interests and needs.

Lesbian, Gay, Bisexual, and Transgender Programs

Most campuses today have lesbian, gay, bisexual, and transgender (LGBT) offices or centers that are committed to providing a safe environment for LGBT students. They organize and host programs and social support groups and advocate for the needs and concerns of LGBT students. In addition, they are committed to educating others about the issues of sexual orientation and gender identity and working to eliminate heterosexism, homophobia, and gender identity oppression on campus. These programs strive to create an inclusive environment to empower all students and can be instrumental in helping your son or daughter feel comfortable, safe, and accepted in the campus community. Due to the recent bullying incidents resulting in the suicides of several young people, many colleges and universities are increasing efforts to ensure that there is a safe environment on campus. If your son or daughter is lesbian, gay, bisexual, or transgender, you will want to encourage him or her to investigate these initiatives and programs.

International Students' Office

If your child is an international student, he or she may want to take advantage of the services provided on campus through the international students' office. Professional staff can offer assistance and advice on cultural adjustment and academic, personal, and immigration issues.

Student Disability Services

Colleges have an office or staff member who serves students with physical disabilities or learning disabilities. This office will provide students with a letter describing accommodations to which the student is entitled, such as extra time on tests. Students can give these letters to their professors who will arrange for the accommodations.

Study Abroad Programs

Your child may want to consider spending a semester or a year in a study abroad program. Many parents are pleasantly surprised to find that study abroad is no longer confined to children of the wealthy. In fact, the cost of a semester abroad can be less expensive than studying back home, although studying abroad is not a guaranteed bargain. If your child is interested in this type of program, he or she needs to start investigating programs early. Planning for such an experience can take a year or more.

Many colleges offer their own study abroad programs, but there are also programs available to all college students through hundreds of American colleges every year. Your child can find out about abroad programs through the college's career center or through the study abroad office on campus. The Internet also offers vast resources for students to explore a variety of study abroad opportunities.

Off-Campus Housing Office

Many colleges and universities do not guarantee student housing after the first or second year of study. And many students prefer to live off campus in apartments. If your child's college has an off-campus housing office, they can provide assistance in locating suitable housing, counseling students on the complexities of signing leases and dealing with local rental agents.

Athletics

Whether your child is involved in organized sports or wants to participate in an informal game of softball or soccer, most colleges offer opportunities for your child to engage in physical activity. Intramural or informal sporting events can provide a healthy way for your child to meet other students, get some exercise, and reduce stress. If your son or daughter is involved in an organized sport, you will no doubt have had contact with coaches and will be aware of services and support available to college athletes.

Student Activities

A major part of your child's experience in college will undoubtedly be his or her involvement in student activities and social events. Most schools have a wide variety of student activities that can help your child find friends with similar interests and make the adjustment to college smoother. Encourage your child to seek out activities and events; you might want to look at the college's Web site to see the variety of opportunities available. Students who are involved in the campus community report that it adds an important dimension to their college experience and it may make them more successful in their academic work as well. Typically, the dean of students' office oversees student activities and organizations on campus and students can easily access information about these opportunities on the Web.

How You Can Get Involved

Parents' Programs

In recent years, there has been an enormous growth in services provided to parents at most colleges and universities. This is, in part, a reaction to the "helicopter parent" phenomenon, but also a recognition on the part of higher education professionals that parents continue to play a key role in the lives of their children throughout college and beyond. Parents' programs or parents' offices on campus typically are charged with providing information to parents about aspects of the college experience and engaging them in appropriate interactions with the institution.

While colleges often have to walk a tenuous line between parent involvement and student privacy and autonomy, the parents' office can provide parents with information and assistance whether that parent has specific concerns about a son or daughter or is simply seeking information on the campus culture and educational program. One way that parents can get involved is to serve on a parents' advisory council. These councils offer invaluable assistance in providing feedback from parents to the university, as well as helping to organize and staff specific programs, such as family weekends, new student and parent orientation events, summer send-off parties for new students and their families and, of course, fund-raising to support campus initiatives that benefit students.

Until relatively recently, parents' offices on college campuses were simply a euphemism for fund-raising efforts directed at parents. This is no longer the case. Most parents' programs today have a broad mission to serve parents as an important constituency. It's important to keep in mind, however, that parents' program staff members cannot "fix" every issue that comes up for you as a parent. What they can do is listen to your concerns and either assist you in understanding the institution's goals in educating your child or to refer you to the appropriate person on campus who can address your concerns.

Getting involved in the parents' program on campus can be a wonderful way for you to feel connected to your child's college experience and you can do some significant good to advance the educational mission as well. If you're not able to make a commitment to serving on the parents' council, many institutions have parents' associations which are open to all parents and do a good job of keeping you informed (often through facilitating e-mail connections with other parents) and feeling part of the campus community. You may be willing to host a summer "send-off" party for new students and their parents or help organize a local get-together with other parents. Ask the parents' office director if he or she can suggest ways for you to participate. There is always a need for volunteers to help out with a variety of programs.

Alumni Clubs

Find out if there is an alumni organization in your town or city. These groups offer a unique way for you to be involved with the college from afar; many clubs offer special memberships for parents. Programs and activities vary, but often include presentations by faculty members, meetings with local community leaders, special faculty-led travel experiences, and sporting events. Alumni clubs often organize special public service projects and participate in fund-raising events. Check with the alumni office's Web site to find out about activities in your area.

Educational and Campus Vacations

Many colleges offer special travel packages, both domestic and international. These often include special seminars and study tours with leading members of the faculty. Some universities offer summer study vacations on campus with activities for the whole family. This can be a wonderful way to get to know your child's campus, learn something, and have the benefit of someone organizing interesting activities for all members of the family.

Athletic Events

You can attend a game or meet in your area. Check on the Web for schedules. If your son or daughter is a college athlete, you may want to get involved with a booster club or ask the athletic office for ways that you can support the team.

Career Services

Consider participating by offering internships or summer jobs at your place of employment for a college undergraduate. You may even convince your company to begin a recruiting program with the college. Be sure to contact the career services office if you have a summer internship or permanent job opening. You might also offer to travel to campus to participate in a program or career fair sponsored by the career office or agree to be a mentor or adviser to a student who is interested in a career in your field.

Chapter 8

$2,000 a Week for a College Education

Dealing with Money Issues and Understanding the Value of a College Education

I know college is a good investment in my son's future, but by the time he and his sister graduate, we'll have a big second mortgage on our house and no savings left. The next few years are really going to be hard on us financially. I sure hope it's worth it!

There is no doubt that paying for college is a major concern for parents, particularly in the face of a troubled overall economy in which many families are coping with job loss and financial instability. As college costs continue to rise and financially strapped states cut aid to higher education, you may question whether a college degree is worth the sacrifice that you must make in order for your son or daughter to graduate from college.

According to a 2008 study by the College Board, there is still a positive correlation between higher levels of education and higher earnings; the income gap between high school graduates and college graduates has increased significantly over time. In 2008, the median family income for those with a bachelor's degree was over $101,099 while the income for those with a high school degree was $49,414.

Although only the most elite colleges carry a $2,000 a week price tag, sticker shock is common when most parents face paying for college. When your generation went to college, it was probably possible to cover a large part of your college costs (at least at a state or public college) through summer job earnings. Now even state schools can cost upward of $12,000 a year.

Why is college so much more expensive today? Many factors contribute to the continuing rise in the price of a college education. Those most often cited in studies are: increased costs for financial aid; utilities; library materials; computer systems and technology; salaries for an aging and tenured faculty; the pressing need to complete deferred maintenance on buildings and laboratories; and the decrease in government support for education. Of course, the recent economic downturn also dramatically affected college and university endowments and that, in turn, affects the cost of providing educational programs and services.

Even though about two-thirds of all students receive some type of financial aid to help defray college costs, the burden on families is still significant. And even though some schools have made a serious effort to maintain stable tuition levels or even decrease tuition, the overall cost of going to college will continue to increase.

Many articles each year in the popular press exhort parents to save early for college, prepay tuition, cash in savings bonds, investigate new tax breaks, take advantage of scholarship opportunities, encourage children to become legally independent, or invest in tax-free education IRAs. We will not try to unravel the complexities of financial aid and scholarship policies, as there are many good resources available to help you understand and take advantage of the best method of financing your child's education.

Our goal is to help you explore two questions:

1. How can I communicate with my child about money issues during the college years?
2. How can I be sure that my child's education is worth the money I'm investing and the sacrifices I'm making?

Money Issues Beyond Tuition

In Chapter 3, we encouraged you to have a frank discussion with your child about how you will pay for the major college costs—tuition, room and board, books, and trips back and forth to school. While your child may still be financially dependent on you, now is the time to help him or her learn the basics of financial literacy. You can do this by working with your student to develop a budget for college costs. Review the basic costs and explain the financial aid package prepared by the college. Talk about what should be in the budget for spending money and "extras" and how much your student can contribute to the budget through earnings from summer or on-campus jobs. If you're unclear about what these costs might be, ask the college's financial aid office or experienced college parents for guidance.

Make it clear to your child what you are willing and able to pay for in addition to the basic costs of tuition, room and board, and books. For example, your child may want to do an unpaid internship in another city during the summer or attend summer school, thereby decreasing the amount that he or she can contribute to the next year's cost of school. Are you willing and/or able to consider this "extra"? Perhaps you can support one summer internship experience, but not two or three. The following scenarios will help you plan for some of the activities and situations that call for additional resources during the college years.

Renting an Apartment

Your son has been living in a residence hall and subscribing to the meal plan. In January of his sophomore year, he calls to tell you that he and his friends have found a great apartment for next year. He wants to sign a lease right away.

What's on Your Mind

> Why can't he live in the dorm?
> What will this apartment cost?
> How will he manage cooking, cleaning an apartment, and studying?

What's on Your Child's Mind

> I really want to get out of the dorms next year. All of my friends are getting out.
> It would be so cool to live in an apartment with my friends.

What's Going On

Many college students choose to live in apartments after the first couple of years on campus. This can actually be a cost-saving alternative if your son chooses the apartment with care and is willing to prepare his own meals. Renting an apartment during college can be a learning experience that prepares your child to take on such responsibilities after graduation.

What to Do

- Remind your child that these are decisions that require thought and time to consider.
- Ask him to get all of the details surrounding signing a lease and give you a proposal, comparing the costs of living in the dorm and renting an apartment.
- Go through the terms and conditions of the lease agreement with your child.
- Many colleges have an off-campus housing office; ask your child to have a staff member review the proposed lease or have a lawyer look at it.

What to Avoid

- Immediately saying no, before you have explored the possibilities.
- Responding to your son's insistence that the lease has to be signed immediately. This is rarely the case, except in major cities.

What You Need to Know

If your child wants to sign a lease for an apartment, it's important that you get all of the pertinent information regarding that lease before making a decision. Rental agents can be aggressive in trying to get students to sign lease agreements, especially if there is ample rental housing available near campus. It's to their advantage to sign up renters early and beat the competition.

Many apartment owners who rent to college students require what is called a "one for all" lease, meaning that each student is responsible for the entire cost of the apartment in the event that one or more of the renters doesn't carry through with the agreement. This could be a problem if one of the renters drops out of school or gets ill and can't return to college for the next year. Ask your child to come up with a fallback plan if this occurs. Many apartment leases have hidden costs, such as utilities and parking charges. Ask your child to gather all the facts and present them to you. If your child is going to rent an apartment with one or more other students, ask them to present a plan detailing how they will share costs. Do not let your son or daughter sign up to assume sole responsibility for utilities or other charges unless there is a written agreement with all of the renters to share equally in the costs.

Spring Break on a Credit Card

Your daughter announces that she wants to go on vacation with her friends over spring break in March. They plan to go to Mexico and spend a week on the beach. She says she can charge almost everything on her credit card.

What's on Your Mind

> Why can't she just come home?
> I've heard these spring break trips are drunken brawls.
> I'm concerned about how she'll pay off the credit card.

What's on Your Child's Mind

> Everyone is going on this spring break trip.
> It will be so great to go to the beach and relax for a week.
> I deserve a break.
> I can get an extra job this summer to pay for this.

What's Going On

Every spring, thousands of college students make the legendary trip to the beach. Others go to ski resorts or take even more exotic trips abroad during spring break. Students plan eagerly for these trips and feel the pressure to go along with friends. Travel companies offer seemingly great deals for these vacations, inundating campuses with special offers and promotional deals throughout the year.

What to Do

- Make it clear if you are unwilling to provide the money for a spring break vacation.
- Ask your child how he or she plans to pay for this trip.
- Discuss your concerns about safety. Ask your child to provide you with details on accommodations and travel.

What to Avoid

- Refusing to let her consider such a plan.
- Regaling her with stories of your drunken brawls "back in the day."

What You Need to Know

Students can get whipped up in a frenzy about going on spring break trips with their friends. Sometimes these vacations are wonderful, relaxing breaks from studying, and sometimes they are disasters with ten students sharing a motel room, cars breaking down en-route, and excessive drinking and partying around the clock. Make sure that your child has thought this trip through and has a fallback plan if things get out of control.

While it's a good idea for your child to have a credit card during college for emergencies, students can get into serious financial trouble by having several credit cards. Although today's students may find it harder to obtain credit cards than students in past years, many come to campus with a credit card. Credit card companies who do offer cards to students generally restrict the credit limit to five hundred dollars. But if a student has multiple credit cards he or she can incur significant debt. These cards usually carry the highest interest rates and annual fees so that students can easily charge far beyond their ability to pay. Even with present restrictions, it doesn't take long for a student to accumulate debt, and often it's the parents who end up bailing that student out because they don't want their child to begin life after college with a poor credit rating.

It's up to you to teach your child about credit cards and money management, helping him or her to be aware of "teaser" offers and inflated interest rates. Moreover, your child needs to understand the importance of establishing a responsible credit history and learning to set budget boundaries. Help your child investigate credit card offers. *Never* cosign a credit card application with your child unless you are willing and able to pay off the balance. Credit card companies are not required to reveal what purchases are made on the card, but if you cosign, you will be liable to pay off all charges that your child is unable to handle.

Fraternities, Sororities, and Social Clubs

Your son told you during holiday break that he wanted to go through rush and join a fraternity when he returns for his second semester at school. You've heard that fraternities are expensive and you wonder what the additional costs will be.

What's on Your Mind

Why does he want to join a fraternity? He seems to party enough already.
What is this going to cost?

What's on Your Child's Mind

I really want to join a fraternity.
All my friends are going to rush next semester.

What's Going On

Fraternities, sororities, and other social clubs can be a good way for your child to feel part of campus social life and to form a close group of friends during his college years. The costs of joining such organizations can vary dramatically from negligible to significant.

What to Do

- Have him give you all of the details about joining the fraternity, including social dues and fees.
- If he plans to live in a fraternity house, ask him to find out what room and board will cost.
- Ask him to figure out how he will cover the costs if they are greater than living in the dorm or in an apartment.

What to Avoid

- Assuming that fraternities are expensive and that you'll have to come up with more money for him to join.
- Telling him that he can't join before you know the facts and have discussed them with him.

What You Need to Know

Social life varies from campus to campus. At some colleges, fraternities and sororities provide a major part of the social life, while at others these social organizations play a relatively small role in life on campus. Just as these organizations vary from campus to campus, the costs of joining can be vastly different as well. It's important to get the information you need to help your child make this decision based on real costs. If your son decides to live in a fraternity house, it may actually cost less than living in a college dormitory or in an apartment. The social dues and fees are usually the costliest aspects of joining a fraternity or sorority. Fraternities, however, tend to throw more parties and, therefore, their social dues are usually higher than those charged by sororities. If your child was an actively social person in high school, this trend will probably continue when he or she goes to college.

Working Away from Home for the Summer

Your daughter is finishing up her sophomore year and wants to go to Maine to work in a restaurant for the summer. She has friends who did this last summer and they earned a substantial amount of money. She plans to go to Maine this summer with two of her sorority sisters who worked there last summer.

What's on Your Mind

Why can't she just come home and work as a waitress here again?
How do we know she'll be able to save the money she needs for next year?

What's on Your Child's Mind

It would be great to see another part of the country.
My friends worked in Maine last summer and made tons of money.

What's Going On

Many college students learn a great deal from living on their own for a summer. If they are willing to work hard, they can also earn as much or more money than they might while living at home and working.

What to Do

- Ask her to do some research on what other students have earned.
- Let her know if you expect her to contribute the same amount to her college costs next year.
- Ask her to do an estimate of her living costs away from home and discuss them with you before she makes a decision.

What to Avoid

- Insisting that she come home and work at the local restaurant again.
- Deciding she shouldn't do this before you find out what's involved.

What You Need to Know

Although waiting on tables has been one of the few high-paying jobs that students can do during the summer to earn money for their college expenses, these opportunities are rare in the current employment climate. If your daughter can find a good waitressing job, it's likely that she can earn enough money to pay for her living costs and save ample money to cover expenses for the next year at school.

It's important, however, that she makes realistic plans for this experience and has written assurance that a full-time job is awaiting her. She should ask her potential employer about what she can reasonably expect to earn and talk to other students who have worked there if possible. Then she needs to arrange affordable living quarters, in order to meet her savings goals for the summer.

The Unpaid Summer Internship

Your daughter, Abigail, calls home excited about applying for a summer internship.

ABIGAIL: Hi, Dad. I have some great news. I just found out about an awesome internship at an ad agency in Chicago, and I was wondering if it's okay with you and Mom if I apply for it. It sounds so cool. It's one of the best agencies in the whole country.

DAD: That sounds interesting, Abby, but where would you live for the summer?

ABIGAIL: One of my friends is going to work in Chicago, too. We thought we could get a place together. I heard that you can sometimes sublet an apartment from another student for the summer.

DAD: Sounds like it might be an expensive summer. How much does the internship pay?

ABIGAIL: Well, that's the bad news, Dad. It's unpaid.

DAD: What? You're going to work for someone all summer and not get paid anything?

ABIGAIL: Dad, there aren't any paid internships in advertising. At least there aren't any that I know of. Lots of students want to intern at this agency because it's such good experience, and I've heard that it's impossible to get a job in advertising after graduation if you don't have any experience. I think it's really worth it, don't you?

DAD: Well, it seems like it's going to cost a lot of money. I mean, you'd have to pay rent, buy your food, probably get some professional clothes, and just getting to Chicago and back is going to cost money. And you won't be earning any money to help with the expenses. What are you going to do for spending money next year at school if you don't earn any money this summer?

ABIGAIL: I don't know. Maybe I could get a higher-paying job on campus next year. I just want to apply for this internship so much.

What's on Your Mind

I can't believe these businesses hire students for the summer and don't pay them anything.
I wonder if it's true that there aren't any paying internships in advertising.
This summer experience could cost a couple thousand dollars.

What's on Your Child's Mind

> I really want to apply for this internship.
> It would be so cool to live in Chicago and work in an ad agency for the summer.
> I hope my parents will let me do it. It shouldn't cost that much if we can get a cheap
>   sublet.

What's Going On

Internships and career-related summer jobs can give students the opportunity to test their interest in a particular field, but students need to research the financial feasibility of these options. If Abigail has a serious interest in advertising as a career, it may be wise for her to try for this internship. If, however, you feel that she's primarily interested in spending the summer in Chicago, you may want to encourage her to try an advertising internship nearer to home for the summer and suggest that she plan for an internship away from home another summer.

What to Do

- Ask your child to provide you with more information about this opportunity and a budget for what it will cost, including the loss of her regular summer job earnings.
- Help her brainstorm ideas for getting work experience at home.
- Discuss what you are willing to support in the way of an unpaid internship experience.

What to Avoid

- Dismissing the idea of an internship without getting all of the details.
- Telling her there is no way she can take a summer job without pay.

What You Need to Know

It can be especially difficult for liberal arts or fine arts students to find summer jobs or internships that relate to their career interests. It's ironic that engineering or business majors, for example, are sought for the well-paying internships while liberal arts students, who also need "real world" work experience, are often unable to find paid internships.

But, there are ways that your child can manage an unpaid internship. It's possible to get an inexpensive sublet in most cities, room with friends, or stay in another university's residence hall. Your child could find a second job at night and earn some money while doing the unpaid internship. Or your child could arrange an internship in a similar organization at home, save the cost of living away for the summer, and work an extra job to earn money for the next school year.

If your child qualifies for federal work-study funds, it may be possible for her to be paid through the summer as well. Many employers who are unable to offer paid summer jobs will consider taking on a work-study student because they will only have to pay a small portion of that student's summer salary. Have your child check with her financial aid office early in the year to see if such an arrangement is possible.

This internship, while unpaid, may be the best choice because it offers a chance to explore a career field and acquire some job experience. Most employers now expect students to have career-related experience on their résumés when they seek an entry-level job after graduation. And in some fields, paid internships are simply not available. You need to discuss the options with your child and remember that an internship experience may be a worthwhile investment in your child's future career prospects.

Students who attend college in a major metropolitan area can often find worthwhile internships during the school year, sometimes requiring only a few hours a week. It may be possible to have an internship and remain on campus in a regular academic program. Students can also gain valuable job-related experiences through volunteer work on campus or in the community during the school year. If your child attends college in a rural area or small town, however, these options may not be available.

Study Abroad

Your daughter is in her sophomore year of college. She wants to spend next year in France with her college's junior year abroad program. She's just chosen French as her major and feels that a year in France, being exposed to native speakers, will improve her language skills.

What's on Your Mind

> This sounds pretty exotic. How much will it cost?
> Will her credits transfer?
> Will she be safe?

What's on Your Child's Mind

> It would be so amazing to spend a year in Paris.
> I could travel all over Europe.
> I can try out my French and I'll meet so many interesting people.

What's Going On

Overseas study by American students is on the rise. Each year thousands of students receive credit for studying in a foreign country. Many colleges and universities have their own study abroad programs or help students to take advantage of the hundreds of programs offered by other institutions. In fact, study abroad is seen as such a positive experience that some colleges offer attractive financial incentives for their students to spend time in another country during their college years.

What to Do

- Ask your child to provide you with detailed information on the program she's considering.
- Talk to her about the advantages and disadvantages of living and studying abroad.
- Find out how the costs abroad compare with the cost of remaining on campus for the year.
- Read all of the literature about the study abroad program.

What to Avoid

- Resisting the idea without knowing all of the facts.
- Assuming that this is going to cost much more than studying in the States for the year.

What You Need to Know

Studying abroad can cost the same as—or even less than—studying in the States. Make a concerted effort to gather all of the information available and discuss the possibilities with your daughter. Be a wise consumer of these offers, and make sure that credits will transfer, adequate housing is available, relative safety is assured, and the costs are manageable for your budget.

Some schools offer short-term study/travel abroad, but, again, investigate the offers and ensure that they are appropriate for your child. Many students experiment with an abbreviated travel program abroad to decide if they really want to study abroad for a whole semester or year. In a rapidly shrinking world, study abroad can be an important experience, adding value to your child's résumé when graduating from college. Refer to Chapter 7 for more information on study abroad programs.

A Car on Campus—Luxury or Necessity?

Your son, Max, insists that he needs a car on campus next year.

> MAX: Dad, I really need a car next year at school.
>
> DAD: Why?
>
> MAX: I'm going to be student teaching next semester and the school where I'll be teaching is a long way from campus.
>
> DAD: How far?
>
> MAX: A few miles at least.
>
> DAD: Can't you ride your bike? Or get a placement nearer to campus?
>
> MAX: No, this is the only school where my professor could place me. And I have to dress up and look professional. I can't be riding my bike to school through the rain and stuff. How would that look?
>
> DAD: We just can't afford to get you a car right now, Max, and your mother and I need our cars to get to work. Isn't there any public transportation? I thought there was a bus system there.
>
> MAX: There is, but it's limited and I'd waste a lot of time waiting around for one to come. I have to study, too, you know.
>
> DAD: How many weeks do you have to student teach?
>
> MAX: I think about ten.
>
> DAD: Well, maybe your brother would lend you his car to take to school for those ten weeks. You know he's worked hard at his after-school job to get his car, but he might be willing to let you borrow it, if it's only for part of the semester. It's kind of an old jalopy, but it should be able to get you back and forth.
>
> MAX: What's Brad going to do?
>
> DAD: He could take the school bus for a while I guess. Why don't you ask him? Maybe he'll make a deal with you if you get it tuned up and serviced for him.

What's on Your Mind

I don't think Max really needs a car on campus.
We can't afford to buy him a car.
We can probably work out something if it's only for ten weeks.

What's on Your Child's Mind

I don't see why I can't have a car.
It would be so much easier if I had a car on campus.
All of my friends have cars.

What's Going On

While it's true that many students have cars on campuses today, usually it is not a necessity but a luxury and a convenience. Rarely do students need a car on campus to fulfill course requirements, but there are extraordinary situations, such as Max's, when a car may be needed for a period of time. Students may find life easier if they have a car, especially if they live off campus and there are no grocery stores nearby. Many students, however, want cars for social or recreational reasons; few really need a car while in college.

What to Do

- Find out if your child really needs a car and why.
- Ask your child to come up with alternatives if a car isn't possible.
- Explore the advantages and disadvantages of having a car on campus. For example, most colleges charge a lot for parking, in part to discourage students from bringing cars to school.
- Remind your child of the responsibilities that accompany having a car and the additional costs involved.

What to Avoid

- Saying no before you find out the specifics. Your child *may* actually need a car for a legitimate reason.
- Being pressured into buying your child a car before you know the situation.

What You Need to Know

Although typically a college student doesn't need to have a car on campus, there may be exceptions and you may need to make a car available to your child for a specific purpose and for a limited time.

If you are in favor of your child having a car on campus, make sure that he knows what this responsibility involves. Cars need servicing and care; your child needs to know how to handle car emergencies. Students don't automatically know that cars need periodic oil checks and fluid replacements. Be prepared for parking and other expenses if your child has a car on campus.

Many cities now have car-share programs through which individuals can have access to a car without having to purchase, borrow, or rent one. These arrangements are most appropriate if a car is needed only occasionally for a specific period of time. You can find more information and usually reserve a car online.

Change in Family Income

You have just been informed that you've lost your job. Your son is in his junior year of college and you feel awful after telling him the bad news.

What's on Your Mind

> What if I can't find another good job right away?
> I can't see how I'm going to pay for college.
> This couldn't have come at a worse time. I should have saved more money.

What's on Your Child's Mind

> This is terrible. What if I can't finish school?
> How is my family going to survive?

What's Going On

Many families, unfortunately, face this problem every year as companies go out of business or have to downsize and lay off workers. In addition to worrying about basic financial survival, parents have to consider interrupting their child's education. This is a very difficult situation for parents; their first reaction may be to shield their child from upsetting news.

What to Do

- Tell your child as soon as you know that you will be losing your job.
- Try to stay calm and confident about coping with this crisis.
- Let your child know what you are doing to find other employment.
- Get in touch with your child's financial aid counselor, explain the situation, and ask for help.

What to Avoid

- Immediately announcing that your child will have to quit college.
- Blaming yourself for not being able to support your family.
- Accepting the fact that you'll be unemployed for a long time and sharing your anxieties about the future with your child.

What You Need to Know

While you may feel anxious about giving your child unpleasant news, it is almost always preferable to keep your child informed about what's going on at home. You need to address your own anxieties about the situation first, and then prepare to explain the circumstances to your child. It's easy for parents to overreact and even go to extreme measures to shield their children from worry. In our experience, however, students who feel included in family decisions and events, even when they are not living at home for most of the year, are able to adjust to changes more successfully. These situations offer opportunities to act as a consultant with your child, treating him or her as an adult. You must take the lead in devising solutions and alternatives, but your child should be kept informed.

Especially in the current economic climate, circumstances change for many families when they have children in college. Because colleges realize that no one has a completely secure job, they are prepared to renegotiate financial aid packages when a family's ability to contribute to their child's education changes dramatically. They may ask students to take on additional loans, work at campus jobs, or even take a semester or a year off to earn money to help pay for college. Whether parents are paying the full cost themselves or helping their child put together a financial aid package that includes grants, loans, and summer earnings, the cost of college is a burden to most families—especially when a family's major wage earner loses a job.

The Value of a College Education

Living a Life and *Earning a Living*

Your son went off to college with the intention of becoming a computer science major. You were pleased that he had chosen a major that would put him in a good position to get a job upon graduation, even though his first love had always been the theater. In his sophomore year of college he found an internship with a local theater company updating their reservations system on the computer. He also worked with the lighting computers and helped design the lighting for a couple of productions. He sees now that he can combine his computer science knowledge with his love of the theater and is thinking of looking for a job with a theater company when he graduates. You're not so sure about theater as a career path.

What's on Your Mind

Will he be able to support himself?
If he accepts a job in computer science, his future might be more secure.

What's on your Child's Mind

I'm really excited about being able to work in the theater.
Now I can see how useful my computer skills will be.

What's Going On

Students who have the benefit of work experience in college often modify their educational goals as they begin to see how they can apply their skills in the workplace. This does appear to be the best of both worlds. Your son will continue his computer science education and add theater courses so that he'll be able to work in a field that interests him.

What to Do

- Encourage your child to explore internships or summer jobs in the theater to obtain more experience.
- Remember that computer science is a good background regardless of whether the theater job works out.

- Let go of your expectations—it's your child's life and he has a right to follow his heart as well as his head.

What to Avoid

- Trying to convince your son that a job with a computer company would be much more stable and lucrative.
- Discounting his interest in working in the theater as a passing fancy.
- Expressing your disappointment in his choices for his future.

What You Need to Know

While it is true that computer science, engineering, economics, and math majors can expect to earn among the highest starting salaries of college graduates, these fields also employ low earners. No specific college major is a guarantee of financial success, especially in a world in which major new career areas are emerging every year. The key determiner of success in any field is the individual's motivation to succeed. You'll find more about academic majors and career expectations in the next chapter.

Majoring in Underemployment

You're upset by the following conversation with your daughter, Paige, who is currently a business major at the state university.

PAIGE: Mom, I've been thinking about changing my major.

MOM: Really? To what?

PAIGE: To fine arts.

MOM: Fine arts? You're kidding, right?

PAIGE: No, Mom, I'm not. I took this great sculpture course as an elective and I really loved it.

MOM: But I thought you wanted to work in a small business.

PAIGE: Well, I like business, but I love art. I've even been doing some painting again, and I'm so happy when I can be creative.

MOM: I know you love art, honey, but you could paint and be a business major, too.

PAIGE: Not really. I checked with the fine arts department and if I want to pursue fine arts, I'll have to change my major and really concentrate on studio courses. You

know, painting, sculpture, and drawing. I can even study printmaking and photography.

MOM: I just don't understand why you insist on fine arts as a career. You can always enjoy
painting in your free time.

PAIGE: But I love art and you always told me that I should do what I love.

MOM: But, Paige, there aren't any jobs for fine arts majors. What will you do when you
graduate?

PAIGE: Well, I could work in graphic arts. You know, in advertising or something like that.
Or I could work in a gallery, or maybe a museum.

MOM: Do you know what people in those jobs earn, if they're lucky enough to get a job in
the first place? I can't imagine you could support yourself. Artists live in hovels and
have to waitress to pay the rent!

PAIGE: So, what would I do with a business major? Work in some boring company analyzing
spreadsheets? I just want to be an artist. I don't care if I have to struggle for a while.

What's on Your Mind

I'm worried that Paige will never be able to support herself.
I'm spending a lot of money for her education, and I want her to have a chance at a good job.
Why can't she see that art is an avocation, not a vocation?

What's on Your Child's Mind

I love art. I want to be an art major.
I can't see myself as a businessperson.

What's Going On

It's natural for parents to show concern when their child switches from a "secure" major to one
that doesn't seem to promise much in the way of career potential. Parents necessarily want to
see a payback for the money they have invested in their child's education. They also want to
know that their child has a chance at being self-supporting after college.

What to Do

- Try to be supportive of your child's love for art.
- Encourage her to explore the career possibilities available to fine arts majors.

- Remember that students who have a passion for their major tend to excel in college and find satisfying work eventually.

What to Avoid

- Insisting that your daughter remain a business major.
- Denigrating fine arts as a major.
- Threatening to cut off support if she changes majors.

What You Need to Know

Regardless of what your child's major is in college, her earning potential is far greater than if she had just graduated from high school. While it may take her longer to find a career niche, your investment in her college education, over time, will yield anywhere from a 10 to 50 percent return, depending on her earnings. It's hard to imagine a better return on investment.

Parents who have sacrificed to put their child through college must balance their expectations with their child's initial earning potential. Especially now, fine arts and liberal arts graduates are likely to go through a floundering period after college and take longer to become comfortably self-supporting. Parents need to keep in mind that the return on their investment in college costs may take several years to materialize if their child chooses a career path that doesn't bring immediate financial rewards. Most students five or ten years out of college are working in careers that do not directly relate to their major. In fact, few work in the career field that they thought interested them in college. Chapter 9 will explore career expectations and academic choices in greater depth.

When faced with high tuition bills, it's easy to forget that there are enormous intrinsic rewards in the pursuit of higher education. The experiences your child has in college—the opportunity to study a field of interest in depth, the chance to interact with students from diverse backgrounds, and the challenge of making decisions and taking responsibility for those decisions—will contribute enormously to his or her ability to live a satisfying life as well as to earn a living.

Chapter 9

So, You Always Wanted to Be a Doctor

Career Expectations, Academic Choices, and the Value of Practical Experience

Marisa always wanted to be a doctor and we were thrilled. Some people have a family doctor, but we have a family of doctors! You can imagine how disappointed and confused we were when she told us that she had decided to drop premed and major in economics. We're really surprised and worried about her decision.

Your Expectations and Your Child's Choices

You've committed significant resources to your child's education and now you're worried about his or her prospects for the future. The job market changes so rapidly it's hard to follow. None of us can predict the future, and very few careers can offer permanent security. Even medical doctors, tenured teachers, and computer scientists fall prey to the changes in national and world economic and employment circumstances.

In our culture, careers indicate social status and social class mobility. Many people define themselves by their jobs, and it's hard not to see your child's career choice as a reflection on you as a parent. You have high expectations that a college education will guarantee your child a personally rewarding and secure future. In a work environment that constantly changes, you may wonder how your child's education will translate into a good job upon graduation and how you can help as your child makes career decisions.

You can do three things:

1. Encourage your child to get practical experience to prepare him or her for a first job.
2. Use your consulting skills and put your child in touch with other people you know who can act as advisers and coaches in exploring career interests.

3. Be open to learning about career areas and how they relate to college backgrounds so that you understand the myths and realities about the world of work.

You don't have to become an expert on every possible job and career field. You don't need to find out if computer software engineers have higher salaries than chemical engineers, or what the five hottest career fields are predicted to be in five years. Even if you had all this information and could choose the ideal career for your child, your child has his or her own ideas. Your child may not be interested in the career fields that you would choose. Your role is to offer support and guidance as your child tries to make sense of the many options.

How Majors Relate to Careers

As students explore the academic offerings of college, they may change majors and career aspirations several times. These scenarios will help you understand the sometimes confusing relationship between college major and career potential.

Changing from Engineering to Liberal Arts

Your daughter, Amanda, is a sophomore and it's time for her to declare a major course of study. She went to college wanting to be an engineer and you're proud that she's chosen such a viable career field. You're surprised and troubled by the conversation you had with her.

DAD: I was just reading *The Wall Street Journal* and came across this article about the challenges that seniors are facing this year in the job market. It made me think of you and whether you've thought any more about what you'll do this summer. Maybe it would be a good idea to apply for an internship.

AMANDA: Yeah, I know. All the seniors I know are really freaking out about getting a job. I'm so glad I'm only a sophomore; I am having second thoughts about engineering though.

DAD: Second thoughts? You're not thinking about changing majors are you?

AMANDA: Well, yes, I am, sort of. I've told you how much I like psychology courses. I met with my psychology professor yesterday and he said I would still have time to graduate on time if I switched my major to psychology.

DAD: What could you possibly do with psychology? I can't picture you as a therapist.

AMANDA: Dad, there are lots of things you can do with psychology besides being a therapist.

DAD: Like what?

AMANDA: My professor said lots of his former students have been successful in business jobs. Psychology involves working with data—it's a lot like science, Dad. But the data in psychology are more interesting to me than the data in engineering.

DAD: You can't be serious. I just read an article that said engineering is one of the hot career fields and that companies are especially looking to hire women. Are you wimping out on me? I know dealing with all that math is tough, but it will be worth it in the end.

AMANDA: Dad, psychology has lots of math, too. It has nothing to do with the math. Besides, my psychology professor says that all the experience you get in quantitative analysis in psychology prepares you for business. And I think psychology is fascinating—all those things about what motivates people and whether intelligence is inherited or depends on your environment. You would love it, Dad. And I think it would prepare me to be a manager in business.

DAD: Amanda, if you're going to abandon engineering then why don't you just major in business? At least you'll be able to get a job when you graduate.

AMANDA: The business courses are so boring. Remember, I took one last semester. I don't think you need to sit through such boring courses to be prepared to go into business. At least that's what my psychology professor says. He says it's better to major in what fascinates you, and as long as you have good basic skills in critical thinking, analytical reasoning, writing, and quantitative analysis, you'll be fine.

DAD: Your psychology professor sounds like he doesn't know anything about the real world.

AMANDA: But I also went to the career center and they said that recruiters look for students who have been in leadership positions in student organizations. They told me that being president of my sorority is giving me experience that I couldn't get just by taking courses. I'm pretty sure I'll be able to get a good job when I graduate.

DAD: Amanda, don't you follow the news? Haven't you heard how difficult it is to get a job—any job—today?

What's on Your Mind

What is Amanda thinking?

This psychology professor has her brainwashed.

Who cares if psychology is fascinating? You can't support a family by being fascinated—you need practical skills.

What's on Your Child's Mind

Dad just doesn't understand that you can get a good job without majoring in a professional field.

I just love psychology. It's intriguing.

I'm not wimping out, am I? Psychology is full of hard math and science.

What's Going On

Amanda's dad tries to keep up with trends in the job market and accurately noted that Amanda will be facing a really tough job market when she graduates. But is her dad taking the short-term view? It's natural that a parent would want to promote a major that seems to guarantee future job possibilities. It may be difficult for a parent to share the enthusiasm for switching to a seemingly less career-oriented major. On the other hand, Amanda is excited about pursuing psychology and has made an effort to explore the skills she can attain that will enhance her career options. Depending on the particular department and the courses she chooses, she will likely be able to graduate with a solid scientific and quantitative background.

What to Do

- Ask your daughter to gather information on what types of jobs psychology majors obtain after graduation.
- Encourage your daughter to research what psychology alumni are doing five to ten years out of college, not just immediately after graduation. Many schools have networks of alumni who are available to talk to students about careers.
- Suggest that she take electives or think about minoring in business.
- Recommend that she talk to some women faculty and alumni in engineering. If she likes the field, but simply needs a mentor and helpful adviser, she may be able to find one this way.
- Be prepared to accept your child's choice of major.
- Encourage your daughter to gain some relevant work experience during the summer and school vacations.

What to Avoid

- Making assumptions about an academic field without investigating it. The career center or Psychology Department should be able to tell you what psychology majors do after graduation.

- Having your daughter believe that she will be a failure if she abandons engineering.
- Threatening that you will not pay for her education unless she majors in something practical like engineering.

What You Need to Know

It's difficult, at best, for anyone to predict the future of employment opportunities, especially during a time of record job losses and uncertainty in the national and global marketplace. It is particularly difficult to foresee what will be in store for the next wave of college graduates. As we witness graduating seniors struggling to gain entry into the professional workforce, many will spend time working as baristas, waiters, and retail salespeople until the job market improves. This "underemployment" will likely have an impact on their career trajectory for years to come.

We have entered a new era in which the Millennial Generation, the largest generation in history, faces extreme competition for jobs at a time when there are vast structural changes going on in the labor market. As the nature of the job market changes, graduates will have to be extraordinarily flexible and tenacious. This job market requires the capacity to specialize and find niche markets in which to employ those skills; the chances of finding an entry-level professional job may depend more than ever on a specific degree. Liberal arts majors can increase their chances of employment if they are willing and able to work at internships and summer jobs that give them specific skills to market when they graduate.

While more generalized skills such as problem-solving, critical thinking, the capacity to work collaboratively, and proficiency in writing and speaking will always be valued by employers, they are, sadly, not sufficient in this hypercompetitive job climate. Graduates need specific skills that are immediately applicable to the workplace. These can include, but are not limited to, computer skills, including knowledge of multiple digital technologies, math and computational ability, and knowledge of foreign languages and cultures.

A liberal arts education encompasses study of the humanities (for example, English and philosophy), the social sciences (psychology, economics, and political science), and the natural and physical sciences (biology, chemistry, and physics). Many parents and students identify the humanities and social sciences, in particular, as impractical in today's job market. While it may take liberal arts graduates longer to find a career niche, it's clear that flexibility and the desire to continue to learn can be the keys to success in the long run, given that the job market will change rapidly in an increasingly global economy.

The Importance of Practical Experience

Your daughter announced over Thanksgiving dinner that she's not sure she wants to attend law school when she graduates, and that she's thinking of changing her major from political science to accounting.

What's on Your Mind

Accounting? She's never been interested in numbers.
She's always wanted to be a lawyer, so what happened?
Is she doing this just because she heard it was easier to get a job?

What's on Your Child's Mind

I love the accounting course I'm taking.
The faculty members in the business school are some of the best teachers here. They
    understand the real world.
Why are my parents so surprised? Everyone I know is thinking of changing majors.

What's Going On

While not everyone changes majors in college, a significant number of students do. In fact, some students change majors several times and often choose a major based on the quality of the faculty members in a particular department. It can be unsettling for parents when their child shifts to another course of study or abandons a goal of pursuing a lucrative and prestigious graduate degree. It's natural to worry about your child's future prospects; after all, you have the benefit of a lifetime's experience and knowledge about work and making a living. However, you can support your child's academic exploration during college and help her to be more "career ready" when she graduates.

What to Do

- Listen to her interests and ask her questions that will help you understand her sudden interest in accounting.
- Ask her to visit the career center on campus and find out more about careers in accounting.

- Talk to her about the career areas that she's interested in.
- Encourage her to apply for an internship or summer job to test out her interests.
- Suggest that she network with alumni who studied accounting to learn more about the field.

What to Avoid

- Refusing to accept her change of major. If you insist on controlling her choice of major, she could be less motivated and do poorly.
- Believing that she'll never go to graduate school.
- Telling her that you think accounting is boring.

What You Need to Know

Your daughter's interest in accounting may be driven by what she's heard about job prospects or it may be driven by genuine enthusiasm or both! Many parents who are committed to the value of a liberal arts degree need to be flexible when consulting with their children. It's important to be sensitive to the very real career challenges facing young people and continue to listen to their concerns and aspirations.

Whatever major your child settles on, you can encourage him or her to try a summer job or internship to help refine those interests and career goals. And don't overlook field studies that can be done during the academic year. Many colleges have work and field study semesters in which students participate in seminars and internships for academic credit. These opportunities for practical experience may be called internships, field study, or coop placements. Graduates tell us that these experiences were the single most useful tool in helping them define their career goals and become more marketable upon graduation.

These experiences can help students focus their career goals and be more attractive to employers who seek a demonstrated interest in a specific career field and an understanding of the world of work. Accounting can provide a solid background for law school and other areas of study if she decides to go to graduate school later. More important, however, is her enthusiasm about majoring in accounting—students who love what they study perform significantly better in college than students who are pressured into majoring in a subject they don't enjoy. You may be concerned if your child chooses a major based on the teaching skills of certain professors, but your child *will* receive a better education from better teachers.

The vast majority of people today change careers many times during their working lives and most people do not ultimately work in a field directly related to their college major. The critical issue is that your child's major engages her and helps her to become an adult who is prepared to continue learning and growing.

Evolving Career Goals

Even students who begin college with clearly defined academic interests and goals often change their focus and decide to pursue a different path. This can be a disconcerting process for students and parents alike. Your consulting skills will be valuable as you help your child explore goals and aspirations during the college years.

Choosing Teaching Instead of Premed

Your son, Bill, has always wanted to be a doctor but now, in his second year at the university, he's having second thoughts about medicine. At holiday break, you had the following conversation:

MOM: So, how was your fall semester?

BILL: Pretty good, but I've been thinking a lot about whether it makes sense for me to stay in the premed program.

MOM: What? You aren't thinking of dropping out of school are you?

BILL: No, I'm not talking about leaving school. I'm just thinking about changing my career goal. You know how I've been having trouble with my premed courses, especially chemistry.

MOM: Yeah, but you told me you had talked to an adviser in the minority students office, who said that it wasn't unusual for kids to struggle with chemistry. I thought you were getting extra help in the learning center with your chemistry. You're still doing that aren't you?

BILL: Yes, I am, and it's helping. My grade has improved. But Bs or Cs are still not good enough to be accepted into medical school. Besides, I started thinking about why I really wanted to be a doctor. It's always been important to me to be able to help people, and I want to be able to come back to Brooklyn and help people in our neighborhood. But I'm really not that interested in being a research scientist.

MOM: Wait a minute. Who said anything about being a research scientist? You've always said you wanted to be a doctor—since you were a little boy. You told me, you told

Grandma—you told everyone at church—that you wanted to be a doctor. You don't want to be a doctor anymore?

BILL: It's not so much that I don't want to be a doctor. I'm just not sure. Anyway, my adviser told me that I should have a backup plan in case I don't get into medical school.

MOM: What's this about not getting into medical school? You were the smartest kid in your high school weren't you? Who thinks you might not get into medical school?

BILL: Mom, that was high school. It's different in college. I'm just not sure that I can get high enough grades in chemistry and physics. I could still study biology and go into teaching. My adviser says there's a need for good science teachers, especially in neighborhoods like ours. I could come back and be like Mr. Williams, my tenth-grade biology teacher. He really inspired me to go on in science.

MOM: What? You're thinking of being a schoolteacher? After all this hard work and sacrifice, you want to be a teacher instead of a doctor?

What's on Your Mind

Bill's always wanted to be a doctor.
Where did he get this idea to be a schoolteacher?
Do you have to have all As to get into medical school?

What's on Your Child's Mind

I never thought about the fact that I might not get into medical school.
I'm not sure if I want to be a doctor or a teacher.
I just know that I want to help people and I could do that either way.

What's Going On

Bill is working hard, but he can't seem to get better than Cs and Bs in his chemistry courses. It's not unusual for students to struggle with science courses in college. College courses move at a much faster pace than high school courses, and students are expected to learn and digest large amounts of information. In high school, teachers often guided students step by step, while in college faculty members expect students to figure out more on their own. This can overwhelm even the best students. At the same time, it's hard to understand why your child isn't the top student he was in high school. If you have little or no experience with college yourself, it's even more difficult to understand why hard work may not result in As.

In small colleges, students can receive individual help and guidance from faculty in science courses, but at large universities, introductory science courses often serve to weed out all but the most talented and best-prepared students from the field. It can be extremely hard to get As. At these large universities, support services and learning centers can help students, but some will need this extra support just to get Bs and Cs. Students who have not been challenged in high school will have to learn new study skills; they will no longer be able to manage on innate ability.

What to Do

- Try to listen to your child and find out what he is thinking and feeling.
- Focus on your son's needs rather than your own desire to have him be a doctor.
- Express understanding about how hard college chemistry must be and give him credit for getting extra help and working hard.
- Encourage him to think carefully about whether he wants to pursue teaching or if he simply feels discouraged about his ability to get into medical school.

What to Avoid

- Insisting that he has to be a doctor to meet your expectations and not disappoint so many people who are proud of him in your family, church, and community.
- Letting him know that you are disturbed that he may become a schoolteacher.
- Acting as if medical school is his only option and he will have failed if he doesn't follow through with his plans.

What You Need to Know

Applying to medical school can be a confusing and daunting process. You may have difficulty determining if your child is giving up his dream of medical school because he's losing confidence in his ability to get in, or if he has seriously thought about the alternatives and decided that he is better suited for a career as a teacher. You may wonder how you can help your child as he struggles with this difficult decision. You may find rereading Chapter 5 helpful in dealing with this situation.

The most effective role you can play is one of helping your son explore the alternatives and urging him to gather the information he needs to make an informed decision. Bill can obtain a realistic assessment of his chances of getting into medical school by talking to the premed adviser and finding out what kind of grades and scores he needs. Encourage him to explain his goals to the premed adviser and map out a realistic plan, including a fallback plan in case he does not get accepted into medical school.

We know of many students who fall short of the stringent requirements to get into medical school right out of college but who eventually do get accepted and go on to successful careers as doctors. If it's clear that your son wants to be a doctor, you need to encourage him to take whatever steps he can to strengthen his case for admission. He may need to take a preparation course for the MCAT exam, or take time off between college and medical school to gain some relevant experience to enhance his application. He could work as a research assistant in a medical school laboratory, join the Peace Corps or AmeriCorps as a healthcare volunteer, or take additional science courses to prove that he can excel in them. Today, increasing numbers of students who want to go to medical school take time after college to do what they can to improve their chances of acceptance to these extremely competitive schools. The average age of entering students at many medical schools today is twenty-five.

If, however, your son persists in wanting to teach, you can encourage him to acquire some experience in a classroom to help him decide if this is the career path for him. Many college students volunteer in local schools for a few hours a week or work in a summer program. He could apply for the Teach for America program, try teaching in a private school, or take the courses necessary to get certified to teach in a public school after graduation. While it's true that few teachers have high salaries, it can be a financially stable and personally rewarding profession. If he decides after a couple of years that he really does want to be a doctor, having worked as a teacher will not hurt his medical school chances; in fact, it will provide support for his interest in helping people.

You can play an important role in helping him explore his options, but you need to be prepared to accept his decisions along the way. It can be hard to give up *your* dreams for your child's career, but you can be most helpful by raising questions, offering guidance, and ultimately supporting the decisions he makes for himself. As difficult as it may be, you need to remember that this is *his* life and these are *his* decisions to make.

In our roles as career counselors, we have had students ask us if they can have their parents call us to talk about why it's a reasonable decision for the student to change plans from medical school to some other field. It may help you to call a staff member at the college to gain a better understanding of your son's situation and options. Don't call the college to take care of your son's business for him, but do call if you want to get some of your own questions answered.

You Want Your Child to Be a Doctor or Lawyer

When your daughter is home over spring break, she says that rather than use her biology background to go to medical school, she thinks she wants to apply to nursing school.

What's on Your Mind

> What am I going to tell the relatives? All of her cousins are in medical school or law school. We've sacrificed a lot so that she could have the chance to become a doctor.

What's on Your Child's Mind

> I'm really interested in nursing.
> My summer job in the hospital was wonderful.
> I don't know why my parents have to be so narrow-minded.

What's Going On

You may not know much about professional jobs, but you know that medicine and law are prestigious and financially rewarding professions. Meanwhile, your daughter, who has done quite well academically and could certainly get into medical school, discovered last summer that nursing was a respected and rewarding profession as well.

What to Do

- Encourage your daughter to learn as much as she can about nursing—its advantages and disadvantages.
- Suggest that she talk to students in the nursing program she's investigating and make an effort to talk to practicing nurses who can help her explore the field further.
- Learn all you can about nursing.

What to Avoid

- Ruling out all fields except medicine and law.
- Giving your daughter an ultimatum: she goes to medical school or you won't pay for her education.

- Putting your daughter in the position of having to choose between your love and support and a career that interests her.

What You Need to Know

While not as prestigious and perhaps not as lucrative as being a doctor, nursing can be a vital and satisfying career. Nurses are currently in great demand, as are other health-care professionals. In fact, nursing is one of a very short list of professions with the potential of career security. Your daughter will no doubt be very employable upon graduation from nursing school and that is an important advantage in this era of joblessness. She could also go to graduate school and become a nurse practitioner, specializing in a particular area of medicine, which will guarantee her a higher salary and increased professional responsibility and credibility.

If you force your daughter to choose between the only two professional fields that you value, chances are she won't be happy. Given the choice of a daughter who is a successful nurse or an unhappy doctor—or even worse, one who can't face her parents or other relatives if she isn't a doctor—we hope you would support her decision to become a nurse. You may have difficulty accepting your child's change in career choice, especially if you have sacrificed a great deal and had one specific dream for your child, but you need to remember that this is your child's decision, not yours, to make.

The Value of Internships

Internships and career-related job experiences make classroom learning more meaningful and eventually help your child make the transition from college to the world of work. Students who have the opportunity to test their skills in a real world setting have a distinct advantage when they search for their first job after graduation.

Internships Help Focus Career Goals

Your son, a sociology major, always thought that he would be a social worker someday. He took a course in urban issues and found out about a summer internship working at a nonprofit community housing agency. Because they couldn't pay him much, the agency agreed to work with his school so that he could get academic credit for his summer's work.

At the end of the summer, he had an entirely different view of his career prospects and began thinking about a career in nonprofit administration. The agency director expressed interest in interviewing him for a permanent position when he graduates.

What's on Your Mind

This summer internship really changed his perspective.
He seems so confident about his future now.
I guess a major in sociology is good for a number of different jobs.

What's on Your Child's Mind

I thought that sociology majors usually became social workers or teachers.
I found out that I can do many different things with my academic background.
I really enjoyed working at Neighborhood Housing Services. I can see the impact that this organization has on people's lives.

What's Going On

Many students find an internship or summer job a great opportunity to learn about a little-known career area. In addition, this internship offered the opportunity to meet with and learn from a variety of related professionals—architects, planners, real estate brokers, and lawyers, as well as community activists. Your son worked on a report to the mayor and his sponsor recognized that he had strong writing skills. He did some preliminary analysis using a spreadsheet, interviewed clients, and gave part of a major presentation to the city's board of zoning appeals. He discovered how useful his writing, research, and presentation skills were in a professional setting. Through this experience, he was able to refine his career goals, expose himself to a whole new field, and add valuable practical experience to his résumé.

What to Do

- Reinforce how useful his academic work will be in a workplace.
- Congratulate him on doing so well that he may be offered a permanent position.
- Encourage him to explore other nonprofit jobs by visiting his career center and contacting alumni who work in this field.

What to Avoid

- Asking him why he's not interested in social work anymore.
- Dampening his enthusiasm for working in a nonprofit job.
- Assuming that his sociology degree is now "wasted."

What You Need to Know

Students with internships or summer jobs in small organizations often have an excellent experience and use a variety of skills. Many small agencies are sparsely staffed and need students who can take on major responsibilities and make a significant contribution to their work.

The difference between a summer job and an internship can confuse parents. Usually an internship implies that the organization will structure the work experience to ensure that learning takes place, especially if they cooperate with the college to offer course credit. Internships for course credit need the support of a professor who will supervise and evaluate the student's experience on the job. Some schools have rather formal relationships with internship sponsors and others handle these requests on a student-by-student basis. Many colleges have or are trying to develop experiential learning programs that place students in work settings throughout their undergraduate career.

While some summer jobs and internships offer significant learning experiences for student employees, others simply expect students to handle routine work and make little effort to see that the job or internship offers the student valuable training or instruction in the field. Students often have to take the initiative by presenting their internship sponsor with written learning goals and requesting weekly meetings to assess their progress.

Some employers insist that students receive academic credit for their internships or summer jobs for liability reasons. A student who receives credit for work is considered primarily a student and not eligible for the organization's workers' compensation insurance if he or she should be injured on the job. If an employer pays a student, the organization has to accept liability for that student, just as they do with their other employees.

In some cases, your child will have to be assertive in convincing his or her department to agree to sponsor an internship for college credit. Your child will also have to invest a certain amount of time in planning, applying, and making sure all parties agree to this arrangement. Some colleges refuse to give course credit for internships and the students may be forced to do the internship as an unpaid volunteer. Even if this is the case, an internship can be enormously valuable in acquiring practical skills and making contacts for future employment. Internships are usually well worth the time and energy required and can make a significant difference in how employable a student is upon graduation. Most employers today expect a certain degree of work experience on a graduating student's résumé and, in some fields that requires a commitment of extra time, energy, and resources during the college years. Students can also explore short-term, informal internships that may be available during the school year or in the summer. These experiences can be valuable even though they are limited in time. Some students gain a great deal of insight by "shadowing" a professional in a particular field, even for a day or two.

Employers often hire student workers in order to assess their performance on the job so that they can recruit these students for permanent positions later. This summer experience can provide a major advantage, especially for a liberal arts student who may otherwise have found his job search at graduation a confusing and frustrating experience.

Job Security

What parent hasn't worried about whether their child will be self-supporting after college? Parents who have lived through years of job market ups and downs may be particularly concerned about their child's prospects for future job security.

The Aspiring Actress—Parent to Parent

The other night Stacy had the following phone conversation with her sister, Marjorie:

STACY: Hi, Marjorie. How are you doing?

MARJORIE: Great. Jed just got his acceptance letter from MIT. We're all so excited. We're going out to dinner tomorrow night to celebrate. Now if we can just afford to pay for it!

STACY: That's great! You must be so proud of him.

MARJORIE: We sure are. He worked really hard for this and he's definitely ready for college. How's Natasha doing?

STACY: Well, she's almost done. We're going down for graduation in late May. As to what happens next, we're kind of clueless to tell you the truth.

MARJORIE: What do you mean? Does she have any job prospects?

STACY: Are you kidding? She's a theater major, remember?

MARJORIE: Yeah, well, I guess that's kind of hard, huh?

STACY: Hard? It almost seems impossible! She's had lots of roles in college but who knows if she'll ever get a paying acting job.

MARJORIE: What's she going to do?

STACY: Well, she wants to go directly to New York and give it a try. To tell you the truth, I'm really scared. It's not only living in New York City, but what if she doesn't find anything? She's so eager and committed to being an actress. I worry about her being disappointed. It's such a hard field to break into.

MARJORIE: I can imagine. I'm so glad my kids wanted to be business and engineering majors. At least I don't have to worry as much about them getting jobs after college.

STACY: Yeah, they probably won't be working in a restaurant waiting for that big break. It's just that Natasha has dreamed of being an actress since she was a little girl, and she's worked so hard at learning her craft. I guess Bill and I are going to have to help support her until she gets on her feet, and New York is so expensive. We've told her that we'll help her for a year and talk about what the prospects are then. Sometimes I wish she had been more like me, content to be a teacher or something more predictable. Maybe they switched her in the nursery at the hospital! She's so different. Everyone else in the family has such practical careers. Mac's in computers and Taylor is in sales. They both had great jobs right out of college.

MARJORIE: Well, you know, you could just tell her that she has to be more realistic and get a regular job. I mean, acting is such a shot in the dark.

STACY: I know, but I can't bear to tell her that she can't follow her dreams.

MARJORIE: I know, it's hard. It sounds like you've accepted the fact that she's going to need a lot of support. But what if she hasn't made it in a year?

STACY: I don't know. We'll just have to see what happens. At least she'll know she gave it a chance. To tell you the truth, right now I'm more worried about her being safe in New York. Sometimes she's so naïve and trusting.

MARJORIE: I don't blame you. I don't know if I'd be so understanding if one of my kids wanted to go to New York and become an actress.

What's on Stacy's Mind

Are we nuts to let Natasha go to New York to pursue her acting career?

What if this whole experience is terrible for her?

Why couldn't she be interested in something more stable?

Marjorie and everyone else must think we're too indulgent with Natasha.

What's on Marjorie's Mind

Stacy and Bill really have their hands full with Natasha and it looks like they will for a while.

I'm sure glad my kids didn't want to study something so impractical.

I don't understand why they can't just say, no, to Natasha. They've put her through college. That should be enough. She needs a little dose of reality I think.

What's Going On

It can be difficult for parents when their child decides to follow a career path that seems impractical or foreign to them. Naturally, you worry about her prospects when a career field such as theater or acting is the only thing she's interested in pursuing. But you can also take pride in your daughter's ambition to tackle a difficult career field. Allowing her to follow her dreams may be a great leap of faith for you, but it is also a great gift to her. It won't be easy for you or for Natasha, but you can support her in this effort while setting clear guidelines for what you are willing and able to do to help her succeed.

It may take several years for her to become self-supporting; a career in the theater may never offer the kind of security that you would hope for, but it's important to remember that no career choice is absolutely secure forever. You need to set aside your fears and recognize that Natasha may never aspire to the kind of job security that you value; that she may be comfortable living a life of constant change and considerable sacrifice if she gets to follow her dreams.

What to Do

- Make it clear to your daughter what you can feasibly do and how long you can support her efforts to become an actress.
- Ask her to think about a fallback plan if she isn't able to support herself as an actress.
- Encourage her, while pointing out how difficult this may be at times.
- Let her know that you are proud of her determination to undertake a tough career path.
- Educate yourself on the realities of a career in acting; for example, find out about the role of an agent in an aspiring actress's life and read about the theater as a career.

What to Avoid

- Standing in the way of her trying to make a career for herself in acting.
- Reminding her constantly of how difficult this choice will be.
- Refusing to support her efforts even if you are able to do so.
- Letting her know that this is a fantasy that you hope she'll outgrow soon.

What You Need to Know

While a career in the theater is a long shot for most people, many actually do make a living acting and find their work satisfying and rewarding. Even though it may seem that everyone you know has children who aspire to more practical careers, your daughter is determined to be an actress. Who's to say that she'll be less successful and happy than your friends' children who work in corporate jobs and may be laid off or become disillusioned in their forties?

While it's hard to accept your child's unusual career choice, it's helpful to remember that a degree in theater (if it includes a liberal arts component) can prepare her for many careers. Natasha has been educated for more than simply a job as an actress, but her passion to work in the theater is worthy of your support. You will have helped her to follow her dreams and that gift will have a long-lasting impact on her life.

You must, however, be clear with her about how far you will support her in trying for a career in acting. You can be realistic about the uncertainties of this field without refusing to help or dampening her spirit and youthful enthusiasm.

What Is *Job Security Today?—Parent to Parent*

A conversation Joe had today with a colleague at work has left him wondering if his son's college major will result in a good job offer when he graduates.

PETE: Hey, Joe. How's it going?

JOE: Pretty good, Pete. I had a talk with my son last night. He's trying to decide if he should get a graduate degree right away.

PETE: What's he majoring in?

JOE: Well, he's in chemical engineering, but some of his advisers have told him that his starting salary will be at least twenty thousand dollars more with a master's degree.

PETE: Hey, let me tell you about my nephew. He started college as a chemical engineering student but by the time he graduated four years later, he had a tough time getting his first job. He's working in sales for an Internet company now. I guess he wishes that he'd majored in computer science. Who knows what kids should study today? Everything changes so quickly.

JOE: Yeah, I know what you mean. I thought an undergraduate degree in chemical engineering would be golden for him. He just finished that coop job with Monsanto and he thinks they're going to offer him a permanent job. But now his professors are telling him he should pursue a graduate degree. Will the tuition payments never end?

PETE: Not in our lifetime! Boy, it's tough to know what to do, isn't it? Look at you and me: working in a company that's constantly threatening to downsize. I've been with this outfit since I graduated from college twenty-five years ago. You've been here almost as long. What kind of job security did that get us? We may be out of a job any day now and we thought we'd signed on until retirement.

JOE: I know. It's really hard to know what *is* secure anymore. He doesn't really want to go to graduate school, but maybe he should while I still have a job myself and can help him out. Maybe he'll be able to support me then!

What's on Joe's Mind

I read about the future of jobs in the papers and magazines, but it's still pretty confusing. How can I know what's best for my son?

Things are changing so fast. It's hard to feel this insecure at my age.

What's on Joe's Son's Mind

That additional twenty thousand dollars a year in starting salary sounds pretty good.

I'm really sick of school, but maybe I should just go ahead and do the grad school thing now.

It may be hard to come back to school once I'm out and earning money.

What's Going On

It gets harder and harder to predict which career fields will be seeking new hires, even in the foreseeable future. Many of us graduated from college in a relatively stable employment market and find it hard to counsel our children about their career prospects. The work world that we've experienced differs drastically from the one our kids will enter when they graduate from college.

What to Do

- Listen to your son's concerns about going directly on to graduate school.
- Ask if he's excited about further study or simply doing it to get it over with.
- Suggest that he get the names of alumni in the field from his college or career office and ask those professionals for advice.

What to Avoid

- Telling him he'd better get the graduate degree now or you probably won't be able to help him.
- Focusing on the higher starting salary and trying to influence him based on that alone.

What You Need to Know

It may be true that a master's degree in engineering will bring a significantly higher starting salary for your son; however, if he takes a job with a large enough company after his bachelor's degree, the company may help him pay for the graduate degree. Your son may be swayed by the prospect of a larger salary, but he doesn't seem very enthusiastic about continuing on to graduate school right away. This is a tough decision and one that doesn't necessarily bring with it any guarantee of future success or job security. If you have experienced corporate downsizing and job insecurity, it's hard to know what to believe and how to advise your child.

If your son sounds hesitant about directly going to graduate school, listen to him carefully. He may be "burned out" by having been in school continuously for so many years and he may need a change. Moreover, he may discover, after a couple of years in a job, that he's really interested in an entirely different field and may want to go to graduate school in another area.

Chapter 12 explores how you can assist your child in making informed decisions about life after college and whether graduate school or full-time employment is the best choice after graduation.

Chapter 10

When to Worry, When to Act

Dealing with Problems and Crises and Knowing the Difference

When Hannah called from college last night, she was crying and unable to tell me what was the matter. She sounded so miserable and unhappy. I didn't know what to do, and she was so vague about what was bothering her. I'm scared that she's really in trouble and can't tell me what it is. I wonder if I should get in the car and go see for myself. It's so hard to tell what's going on over the phone.

How Can You Know What's Really Going On?

There is nothing more frightening than the feeling that your child is in trouble, especially when that child is away from home and you're not sure what's going on. As we've said before, college students tend to unload their worries on parents and then they feel better and go on about their lives. How can you tell from afar when there *is* a serious problem?

Whether your child is going through a normal developmental struggle, dealing with a serious problem, or in the midst of a dangerous crisis, you need to know how to identify, distinguish among, and respond to these situations. It is important to recognize when you are being used as a sounding board for normal confusion and unhappiness and when problems are serious and need outside intervention. You also need to know what resources are available on most campuses to assist with problems and crises. This chapter will help you evaluate your child's situation and offer strategies for dealing with typical problems or crises.

Normal Developmental Struggles

Most students go through personal struggles during the college years. These struggles, while troubling to you and your child, rarely call for more than understanding and a sympathetic ear. Relationship issues and managing routine stress can consume a great deal of your child's energy and cause you to worry. It's important to recognize, however, that struggles like these are a natural part of your child's development. The following situations illustrate how you can use your consulting skills to guide and support your child during difficult times.

Breaking Up

Your daughter has called you every night for the past two weeks. She sounds so listless and unhappy since she broke up with her boyfriend. You suspect that she's spending most of her time alone in her room, skipping classes and meals. Now *you're* beginning to lose sleep worrying about her.

What's on Your Mind

> I'm really worried about her.
> She sounds so unhappy.
> What can I do to help her?

What's on Your Child's Mind

> I'm so depressed.
> I don't feel like doing anything.

What's Going On

The breakup of a long-term relationship is a big deal for most college students. It's not unusual for your daughter to call home for support and comfort. She probably needs to unload her feelings and be reassured that you love her. These situations are usually hard on parents because they feel helpless. How can you tell from afar if this problem will resolve itself over time or if your daughter is seriously depressed? She may simply need reassurance and care from you for a relatively short time until she can get past this period of sadness. It's difficult for you, too, because you can't see her, give her a hug, and reassure yourself that she's basically okay.

What to Do

- Listen, listen, and then listen some more.
- Let her express her feelings of sadness.
- Reinforce how much you care about her.
- Tell her how sorry you are that she feels so sad.

What to Avoid

- Minimizing her sadness now by telling her she'll get over this relationship in time.
- Telling her that you expect her to deal with this and tend to her studies.
- Taking it on as your problem.
- Trying to "fix it" for her, by offering *your* solutions.

What You Need to Know

It is a major task of late adolescence to form and commit to intimate relationships. Friends and relationships are critical to college students; in fact, when most people are asked what meant the most to them in college, they mention friends immediately. When these relationships end, your child may be temporarily devastated. Your job is to listen and attend to the feelings of loss and sadness that your child expresses. Hopefully, your child will also have close friends at school with whom he or she can share these feelings. While relationship breakups in college are painful and difficult to experience, most are not of a crisis nature. That doesn't mean they are not significant events and important to your child; it simply means that you probably don't have to worry about serious consequences and that your role is to support your child and listen. If your child persists in sleeping most of the time and not attending classes for more than a week or so, you may want to suggest that he or she get some counseling.

Stress

Every time you speak with your daughter she's in a near panic about something going on at school. Your conversations never last long because she's always in a rush to get somewhere or complete something on time. She always exclaims that she's totally stressed out.

What's on Your Mind

Is it normal for her to be in such a frenzied state all the time?
She seems pretty overwhelmed by her responsibilities.
I wonder if this college is too much pressure for her.

What's on Your Child's Mind

I never have enough time to complete my work.
I can't remember the last time I relaxed and had fun.
If I don't keep up, I'll fail my courses and never get into graduate school.
My friends have started calling me a "stress case." I never have time to go out with
    them.

What's Going On

Many bright and capable students who seemed to breeze through high school find the competitiveness and adjustment challenges of college difficult to negotiate. Perhaps because of their intelligence, they take on the pressures and stresses of a highly competitive environment even more than less achievement-oriented young people. Moreover, many students don't realize how much they relied on the comfort and security of home and being around people who cared about them on a daily basis. All of these factors add to the already stressful change of being at college and away from home.

What to Do

- Try to remain calm. Don't absorb her stress and anxiety.
- Empathize with how hard college life can be.
- Remind her that you love her and that you don't expect her to be perfect.
- Ask if she's thought of any ways she could make her life more manageable. Mention things that you do to relieve stress.
- Suggest that she may want to look into taking a class in stress management or talk to someone who understands the pressure she's under.

What to Avoid

- Feeling rejected because she cuts your phone calls short or overly concerned because she calls all the time.
- Telling her she's always making mountains out of molehills.
- Reminding her that she's not the only one who has a lot to do.
- Assuming that she's this way all of the time.

What You Need to Know

Feeling stressed out and tense is a natural response to trying to manage the many demands of college life. There are papers to write, classes to attend, reading and lab assignments to complete, tests to prepare for, roommate conflicts to resolve, friendships to develop and maintain, social pressures, worries about doing well in school, and anxieties about the future, in addition to managing all the daily physical needs—feeding yourself, doing the laundry, getting enough sleep, and getting up and showered in time for class.

A certain amount of stress is unavoidable and usually manageable, but when stress becomes excessive, it can lead to great anxiety and actually make you physically sick. If your child is under too much stress, you may notice the following signs.

He or she:

- Is always late and rushes to accomplish daily activities.
- Is moody and irritable a lot of the time.
- Can't avoid striving for perfection in everything she does.
- Can't sleep well and almost never relaxes for any period of time.
- Always seems to have too much to do and can't stop worrying about everything.
- "Catastrophizes" everything and is sure that something awful will happen if any responsibilities are put off.
- Often complains of a headache, an upset stomach, and/or assorted aches and pains.

Most campuses have counselors and programs to help students deal with excessive stress and anxiety. Of course, it's usually the most stressed out students who don't feel they have the time to get help. As a parent, the best you can do in this situation is to encourage your child to get help and remind her that she is a valuable and worthwhile human being even if she isn't perfect. You can also model behavior that assists you in stress reduction—taking time to relax and have fun, accepting the fact that you cannot be all things to all people in your life, reinforcing the importance of behaving like a "human being," as well as a "human doing," and trying to avoid all-or-nothing thinking, such as "If I don't complete this task perfectly, I'll never have another chance."

Serious Problems

It may be hard for you to assess from afar when a situation becomes a serious problem. The following scenarios can help you determine whether a serious problem exists and if you need to get involved.

Depression

Recent phone calls with your daughter have left you concerned. She seems to be going through a tough time at school. Even her voice sounds different. You're worried that she may be seriously depressed.

What's on Your Mind

> Should I be really worried?
> I can't get any information out of her. She seems so listless.
> How can I tell just how bad this is?

What's on Your Child's Mind

> I am so bummed about everything.
> I just want to sleep all the time.
> Going to class is just too hard and studying is impossible.

What's Going On

Your daughter certainly seems depressed, but it's difficult to determine the severity of her depression. You wonder if she feels this bad all of the time, whether she attends classes and studies, and if you can help her in any way. College students commonly do feel depressed; in fact, a recent study by the American College Health Association revealed that 45 percent of college students report some level of depression that interferes with their ability to function from time to time. The highs and lows of adolescence do not lessen during the college years; in fact, they often intensify. Great stimulation, excitement, and challenges are often followed by frustrations, fears, and disappointments. And students usually struggle with these highs and lows without the benefit of adequate sleep, regular nutritious meals, and the care and nurturing that sustained them during times of stress at home.

What to Do

- Listen carefully and nonjudgmentally to your child's feelings. Keep your voice and manner calm even if you feel alarmed.
- Be patient if your child has difficulty articulating exactly how she feels.
- Ask when these feelings began and how intense they are.
- Empathize with the feelings expressed; accept them at face value even if you find them exaggerated, embarrassing, or painful.
- Ask how these feelings are affecting your child's daily life: "Are you finding it difficult to sleep, eat, go to class, etc.?"
- Ask how you can help.
- Stay in close touch with your child until you feel she is better. A short phone call each day to check in and let your child know you're thinking of her can be a great help to both of you.
- Remind her that depression is treatable and that she may want to talk to a professional counselor or therapist.

What to Avoid

- Overreacting, thus making *your* feelings an extra burden for your child.
- Judging and evaluating the situation: "No wonder you're depressed; you don't eat well and you never get a decent night's sleep."
- Trivializing her feelings: "Everyone has their ups and downs. I'm sure you'll feel better soon."
- Taking on the problem yourself or getting angry if your efforts to help are rejected.

What You Need to Know

On college campuses across the country more students than ever before are seeking psychiatric help, according to Daniel Eisenberg, who directs the Healthy Minds Study at the University of

Michigan. Better screening and earlier diagnosis of mental illness in high school may partially explain why college counseling centers are busier than ever and sometimes overwhelmed by the number of students seeking services.

Depression can come in many forms, from mild to full-blown major clinical depression that may require immediate intervention, treatment, and even hospitalization. The National Institute of Mental Health describes three forms of depressive illness:

Major depression usually entails a combination of symptoms that interfere with the ability to work, sleep, eat, and enjoy once pleasurable activities. Symptoms include:

- Sadness, anxiety, or empty feelings.
- Decreased energy and fatigue.
- Loss of interest or pleasure in usual activities.
- Appetite and weight changes (either loss or gain).
- Sleep disturbances (insomnia, oversleeping, wakefulness).
- Feelings of hopelessness, guilt, and worthlessness.
- Thoughts of death or suicide, or suicide attempts.
- Difficulty concentrating, making decisions, and remembering.
- Irritability or excessive crying.
- Chronic aches and pains not explained by other physical conditions.

Dysthymia refers to a long-lasting but comparatively mild form of depression. Dysthymic persons manage to get by from day to day, they can bring themselves to study and socialize, but they view whatever they experience through gray-colored glasses. One psychologist compared dysthymia to a "low-grade infection." Dysthymics never really feel good.

Bipolar illness (also known as manic-depressive illness) is characterized by alternating cycles of depression with cycles of elation and increased activity, known as mania. We discuss this form of depression in more detail in the next scenario.

Students are particularly vulnerable to feelings of depression because of the significant developmental tasks and the enormous challenges and uncertainties of late adolescence. Anyone, students included, can go into a tailspin if the stresses in their lives exceed their coping abilities at the time. Most students experience some sadness during the college years, but usually the mood passes within a few days. Sadness, however, is a temporary state and a normal human reaction to a loss, such as a romantic breakup, a failure in class, the divorce of one's parents, or the death of a loved one. In these instances, anyone might experience sadness and a depressive reaction to the negative events. It's important to be able to differentiate, however, between a depressive reaction to a specific cause, which will likely abate over time, and a serious debilitating depression, which may be due to underlying biological and/or psychological vulnerability.

You may have difficulty determining if your child is merely temporarily sad or seriously depressed and in need of help. In general, if you feel that your child is struggling to cope, it's a good idea to suggest that he or she talk to a counselor or another trusted adult. Certainly no harm can come from a visit to the college counseling center, and it may help your child to be evaluated by a trained professional. While it is positive that your child is confiding in you, it is also important that he or she see someone who can assess whether therapy and/or treatment on an ongoing basis is required.

Assessing whether your child needs help is not an easy task, especially from afar, but if you observe one or more of the symptoms listed above over time, you will want to pay close attention. Don't be afraid to ask if she ever thinks of hurting herself or others and don't be frightened if there is an intense emotional response. Keep talking. Talking about a problem or crisis does not make it worse; it is the first step toward finding a solution.

Bipolar Disorder

Your son is home on break after his first semester at college. His appearance and general attitude alarm you. When he isn't sleeping, he seems wound up and irritable. One minute he raves to his friends about how great college is; the next minute he refuses to talk about it and retreats to his room.

What's on Your Mind

He seems either super happy or down in the dumps.
He looks awful, like he's lost weight and has never seen the outdoors.
Is this normal adjustment to college or is he in trouble?

What's on Your Child's Mind

I am really freaked out about the pressures at school.
All I want to do is sleep and my parents keep bugging me to talk about school.
Last night was awesome, dancing and partying with my friends. It was crazy fun!

What's Going On

Your son's behavior may indicate that he suffers from bipolar disorder (sometimes called manic-depression), although some of the symptoms may simply be the result of exhaustion or normal developmental struggles. Bipolar disorder is characterized by episodes of being uncontrollably high or manic alternating with episodes of depression. Both the up and down extremes are grave problems, although in the high phase the person has little or no insight into the dangers. In the manic state, an individual feels superhuman, able to function on no sleep and tackle any situation; he or she might also go on a spending spree or "act out" sexually. In the depressive state, he or she feels profound despair and may contemplate suicide.

Review the list of symptoms of depression given earlier to begin to assess whether he needs help. For example, do his behaviors prevent him from living his life in a reasonably healthy and orderly way? Are his moods either excitedly high or dreadfully low with little in-between?

What to Do

- Find out the symptoms of these illnesses and observe him to determine if he manifests any of these symptoms.
- Ask him if he is experiencing any of these symptoms.
- Reassure him that this disorder is treatable but that he needs help.
- Suggest that he see a counselor at school and follow up on whether he has done so.
- Keep talking about these behaviors in a nonjudgmental way: "I notice that you're sleeping a great deal and not eating well. That worries me. Can I help in any way?"
- Remember that it's important for your child to take the initiative in getting help, but you can intervene and insist that he get treatment if you feel he is in danger.

What to Avoid

- Ignoring or criticizing his behavior.
- Keeping it a secret if your family has a history of mental illness.
- Assuming this is only a first-year-in-college adjustment issue.

What You Need to Know

College students are at an age when serious mental illnesses such as depression, bipolar disorder, and schizophrenia are most likely to appear. It can be hard to distinguish if your child is becoming seriously ill or merely reacting to the kinds of stressful habits and lifestyles that are so typical of college students—routine lack of proper sleep, poor eating habits, sleep deprivation brought on by last minute cramming for exams, and overindulgence in drugs or alcohol. Parents need to be on the lookout for these behaviors and this can be especially difficult when they don't have much direct contact with their college child. Even if your child suffers from something serious, such as bipolar disorder, these conditions are highly treatable, especially if they are diagnosed at an early stage. Students who receive professional help can learn about the habits that put them at risk and avoid spending their college years in the grip of mental illness.

College medical or counseling centers usually are not equipped to handle serious mental illness, and even if your child goes to the counseling center, he or she might not see an expert who can diagnose the condition accurately. Most colleges have therapists or social workers who deal with temporary problems, but few have staff with the time or qualifications to diagnose and provide long-term treatment and care for serious conditions. Most students with serious mental health problems are encouraged to take a medical leave of absence (this is a strictly confidential medical record and will not affect your child's future prospects negatively) for as long as it takes to get appropriate treatment.

The best thing you can do as a parent is to facilitate your child getting the necessary help. In most cases, treatment works and can provide relief from symptoms in just a few weeks. Treatment may include psychotherapy (talk therapy), medication, or a combination of the two. Stay informed, ask questions, and remind your child that this is a not a personal failing but a condition that requires treatment and patience.

Sexual Harassment

Your daughter called last night to tell you that she has decided to file sexual harassment charges against her biology professor. She had already met with an adviser in the college's equal opportunity office and called to ask if you would support her in taking the professor to court.

What's on Your Mind

> What in the world is going on?
> I'm really angry that the college allows creeps like this to teach young people.
> Is she taking on more than she can handle?
> I worry about the consequences for her whether she wins or loses.

What's on Your Child's Mind

> I'm so glad I talked to that person in the equal opportunity office.
> I want to do something so that other students aren't subjected to this horrible experience.
> I hope the professor gets fired for what he's done.

What's Going On

Sexual harassment and the handling of such incidents is a hotly debated topic on most college campuses. Attitudes and behaviors that may have been tolerated when your generation was in college are no longer acceptable. Moreover, most colleges have taken a firm stand with regard to treatment of faculty, staff, or students who are found guilty of sexual harassment. Title VII of the Civil Rights Act of 1964, as amended, has identified sexual harassment as an act of discrimination on the basis of sex. In accordance with Title VII and Title IX of the Civil Rights Act, most universities have adopted the following definition of sexual harassment:

> *Unwelcome sexual advances, requests for sexual favors, and other verbal or physical conduct of a sexual nature constitute sexual harassment when (1) submission to such conduct is made either explicitly or implicitly a term or condition of an individual's employment or academic status, (2) submission to, or rejection of, such conduct by an individual is used as the basis for an employment decision or academic decision affecting that person, or (3) such conduct has the purpose or effect of substantially interfering with an individual's work or academic performance or creating an intimidating, hostile, or offensive working or learning environment.*

Most colleges have a policy manual and procedures in place governing such infractions and will support any individual member of the academic community who wishes to file sexual harassment charges through the campus review and judicial system.

It's still difficult and humiliating for most students to file charges against a faculty member and parents may need to get involved if such a charge is taken to the public legal system. Your child is entitled to a safe living and learning environment in which he or she is treated with dignity and respect by faculty, staff, and students. Unfortunately, this is not always the case; conduct that constitutes sexual or gender harassment occurs on many campuses, but it does not have to be tolerated.

What to Do

- Listen to your child's anger with respect and empathy.
- Keep reminding her that she is entitled to respectful treatment.
- Help her to assess what type of action is appropriate.
- Commend her for being courageous enough to address this issue.
- Recognize that she will probably waver and question herself during this process no matter how strong she is in the beginning.

- Be prepared for the fact that this may be a long and painful process and that it may require extensive emotional and financial support.

What to Avoid

- Asking her to drop the charges and just stay away from that nasty man.
- Suggesting that she may have done something to elicit this conduct.
- Telling her she will only intensify her pain by taking this public.
- Threatening to take her out of school and sue the college.

What You Need to Know

Nearly every college and university in the country is dealing with the issue of sexual harassment and has established a policy to respond to complaints by students. If your child brings a charge against a faculty member within the college system, a confidential review board will hear this complaint, determine whether there is cause, and recommend sanctions or penalties if the complaint is upheld.

This poses a difficult situation for a student, as the complaint will be the student's word against the professor's. Although these review processes are designed to be fair and impartial, the power imbalance between a faculty member and a student is a real concern in trying to effectively adjudicate these situations within the college system. Very few faculty members are dismissed for alleged sexual harassment, especially if they have tenure. On some campuses, however, the process can work in favor of the student, because a college can sanction and punish members of their community without the more stringent rule of law requiring the standard of "beyond a reasonable doubt" in applying penalties for wrongdoing.

If the student decides to take the matter to a public court of law, the process could be quite different. Lawsuits of this type tend to be drawn out, expensive, and extremely painful for both student and faculty member. College officials may try to discourage your child from taking her complaint to a public court of law, given that they have to look out for their own interests and would rather not have this matter made public. If your child persists in wanting to go to court, she may have to contend with both the college and the faculty member. Having to rely on limited family resources, she may be compelled to settle the suit without getting the satisfaction he or she sought, and may suffer from the humiliation and exposure to public scrutiny. Taking public legal action to redress sexual harassment is a step that requires resources and commitment.

Parents should talk to their children about the consequences of sexual harassment and sexual assault before they leave for college or early in their college career. If you have a daughter, make sure she knows that she has a support system if she is ever the victim of sexual harassment and that you expect her to take advantage of that support if she needs it. Ensure that she knows she does not have to tolerate any form of harassment based on her gender, including overt acts: a fellow student using an offensive term to refer to females, a faculty member making sexist remarks in class, sexual propositions, innuendoes, or negative stereotypes and attitudes based on gender. Make sure that she knows she is not to blame when these events occur and that she is entitled to a safe environment in which to live and learn. If she is the victim of one of these acts, she will need your love and support to recover and carry on. She will need a calm and rational adult presence, not a hysterical, revenge-seeking parent who takes on the anger and humiliation that belong to her.

Parents also need to remember that recovery from these incidents, depending on the severity of the harassment, may take a long time. Be patient and keep reminding your child that you love him or her and that he or she deserves great care and respect.

Eating Disorders

You noticed over Thanksgiving break that your daughter was acting strangely. She ate some of the family holiday dinner but later you heard her vomiting in the bathroom.

What's on Your Mind

> Why is she throwing up?
> She doesn't seem sick.
> Should I approach her about the vomiting?

What's on Your Child's Mind

> I am so fat; I hate my body.
> All of my friends are thinner and better looking.
> If I could only lose another five pounds.

What's Going On

Disordered eating is all too common among college students today. While serious eating disorders affect a relatively small percentage of the college population, disordered eating—severe dieting, unusual eating patterns, preoccupation with eating choices, troublesome though not frequent binge eating, anxiety about weight gain, and shame or guilt about one's body—is estimated to affect nearly 50 percent of the college population and can include men, particularly athletes. Serious eating disorders—anorexia nervosa, bulimia, binge eating, and combinations of these—are found in perhaps 5 percent of college students and nine out of ten of these are women. These conditions, particularly anorexia, can have serious consequences and even result in death if not treated appropriately.

Most schools today have counselors on hand who are experienced in dealing with eating disorders. In some cases, students who exhibit symptoms of eating disorders are referred to a school psychologist or social worker by a friend or roommate who has become aware of and alarmed by the student's physical condition or behavior. The staff member would then call in the student for a counseling appointment and evaluation. At large colleges or universities, however, this level of attention to individual students may not be present, and you may need to take steps to ensure that your child receives the help she needs. Some small colleges may not have adequate resources to deal with these problems, but the dean of students' office staff should be able to make a referral for your child.

What to Do

- Confront your daughter if she exhibits erratic and/or unusual eating patterns.
- Describe the behavior that concerns you in nonjudgmental terms: "Since you've been home, I've noticed that you eat very little at meals and yet I've heard you vomiting later in the day. I'm concerned about your eating habits. Are you eating a lot between meals? What's going on?"
- Find out all you can about eating disorders.
- Suggest that your child seek counseling and treatment at school.
- Reassure her that you love her and have confidence in her ability to make wise choices.
- Keep talking about this issue with your child.
- If the behavior continues and/or escalates, make sure that she seeks professional help immediately.

What to Avoid

- Ignoring the behavior and assuming that it is just a phase.
- Letting your fears get in the way of finding her help.
- Nagging your child about eating properly.
- Threatening her or judging her behavior.

What You Need to Know

A tremendous amount of written material can help you understand the nature and complexity of eating disorders. Anorexia is self-starvation and can be extremely dangerous, resulting in death in as many as 10 percent of the cases. Bulimia is a disorder in which the individual alternates between binge eating and purging, usually through self-induced vomiting. This purging can also take the form of excessive use of laxatives, diuretics, or diet pills and extreme exercise efforts to burn off calories. Compulsive eating, without purging, is known simply as binge eating disorder.

Two factors conspire to make dealing with eating disorders difficult for parents of college students. First, the child is away from home and cannot be observed on a daily basis and, second, eating disorders are usually accompanied by extremely secretive behavior. It's possible for a child to have a fairly serious eating disorder for a long time and keep it hidden from parents and friends. Moreover, individuals who suffer from eating disorders are usually embarrassed and ashamed of their actions and will often vehemently deny this behavior. Because of these feelings of shame and guilt, it is crucial that the child be reassured that any treatment or discussion of this disorder will be strictly confidential. Parents need to be vigilant about respecting their child's right to privacy on these issues.

Eating disorders are often tied up with feelings of shame, guilt, and lack of control over oneself. Families need to prepare for participating in counseling and/or treatment. Students whose parents are actively involved in dealing with the treatment of eating disorders have a better chance of overcoming this condition. Treatment can be painful for parents and children alike, as eating disorders are often symptoms of family dysfunctions that are difficult to address. For example, a child who witnesses her parents fighting constantly may see food as the only area of her life over which she has control. Hence, the eating disorder becomes a symptom of an unaddressed and unresolved family problem.

Bulimia is harder to detect than anorexia because many bulimics maintain a normal body weight even though they regularly binge and purge. The common symptom is uncontrollable eating—a hunger that stems from psychological rather than biological cravings. Bulimics are often excellent students, highly popular, talented, and extremely clever at hiding their eating disorder. In fact, a drive for perfection and achievement is at the heart of many eating disorders; therefore, it is a significant problem on college campuses filled with intelligent, achieving young people. Students who find themselves in a competitive environment may feel they have lost control over the academic part of their lives and may turn to eating as an area they can master.

In fact, on some campuses there is an alarming behavior that experts call "fad bulimia." In dorms and sororities, women get together and gorge themselves and then vomit or abuse laxatives, diuretics, and enemas or engage in excessive exercise to shed the pounds.

Your role as a parent is to help your child acknowledge and accept that she has a problem. Denial is the biggest hurdle in overcoming eating disorders. Compassion, reassurance, love, and support, along with a firm insistence on seeking help, is the surest route to helping your child conquer an eating disorder.

Illness

Your daughter has been sick for a week or more with severe stomach cramps. She has been to the college health center for an examination but the symptoms continue. She's gone back to the health center a couple of times but the nurse insists that she's just suffering from the intestinal flu bug that's going around campus. She's been told to rest and drink liquids, but she's still in a lot of pain.

What's on Your Mind

Is she in danger?
What if something serious is wrong with her?
Should I go see what's happening?

What's on Your Child's Mind

My stomach really hurts.
I don't see how this could just be the flu.
The health center nurse made me feel like a whiner, but I'm really in pain.

What's Going On

It's possible that she is suffering from an intense case of the flu, but it's also possible that she has something else. It's hard for students, especially when they are sick, to be assertive about receiving adequate healthcare. Friends and roommates may or may not help a student who is too sick to get out of bed to get food and medicine. This is especially true for an illness that is not minor, but is not a crisis, either.

What to Do

- Trust your instincts. You know your child.
- If you feel she is in danger, take action to get her some help.

- If you can't get to campus, get in touch with the residence hall adviser or director and have them check on her.
- Ask the RA to help get your daughter to a physician or emergency room where she can get a second opinion.

What to Avoid

- Ignoring your child's complaints and insisting that she handle this herself.
- Calling the health center and complaining about your daughter's care.
- Telling your daughter she has to go back to the health center until they get to the bottom of this problem.

What You Need to Know

Health centers at colleges are often overburdened and understaffed. Some have excellent resources and services and some may not even have a physician on hand to diagnose and treat serious illnesses. Students' complaints can go unheard in a busy health center.

It's difficult and frustrating to have to figure this out from a distance, but if your child isn't improving and you are worried that he or she is in danger, you may have to become directly involved, at least to make sure that your child has the best professional help available.

Loss and Grief

Your husband has just been diagnosed with terminal cancer. You wonder if you should tell your son who is a junior in college and halfway through the spring semester.

What's on Your Mind

I can barely deal with this news myself, how am I going to tell our son?
Should I just wait until he's home for the summer?
I'm worried about how he will take this news and how it will affect his studies.

What's Going On

The death or serious illness of a parent is a major issue for a college student. A college student, above all, needs to know that there is a secure base at home and news of this kind can create tremendous stress and anxiety. The serious illness and death of a parent is difficult at any age, but may be most unsettling just as a late adolescent is away from home and really needs everything at home to stay the same.

What to Do

- Tell your child as soon as you can. It's better to do it in person; you may want to visit him at school to break the news.
- Be as clear as possible about the prognosis.
- Ask your child what you can do to help him through this crisis.
- Offer to allow him to take a leave of absence for a while if your child expresses the need to spend time with his or her parent.
- Honor his feelings even though they may be hard to accept.
- Give your child time and space to adjust to this news.
- Suggest that your child might want to seek counseling on campus.

What to Avoid

- Keeping this news a secret in hopes of protecting your child.
- Insisting that he go on with life, despite the parent's illness.

What You Need to Know

The death of a parent is a significant life event no matter what the age of the child. When this happens during the college years, your child will need an extraordinary amount of care and compassion. Be prepared for a variety of reactions from your child. Experiencing and accepting feelings of grief, such as sadness, helplessness, loneliness, guilt, or anger can help your child recover from this loss. He or she may be in denial or shock at first. After the shock has passed, your child may be depressed, panicked, remorseful, angry, and/or experience a variety of physical ailments for up to eighteen months. He or she may need to talk about this experience, tell stories, and reminisce, or recall events over and over.

This can be extremely difficult when you, too, are trying to work on your own feelings of grief, anger, and sadness. Be patient and gentle with yourself and your child. Expect this process of grieving to take a long time and give yourself and your child as much time as it takes to come to terms with this tragedy. This may be even more difficult with an accidental or sudden death.

Dealing with Crises

Although extremely rare, some situations become crises and require an immediate response. Sometimes you are the person to intervene and other times you will need to rely on professional help for your child. In either case, you may be the first to recognize how serious the problem is. We hope the following scenarios will help you respond.

Suicide

When your daughter was home for spring break, she appeared extremely depressed. She complained about how hard it was to do well in school and that she didn't feel she had any real friends at college. She seemed so listless and discouraged. When you asked about her plans for summer break, she replied, "Who cares? I may not even be around by then."

What's on Your Mind

> I'm really worried.
> I wonder if she's depressed enough to be suicidal.
> What should I do?

What's on Your Child's Mind

> Life is just too hard.
> I feel like giving up.

What's Going On

College students are among the highest risk group for suicide. The college years are a time in which individuals strive to create an individual identity, adjust to life away from home and family, form intimate relationships, and plan for the future. These are not easy tasks.

Suicide is the third leading cause of death among young people between fifteen and twenty-four years of age; every year 5,000 young people commit suicide and more than 400,000 have made serious attempts that require medical attention. Although completed suicide rates are higher for men, attempted suicide is far more common among adolescent girls than boys. About 60 percent of teens report that they know another teenager who has attempted suicide.

There are several risk factors that have been identified through the study of adolescent behavior. Those young people who are at greatest risk are those who: suffer from psychiatric problems, especially depression or substance abuse; have a family history of suicide; experience family disruption, significant family conflict or parental rejection, or are under extreme stress, especially in the areas of achievement and sexuality. If a child has one of these risk factors, he or she is more likely to attempt suicide than his or her peers and if more than one risk factor is present, he or she is dramatically more likely to succeed. Moreover, adolescents who have attempted suicide once are at greater risk for another attempt.

What to Do

- Take any expression of hopelessness or desire to "go away" very seriously.
- Don't be afraid to ask your child if she has thought about hurting herself. Asking about suicidal feelings never encourages a person to take that step—it may open the door for saving that person's life.
- Ask your child what makes her feel so hopeless, and allow your child to speak even if what you hear is painful and frightening.
- Act quickly to get her professional help. Better to overreact than underreact in these situations.
- If your child can't find professional help on campus, arrange for a medical leave of absence.
- Think about getting some help for yourself. This is a traumatic experience for you as well and you will need a safe place to talk about your fears and anxieties.

What to Avoid

- Ignoring the behaviors and symptoms.
- Underreacting when your child's life may be in grave danger.
- Becoming hysterical and needy yourself.

What You Need to Know

If your child suffers from serious mental illness or behaves suicidally, act decisively to get that child some help. Even if your child seems "recovered" after a bout of serious depression or suicidal behavior, you need to remain vigilant. Once people have decided to take their life, they often feel a period of calm before actually committing suicide. It is easy to misinterpret this period of calm as recovery, especially when you so desperately want that to be the case.

While all expressions of wanting to die should be taken very seriously, there are varying levels of risk. An individual who has a plan and a method of committing suicide is a high risk and an individual who has attempted suicide in the past is an extremely high risk. If your family has a history of mental disorders or suicidal behavior, you should pay especially close attention to your child's mental health. One of the strongest protective influences against adolescent suicide is a cohesive, supportive family that provides a sense of stability. Even one family member who reacts responsibly with love, support, and intervention, if necessary, can make the difference between a student struggling through a rough period and a tragic death.

Rape

Your daughter had been acting unusually withdrawn and uncommunicative since she arrived home for spring break. You finally asked her if anything was wrong and she broke down and told you that she had been raped by a guy at school.

What's on Your Mind

> I am so angry I could kill this guy.
> What can I do to help her?
> Will she ever get over this terrible violation?

What's on Your Child's Mind

> Maybe I should have told him earlier that I didn't want to have sex yet. I must have led
>   him on.
> This has turned into a real nightmare.
> I feel so ashamed and embarrassed.
> I'm glad I told my mom, but now she's really upset, too.

What's Going On

Unfortunately, rape is a common problem on nearly every college campus today. One study found that one in four college women have been victims of rape or sexual assault; about 10 percent of sexual assault victims are men. Sexual intercourse forced by an acquaintance or a date is rape. In some ways, it is more traumatic than by a stranger because it can seriously damage the victim's trust in others and in her own judgment.

It is a positive sign that your daughter has shared this trauma with you. Too often, victims of acquaintance rape blame themselves and do not get the help they need to deal with the aftermath of this assault. Victims can feel ashamed, dirty, embarrassed, and responsible for the assault, especially if alcohol or drug abuse was involved.

Every college has to deal with this growing problem and most have health services and counselors to assist victims of sexual assault and rape. Moreover, nearly all colleges have a policy about acceptable and unacceptable behavior in intimate relationships, and a judicial or review process to address these infractions in a formal way. A rape victim can also avail herself of the public legal system and press charges that will be heard in a courtroom.

What to Do

- Listen with empathy to your daughter's pain.
- Reassure her that you love her and that she is lovable.
- Let her know how important it is that she is able to talk about this horrible experience. Ask her if she has someone to talk to who has experience in dealing with rape victims; if not, suggest that she see a counselor.
- Remind her, often, that this is not her fault and that her feelings, no matter what they are, are appropriate and acceptable.
- Ask her how you can help. Offer to go with her if she wants to seek medical attention and/or counseling.
- Be patient if she seems to be indecisive and confused.
- Support her if she decides to press charges or take any other action.
- Realize that it will take months, and maybe years, for her to recover from this experience.
- Respect her right to absolute confidentiality. Don't tell anyone about this event without her permission.

What to Avoid

- Becoming hysterical and threatening to take action against the boy yourself.
- Questioning your daughter about how this could have happened.
- Blaming her for getting drunk and being out of control.
- Asking questions that imply that the rape was your child's fault: "Why did you go to his room?" or "Why didn't you scream and run away?"
- Telling her that she must press charges and make sure this guy pays for what he did.

What You Need to Know

If your daughter is the victim of sexual assault, the recovery may take a long time. She may have flashbacks, nightmares, and bouts of depression and fearfulness for many years after such an experience. Counseling is extremely important for victims of sexual assault or rape, and parents of victims often avail themselves of counseling as well. If you learn about the rape directly after it's occurred, ask her to consider contacting a local rape crisis organization for information, advocacy, and support. In addition to offering vital emotional support, they will reinforce the importance of immediate medical attention and assist her in reporting the crime to authorities in case she wants to press charges later. Notifying the police, however, does not obligate your child to press charges later.

You may need to support her if she decides to press charges, either formally or informally, within the college system. But you also need to respect your child's right and responsibility to make those decisions herself.

Show your support and love for your daughter, reminding her constantly that it is natural and normal to feel confusion, rage, guilt, shame, insecurity, and depression. You may need to remind her often that she is lovable, precious, and entitled to be treated with dignity and respect, and that she is not responsible in any way for what happened to her.

If you have a son in college, there are a number of issues he needs to keep in mind. College men can be victims of sexual misconduct as well, although it is uncommon. Most often, however, college men need to be aware of their behavior when they express sexual interest in another student. Negotiating a sexual relationship can be confusing, clumsy, and embarrassing, but young men need to be reminded that they are responsible as well to make sure that consent is present before any sexual behavior takes place. Men are rarely the victim of sexual assault by a woman but many college men regret having sex with a woman they have just met or with a woman who has been drinking too much. Cultural pressure makes it difficult for men to turn down sexual opportunity. Remind your son that it is okay to remain a virgin until he is ready to have sex or to abstain from sex if the situation is not appropriate for him. You can reassure him that making sound choices and acting with respect and constraint is the mature thing to do.

Parents of college men need to be especially clear on their expectations regarding consensual sex. Modeling respectful behavior is a parent's best teaching tool, but it is also necessary to talk about unacceptable and illegal behavior and the consequences of using pressure or force in sexual relationships. He needs to be reminded that under no circumstances should he ignore a "No!" when he hears it and that it is never his "right" to engage in sex with an unwilling partner, no matter what the circumstances. Being drunk and, therefore, unaware of whether the woman has given consent does not absolve him of responsibility. Neither is he absolved if the woman is too drunk to give consent.

If your son is accused of sexual misconduct, make sure that he gets all of the support he can. This is a terrifying process for most young men and you should encourage him to seek counseling so that he doesn't have to experience this alone.

Alcohol Abuse

Your son has been charged with driving while intoxicated and has to appear in court to answer these charges. You've felt for some time that his drinking is out of control.

What's on Your Mind

I wonder if he is an alcoholic.
What can I do to support him even though I am appalled by his behavior?
Where can he get help?

What's on Your Child's Mind

I am so bummed out that I got caught driving drunk.
I'm not the only one who drinks a lot here. Everyone does.
I can't be an alcoholic, can I?

What's Going On

Underage drinking and alcohol abuse is an enormous problem on most college campuses. If you've read a newspaper or magazine lately, you probably have seen articles on binge drinking and how colleges are trying to limit/prevent alcohol abuse. Despite alcohol awareness and other programs to alert students to the dangers of alcohol abuse, studies indicate that nearly half of all college students engage in binge drinking. Colleges are faced with two unattractive alternatives: one, to clamp down on underage drinking on campus, thereby forcing students to drive to remote drinking locations, or two, to turn the other way and ignore illegal and dangerous drinking behavior on campus.

What to Do

- Confront your son about his drinking behavior. Let him know that you take this seriously and that you are concerned.
- Allow him to experience the consequences of his behavior.

- You can impose consequences, such as taking away his car or limiting his spending money, if that feels appropriate.
- Ask him if he needs help.
- Suggest that he find a counselor and/or attend an Alcoholics Anonymous meeting.
- Let him know that you love him and will support him in getting the help he needs.
- Model responsible drinking behavior. If you abuse alcohol or condone its abuse, it's likely that your child will, too.

What to Avoid

- Blaming and threatening.
- Ignoring his destructive drinking behavior.
- Assuming this is just a phase that all college students go through.

What You Need to Know

Underage drinking has been a major concern for college administrators for some time. College students who have not reached the age of twenty-one are legally not allowed to purchase or possess alcoholic beverages, but most students break that law. The problem has become so severe that schools have asked Congress to add an amendment to the Higher Education Act allowing them to inform parents any time a student under twenty-one violates drug or alcohol laws. This amendment was passed in the fall of 1998 and is a departure from the post-1960s recognition that college students who have attained the age of eighteen should be treated as legally independent adults. At a time when extensive efforts to curb alcohol use and abuse on campuses have largely failed, colleges are now turning to their last resort—parents—to help them reverse the often tragic results of excessive drinking.

Some colleges have instituted a "zero tolerance" rule that results in a student's suspension or expulsion after three alcohol offenses. Some notify parents after a serious violation (such as fighting or requiring medical attention due to excessive drinking) or after two minor violations (such as possession of alcohol). The parental notification plans for most colleges are aimed at high-risk behavior, the kind that may result in accidental death or serious injury to self or others.

As we described in Chapter 4, there is growing evidence that drinking may cause irreversible brain damage, particularly in young people. We now know that key areas of the brain are still under construction during adolescence and are more sensitive to the toxic effects of drugs and alcohol. The impulsivity of adolescents is well understood, but the negative consequences of alcohol and drug abuse are just now emerging. Initial studies have shown a marked difference in the brains of binge drinkers, even if they only engaged in binge drinking once or twice a month. These abnormal brain scans revealed poor, inefficient communication between brain cells. What is unknown yet is if this cognitive downward slide found in drinkers is reversible.

Drug Abuse

Your son called you last night at the urging of a nurse in the college's medical center. He explained that he had blacked out at a party on Saturday night and that tests revealed that he had a high level of cocaine in his system. The staff at the medical center has recommended that he take a leave of absence and go into a rehab program.

What's on Your Mind

> Is my son a drug addict?
> What can I do to help him?

What's on Your Child's Mind

> I guess I really screwed up this time.
> I don't understand what everyone's so freaked out about. I've only used cocaine a few
>   times.
> Are they going to make me leave school?
> A lot of kids use drugs here.

What's Going On

While alcohol is usually the drug of choice on campuses today, the use of other drugs—marijuana, cocaine, hallucinogens, opiates (like oxycontin), and amphetamines (like crystal meth, and ecstasy)—is also a huge problem. Depending on who their friends are, there can be significant pressure on students to experiment with illegal drugs in order to be a part of the social scene on campus. Most colleges have extensive programs and other outreach efforts to educate students on the dangers of drug use and abuse, but each year students are harmed by drugs, and the danger can be even greater if drugs are combined with alcohol.

What to Do

- Take this incident seriously.
- Accept the fact that your son may have a serious drug problem.
- Make sure that he gets medical treatment and care to address this problem, even if it means he needs to take a leave of absence from school for a while.
- Let him know that drug abuse is absolutely unacceptable to you.
- Remind him that you care deeply about him and expect him to take the necessary steps to deal with his problem.
- Be prepared to do anything required to help him recover.
- Educate yourself on the effects of this drug.
- Prepare yourself for the fact that this may take extraordinary amounts of time, effort, and love.

What to Avoid

- Assuming that this is just a one-time event and that he's learned his lesson.
- Reacting with outrage and anger and refusing to help.
- Blaming the person who gave him the drug.
- Refusing to address the seriousness of his situation.

What You Need to Know

Drug use that results in blackouts is evidence of potentially serious drug abuse. It's important that you recognize this problem and do everything you can to get help for your child. This kind of abuse can have long-term negative and even tragic effects on your son's life and future. The health risks are significant, with the possibility of causing both physical and emotional trauma and damage. It's imperative that you make sure that your son gets evaluated by a professional and that steps are taken to get him into a recovery program if necessary. It's customary for the family to be engaged in the counseling portion of rehabilitation and this can be an enlightening, if painful, experience.

Coming to terms with serious drug abuse in a child can be an excruciating experience for parents. It's normal for parents to want to deny what is going on, partly because of the social stigma of dealing with a child who has a drug abuse problem and partly because the prospect of acknowledging that you have a drug-addicted child is so terrifying. Now is the time, however, to set your fears aside and do everything you can to help your child through this crisis. Failure to do so could result in real tragedy down the road.

Violence/Crime

Your daughter called you at one o'clock in the morning to tell you that one of her sorority sisters had been found dead in the park near the sorority house. Your daughter thinks she was killed by her former boyfriend who had been threatening her and acting very strangely.

What's on Your Mind

Is my daughter safe?
What if this is some crazed serial killer?
I want her to come home where we can protect her.

What's on Your Child's Mind

How could this have happened to one of my friends?
I am really freaked out about this.
I don't feel safe here anymore.

What's Going On

Although rare, violent crime does occur on campuses. Just as domestic violence plagues the larger culture, violence on campus can occur between estranged boyfriend and girlfriend, and usually the boyfriend is the perpetrator. This is a terrifying situation for student and parent alike. Families don't expect that violent crime will be a part of their child's college experience and, therefore, many students come to college unprepared to adequately protect themselves.

What to Do

- Listen to your child's fears without sharing your anxiety and alarm with your daughter.
- Ask her if she feels safe.
- Encourage her to take advantage of any counseling offered by the college as a result of this tragedy.
- Urge her to talk about her fears and sadness with you and others.

What to Avoid

- Becoming distraught yourself and insisting that she come home until you're sure she's safe.
- Focusing on the crime instead of on the death of your daughter's friend.

What You Need to Know

Most students and their parents do not expect to have to deal with violence and crime but college campuses are no longer protected enclaves immune to the ills of the wider world. Until recently, colleges did not routinely make their violent crime statistics public nor did they share these statistics with incoming students. In 1990, however, the federal government passed the Jeanne Clery Disclosure of Campus Security Policy and Campus Crime Statistics Act that required that colleges and universities publicize their annual crime statistics to students, prospective students, and employees.

It is important for parents to talk to their children about what they can do to increase their personal safety on campus and off during the college years. Seemingly obvious measures such as locking doors, avoiding walking alone at night in secluded areas, and moderating drinking behavior can go a long way toward ensuring safety in a variety of situations.

While most college women will not be victimized by violent crime, one in twenty women can expect to be stalked at some time during her life and the stalker is usually a man she knows or has dated. If your daughter has ended a relationship with a man (or woman) you feel is dangerous and unbalanced, it is important that you talk to her about what she can do to avoid a confrontation. Any behavior that is out of line should be taken seriously and responded to with absolute consistency.

Although your daughter should strive to protect herself by keeping her address, telephone number, and e-mail address private, this is not easy in the Internet age, especially with Facebook and other social networking sites. If she is the victim of threatening behaviors, she should keep a diary recording incidents with names, dates, and times of every contact, and save phone messages or copies of anything sent by the offending party. She should be careful about locking her dorm or apartment doors and securing her car. She should also contact her campus security office and police force if she receives threats or has experienced any type of threatening behavior.

Pregnancy

Your daughter is in her senior year of college. Over holiday break you overheard her telling her younger sister that she had an abortion when she was a sophomore.

What's on Your Mind

Why didn't she tell me about this?
Should I tell her that I know?
I'd like to know if she's okay.

What's on Your Child's Mind

Should I have told my sister about my abortion?
I thought she should know what can happen if she has unprotected sex.
I wish I could tell Mom and Dad, but I'm afraid they would be so upset.
I still think about that abortion. Did I do the right thing?

What's Going On

Unwanted or unplanned pregnancies are a serious crisis for many young women in college. They often feel guilty and ashamed, and they may wonder for many years if they made the right choice if they have an abortion. Although there are fewer unplanned pregnancies on campuses than there were in the 1970s and 1980s, it is still a major dilemma for those young women who become pregnant. Many are afraid to tell family and friends and, hence, have to shoulder this emotional burden alone. This can be a tremendous source of guilt and pain, especially for those students whose religious or ethical beliefs make terminating a pregnancy a difficult choice.

What to Do

- Let her know that you overheard her conversation with her sister.
- Make it clear that you respect her right to privacy but that you'd like to offer support and a chance to talk about it if she wants to. Be open to discussing this issue nonjudgmentally.
- Recognize and honor her right to have made this decision, even if you do not agree with it.
- Empathize with the difficulty she's been through and offer her unconditional love and support.
- Ask her how she is dealing with this decision now. You may want to suggest counseling if she's continuing to have feelings of grief, guilt, or self-doubt.

What to Avoid

- Confronting her with having had an abortion.
- Moralizing and preaching about having premarital, unprotected sex.
- Asking your younger daughter to tell you what she knows about the abortion.

What You Need to Know

While most colleges do not have adequate resources to support a young woman through pregnancy and child rearing, many student health plans cover abortions. Insurance requirements usually make it mandatory for family planning practitioners and pregnancy counselors to discuss carrying the child to term as well as the option of terminating the pregnancy. This can be a complicated decision, fraught with emotional and financial worries for a college student. Carrying a child to term will often mean having to take a leave from school for a semester or a year and it can be difficult to return to college while raising an infant. Choosing an abortion is also a tough decision.

If your child decides to carry through with an unplanned pregnancy during the college years, you may need to provide a lot of support, both emotionally and financially, for a number of years. This can make it difficult for you to respect her decision and honor it, knowing what hardships may be down the road for all of you. Good counseling is absolutely essential when your family is dealing with this issue.

The incidence of Sexually Transmitted Diseases (STDs) and concern about contracting the AIDS virus has encouraged many young women and men to be much more careful about protecting themselves. Some also abstain from vaginal intercourse because of these fears, choosing to practice oral sex instead, although oral sex is certainly not risk-free. Many colleges offer free and confidential AIDS testing, as well as infection checkups to detect any one of a number of sexually transmitted diseases (STDs).

Parents need to be proactive about discussing these issues with their college-aged daughters and sons. Even if the conversation is one-sided, make the effort to inform yourself and talk about pregnancy, AIDS, and STDs with your child. Discuss abstinence as an option, but also encourage your child to practice safe sex and to discuss any risk factors with a partner before having intercourse. Stress the importance of making careful decisions about when and with whom to have sex.

Above all, let them know that you are available to talk about these difficult topics. You may not know if your daughter becomes pregnant, contracts an STD, or becomes infected with HIV, but you can take the initiative to discuss these concerns with her and be clear about your values and the behaviors that you expect her to adopt when and if she becomes sexually active.

Other Problem Areas

During the college years, many issues can arise. Your consulting skills, coupled with your ability to assess situations and determine whether you need to be involved, will help you weather these temporary situations and problems. If you suspect your child is involved with cult activity, is gambling or irresponsible with money, or is behaving in any way that you feel might endanger his or her life, the first step is always to listen to your child and ask questions nonjudgmentally and with love, even if he or she is defensive. This technique alone will go a long way toward opening up communication about difficult topics.

How to Obtain Help from the College If There's a Problem or Crisis

You're not alone if you are puzzled about what to do if you feel your child is in danger or needs help with a serious problem. Every parent sending a child off to college has high hopes that their child will have a successful and rewarding college experience; however, most undergraduates encounter some distress and unhappiness during their college years. Usually, these are temporary bumps on an otherwise relatively smooth path. While it's important to allow your daughter or son the opportunity to deal with minor problems and adversity, and learn from those experiences, it's also important to know how to get assistance when you're concerned with your child's safety and well-being.

While we nearly always suggest that parents allow their children to experience the consequences and learn from their mistakes, there are times when parents need to get involved and call upon the resources of the college. The first involvement, however, should be directly with your child. Ask him or her to share specifically what is going on, and be ready to share your opinion and offer guidance without judgment or criticism. Be wary of "taking over" your child's dilemma, but be prepared with resources and information. It's appropriate to share your values, but then let your child make his or her choices free from your admonishments.

If you feel that intervention is justified, respect your intuition. You know your child and you will likely be able to sense if things are not right. Start by listening to your child carefully and in a calm, nonaccusatory way. Describe the signs or signals that you've observed. Let your child do most of the talking, and assure him or her of your full support, but be ready to deal with rejection if your child refuses to discuss what's going on. If your child slams the door in response to your concern, it may be that there is more going on than he or she wants to admit.

You may want to enlist the help of someone on campus to assess your child's situation and provide support. Ideally, you would inform your child before contacting someone on campus. In a crisis situation, however, it may be necessary to consult someone on campus without your child's knowledge. If you do this without your child's approval, there is a good chance that your child will eventually find out and may be antagonistic about your intervention. Hopefully, your child will realize sooner or later that you acted out of love and concern, but you may need to risk rejection or hostility in the short term.

If you decide to seek the help of campus administrators or counselors, you need to come across as a calm, thorough, and systematic person who has a reasonable attitude about determining whether a serious problem exists. Before you contact the college, make notes describing specific aspects of your child's behavior that concern you. Try not to exaggerate or jump to conclusions before enlisting help in assessing the situation.

The dean of students' office is usually a good place to start. Ask for a referral to another office if necessary. The college's dean of students' office is usually administratively responsible for dealing with most aspects of student life outside of the formal classroom or academic setting. This may include offices of health services, counseling, campus security services, and residence hall life. Larger colleges may have an assistant dean dealing with specific aspects of student life, such as fraternities and sororities, women's affairs, student activities, minority affairs, and other campus programs.

When you contact a staff person, tell them who you are and who your child is. Then simply lay out your concerns in a systematic and specific manner. Emphasize that you are trying to assess if there is a serious problem and that you are seeking advice on how to proceed. Have a paper and pencil ready to take notes. You should, at this point, receive a caring, professional response and be taken seriously. This does not mean, however, that the staff person will be able to give you any specific information about your child's behavior or activities. Chances are, this person will not even know your child, but he or she is bound legally to maintain your child's right to confidentiality. This doesn't mean that he or she cannot help you with your concerns or offer support and suggestions on dealing with those concerns. Staff members can listen to your worries, advise you on ways of dealing with your son or daughter, and, most importantly, help you assess whether there is a serious problem present. They cannot, however, share with you any information that would compromise their ethical and legal relationship with your child.

Many college counseling staff and residence hall advisers will be willing to contact your child and ask him or her to come to see them if they are convinced that a serious problem or crisis is looming. If this intervention is unwelcome by your son or daughter, however, it may not do any good or may even exacerbate the problem. At this point, you may have to go back to your child and be assertive in getting help for him or her. This should be a last resort effort and only used if you sense there is grave danger to your child.

In general, it makes sense to rely on the professional advice and support that you will receive from college staff members. In most cases, they have the experience and expertise to help *you* through a difficult time, even if they are unable to share specifics about your child's life on campus.

Chapter 11

If They Leave College, Will They Ever Get Back on Track?

The Challenges and Benefits of Taking Time Off

When my son flunked out of college, I thought it was the end of the world. I didn't know what to think. He'd always been such a good student. I was really worried for him and what this would mean for his future. I have to admit, too, that I was embarrassed and wondered if I could keep this a secret from his grandparents and my friends.

You may be surprised and alarmed when your child decides to quit school, is asked to leave, or wants to take a break from college. Most parents assume that their children will be successful and happy in college, and they never think about how they would respond if their child decides to quit or flunks out.

We've found that students who take time off, for whatever reason, usually come back with renewed and focused energy to do well in college. Many students can benefit from time off. It gives them time to mature, explore the "real world" through volunteer work or a job, test their academic ability in another setting, reevaluate their reasons for going to college, and learn from the opportunity to reflect on their skills and interests. Parents can play a key role in helping their child through this experience. Using your consulting skills, you can discuss the options with your child and suggest activities that will ensure that the time off is productive.

This chapter will help you deal with this highly charged issue and understand some of the alternatives available if your child leaves college, including the possibility that he or she may decide not to return to school.

Being Asked to Leave

Few events are more disturbing than having your child fail. You will probably feel embarrassed, disappointed, and helpless. While you cannot control your child's academic performance, you can respond as a consultant, helping your child learn from this experience and make decisions about his future.

Flunking Out

When your son, Will, called to tell you he'd flunked out of school, you were shocked.

> WILL: Hi, Dad. How are things?
>
> DAD: Okay, son. How are you?
>
> WILL: Well, not so good actually. I got a letter from the dean today asking me to take a year off. The letter says, "so that I can rethink my priorities and prove to them that I'm capable of doing college-level work."
>
> DAD: I don't believe this! What happened?
>
> WILL: Well, you know last semester I got a 1.5 GPA and they said if I didn't bring it up to a 2.0, they were going to ask me to leave. My grades came with the letter and I only got a 1.8 GPA this semester. I would have gotten a 2.0 if I hadn't blown my chemistry final. I'm sorry, Dad.
>
> DAD: What does this mean?
>
> WILL: It means I flunked out! What do you think it means?
>
> DAD: I know that, but what are you going to do?
>
> WILL: I guess I'm coming home. They said I have to take courses somewhere else to prove that I can get at least a B average before they'll consider letting me back in. I guess I'll have to go to the community college next year.
>
> DAD: I guess so. Gosh, I don't know what to say, Will. I find this so hard to believe. You were always such a good student.
>
> WILL: I know, but college is really different. There are so many smart kids here; I guess I just got discouraged and stopped trying.
>
> DAD: Why didn't you say something sooner? Maybe you could have gotten some help.
>
> WILL: I just thought I could catch up, but I guess I was wrong.
>
> DAD: I'm really sorry, Will. You must feel awful.

WILL: Yeah, pretty much.

DAD: So, do you want me to come up on Saturday?

WILL: You can come earlier if you want. No need to stick around here any longer.

What's on Your Mind

This is a nightmare.

How is my wife going to take this? I hate to have to tell her when she gets home from work.

What will happen to Will? He sounds so discouraged.

Could it be that my kid isn't capable of getting a college degree?

What's on Your Child's Mind

I can't believe I actually flunked out.

What's wrong with me?

I'm so embarrassed and my dad sounded so ashamed of me.

What's Going On

The first year of college is a real trial for many students. While there are a number of reasons that a freshman may not return for his sophomore year, a significant one is failure to achieve a sufficient grade point average to remain in good academic standing. When students do not receive the minimum grades required, colleges typically will ask them to take a semester or a year off and take courses at another institution to prove that they are capable of doing college-level work. This can be a real crisis of confidence for your child and a difficult struggle for you as a parent.

What to Do

- Listen to your child with empathy.
- Ask him what you can do to help.
- After both of you have come to terms with this situation, sit down and talk about what will happen next.
- Engage him in a discussion of the options available. He may want to enroll at a college near home to save money.

- Make your expectations clear. If he's coming back home to live, you will want to discuss what his responsibilities will be and what you expect in the way of help around the house and adherence to family schedules and rules.
- Try to focus on the next few weeks and months to help your child get through this crisis.
- Pay attention to any indicators that may point to psychological or substance-abuse problems that contributed to his failure.
- Schedule an appointment with a family therapist to talk about how you will manage this new arrangement.
- You may have to take the initiative in getting your son some tutoring and/or counseling help as well.

What to Avoid

- Dumping all of your feelings of disappointment on your child. He feels humiliated and embarrassed enough.
- Telling him how he's let you and the family down.
- Calling the college and trying to get the dean to reverse the decision.
- Losing faith in your child's ability to do college work.

What You Need to Know

In 2008, an average of about 25 percent of first-year college students nationwide did not return for their second year. That number is significantly higher in some states and may be due to academic and/or financial difficulties. Because so many students do not finish college in the traditional four years, most studies look at the rate of graduation over a six-year period. In 2008, according to the National Center for Higher Education Management Systems, states range from 22.1 percent (Alaska) to 69.1 percent (Massachusetts) in six-year graduation rates for bachelor's students. Overall, just over 50 percent of American students finish college, but graduation rates vary a great deal from college to college.

Failing out of college can be a real crisis for families who sent a confident, bright child off to school and never expected to bring a defeated child home at the end of the year. There are many reasons why students may fail to achieve in college. Although they are bright and capable in high school, some students experience enormous challenges academically, personally, and socially in college. Some are simply not ready for the freedom and responsibility that are a part of college life and need more time to mature into successful students. This can be especially true for students who are not used to taking care of their daily physical needs and are overly dependent on parents to set guidelines and rules for their behavior.

Some students just need more time to grow up and learn to accept responsibility for the many demands of college life. A semester or year at home can provide that extra time and can be productive, if there are clear, realistic goals and expectations set.

Many colleges, realizing that some students come to school ill prepared to tackle the rigors of college course work, have made concerted efforts to provide additional support to students having difficulty adapting to college work and offer information on where students in academic trouble can get help. If your child is enrolled at a large university, however, he or she may fall through the cracks and not take advantage of the assistance available.

A Leave with a Silver Lining

Your daughter was not doing well in her English major at the state university and she was asked to take an academic leave. She found a job at a local resort and loved her work in the hotel manager's office. She's now decided to go back to school and to transfer to the university's hospitality program.

What's on Your Mind

I'm glad that her time off was so helpful to her.
I'm relieved that she's going back to school.

What's on Your Child's Mind

I love the hotel business.
Taking this leave was the best thing I've ever done.

What's Going On

As we've said before, there are often great benefits when a child drops out of school for a time. In fact, we have never met a student who didn't feel later that his or her time off, for whatever reason, was a good thing. Students who come back from a leave are usually the most motivated and enthusiastic learners and many find that their time off has given them a whole new academic direction and career focus.

What to Do

- Encourage your child in her new major.
- Congratulate her on the successful job she's done.
- Let her know how proud you are that she made such good use of her time away from school.
- Remind her of how courageous it was for her to make something positive happen from this initially negative experience.

What to Avoid

- Dampening her enthusiasm for her new career interest.
- Telling her how hard the hotel business is.
- Thinking this is not a very rigorous major and trying to convince her to stick with a liberal arts curriculum.

What You Need to Know

There are so many success stories to be told about students who take time off and come back to school ready and able to excel in their college work. Some find themselves dissatisfied with the major they've chosen, some don't yet have the maturity to manage the competing demands of school and social life, others need a bit of extra time to explore their interests.

While we don't want to downplay the disruption and anxiety that time off from college can cause parents and students alike, we do want to emphasize how valuable this experience can be and how important it is that parents support their children in considering alternatives and discovering ways to make time off a productive hiatus.

As one college administrator put it: "College is the most expensive buffet in the world; you'd better be sure you're hungry." The truth is that many young people are not ready to begin college right after high school and are not capable of taking advantage of the sumptuous array of offerings available to them. Given the cost of college, it's better that they take time off and come back when they are ready to make this enormous investment of money and time worthwhile.

Choosing to Leave

You will probably be surprised and confused when your child decides to quit college or interrupt his or her college career. When your child is doing well academically, it's difficult to understand why he or she chooses to leave. You wonder if he or she will ever go back and finish a degree. You may also be annoyed about all of the money you've invested and question if your child appreciates how much you've sacrificed to make college possible.

Dropping Out

You were shocked when your daughter announced that she has decided to drop out of school in her junior year to work at a Zen meditation center in Upstate New York where she had a summer job.

What's on Your Mind

> Has she become so enchanted with life at the Zen center that she'll never be able to cope in the "real world" again?
> She can't live in a meditation center forever.

What's on Your Child's Mind

> I really feel at home at the center.
> I can always go back to college if I want to. Not everyone needs a college degree to be happy.

What's Going On

Your daughter may be experiencing an identity crisis that is difficult for you to understand. The meditation center may offer her the time she needs to tackle the important task of deciding who she is in the world. She had a wonderful summer at the meditation center and began to develop a part of herself—her spirituality—that she found rewarding and compelling. In the college world of achievers and strivers, she may have felt out of place. A year working in the bakery at the Zen center may be exactly what she needs to continue her identity and autonomy quest.

Although this may not be the plan you had in mind for your child, it's very important that you learn to accept and support this choice. Even though she's chosen to live in a cloistered community, she will learn life skills that will benefit her down the road, whether she chooses to stay or return to school.

What to Do

- Listen to her reasons for wanting to drop out of college.
- Try to be as supportive as possible of her choices.
- Recognize that this may be a necessary and productive part of her development.
- Find out more about the meditation center. Offer to visit her there and learn about the community.
- Remember that this is her choice and that your role is to raise questions but ultimately to be supportive.

What to Avoid

- Telling her that you think she's crazy.
- Reminding her that people who live in these places are losers who can't make it in the "real world."
- Jumping to the conclusion that she has joined some dangerous cult.
- Making your expectations more important than her explorations.

What You Need to Know

Students who are not motivated to learn in college can benefit from time off. In fact, many students who simply stick it out in college would be better served by taking some time off and exploring their interests and passions. Parents can't give their kids motivation; in most cases, students who take time off return to college with increased energy and more focused goals.

Most colleges have a voluntary leave policy, in addition to medical and academic leaves. It's usually a good idea to take a leave of absence instead of just withdrawing; taking a leave makes it easier to return later.

College Seems Meaningless

Your son has always been a self-starter with an uncommon curiosity about the world. He decided after his freshman year that college wasn't for him. Although he'd always done well in school, he didn't seem excited about the courses of study offered at the university and wanted to spend some time working with a not-for-profit development group that works on refugee re-settlement in central Africa.

What's on Your Mind

> He's always been interested in what he calls "real people and real work."
> I guess we can't force him to stay in school.
> Will he be safe in Africa?

What's on Your Child's Mind

> There aren't any courses here that I really want to take.
> I want to learn by doing, not by studying and taking tests.
> I hope my parents will understand.

What's Going On

College can seem cloistered and unreal to some students. Some don't relate to the "careerism" found on most campuses and wants to do something meaningful in the world. This student might have been a good candidate for taking a year or two off after high school and doing community service work. Now, much to his credit, he has realized that he isn't motivated to do college work and needs to pursue his education in another way.

What to Do

- Support your child, even though you may find his ideas unorthodox.
- Let him know that you are proud of his values and his desire to make a difference in the world.
- Ask him to share details of his plans with you.
- Review with him the pluses and minuses of his decision and ask him if he's thought about alternative plans.

What to Avoid

- Telling him that he's gone too far.
- Trying to convince him to stay in school.
- Letting your fear of uncertainty thwart his spirit and passion.

What You Need to Know

The traditional college experience is not for everyone. While you may not be surprised if your child has come up with an unconventional alternative to staying in college, it still may be hard for you to understand and accept, knowing the risks and possible pitfalls of his or her decision. Your consulting skills can be useful in helping your child assess choices. A child who leaves college with well-defined goals will learn a lot more than one who drifts aimlessly about, becoming more and more dependent on his or her parents to set the agenda.

We recently read about a young man who dropped out of Oberlin College to enroll in what he called "the University of Planet Earth." He became an enthusiastic participant in a growing self-schooling movement, following his realization that "there were no courses in college covering the things I most wanted to learn."[1] His self-styled curriculum is to "Live in a different city every year. Attend a different place of worship every week. Seek out hundreds of mentors to help me find answers to my thousands of questions. Spend the rest of the time in the library and on the Internet. Create lists, make charts, and undertake the most ambitious projects I can think of. Create my own personal bible, almanac and telephone book. Live in the poorest neighborhoods in order to learn how to get along in the world and to save money. . . ."[2]

While this young man's story is an unusual one, it's also an indication of his curiosity, initiative, and desire for self-knowledge. His parents were not willing to give him the money they would have spent on his education, so he is working to support himself and accepting responsibility for his choices.

Although hard for parents to accept, there is no doubt that students who leave college to pursue an unconventional, but well-conceived, alternative can have some extraordinary learning experiences. It's normal to wonder what your child's future prospects will be without a college degree, but parents have at least as much reason to be proud of a child who exhibits such passion and motivation to take charge of his or her learning as they do a child who takes a more traditional route. And, remember, your child can always return to college later.

Financial Difficulty

You recently lost your job and have come to the conclusion that you have to ask your daughter to leave college because you can no longer afford to pay her tuition. She's just completed her first year and you're very concerned about what this decision will mean for her future.

What's on Your Mind

I'm so embarrassed and sad that I have to spoil her dreams of a college degree.
I wonder what she'll do now.
Maybe she can return when I get a new job.

What's on Your Child's Mind

I had no idea that my family was in such trouble financially.
I guess I'll have to go home and try to find a job.
This is so depressing.

What's Going On

While distressing, this is an increasingly common situation for many American families. Some parents are not able, even with financial aid, to come up with their share of college costs or qualify for loans. This can be a real crisis for parents and students alike. Parents who have dreamed of a college education for their children can feel embarrassed, humiliated, and worried about what the future may hold for their family. Students who have just settled in to college life have to disrupt their plans and face the prospect of moving home and taking a low-paying job just to help the family out.

What to Do

- Try to explain this change in family circumstances as clearly as possible.
- Make an effort to remain positive about the future, even if you are anxious about the prospects for getting another job.
- Be honest with your child about what is possible and what you're doing to change the situation.

What to Avoid

- Promising your child that she'll be able to go back to college soon.
- Feeling that you have ruined everyone's lives in the family.
- Refusing to talk about the realities of the situation.

What You Need to Know

You are not alone in facing this most difficult of financial circumstances. Many families are dealing with job loss, home foreclosure, and the inevitable challenges that those events cause. This can be a real crisis for all family members and one that may take months or years to recover from.

Earning a college degree is an important goal for many young people, but families have to be realistic about what's possible when they are struggling with financial setbacks. While no one can predict the future, there may be ways to help your family get through this tough period that will result in more promising outcomes. As we've described before, many students rise to the challenge when they're faced with difficult circumstances and actually learn a great deal by spending some time in the workforce before returning to college. Situations that require extraordinary effort and selflessness can contribute to maturity and the sense of the accomplishment that comes from doing something really hard. These crises can be as much about building a stronger family as they can be about destroying hopes and dreams.

Transferring to Another College

Your son, who is a sophomore at the state university in a nearby town, wants to transfer to a small, private college in another state.

What's on Your Mind

Why can't he get what he wants at the state university?
This is going to cost a lot more money and he'll end up having to take out loans.

What's on Your Child's Mind

I don't fit in here.
I should have gone to a small college in the first place.

What's Going On

Your son has found that the college he chose is not a good fit for him. While this means a disruption in his plans and the necessity of readjusting to a new place, it's a good idea if you can support his desire to transfer. Feeling at home is an important part of doing well in college and feeling in synch with a peer group is a critical aspect of the college experience.

What to Do

- Talk to him about his reasons for wanting to transfer.
- Listen to him and accept that he is the best judge of his comfort level.
- Support him in finding alternatives to his situation.
- Reinforce the importance of planning this move carefully to make sure as many credits as possible will honored by the new school.

What to Avoid

- Dismissing his feelings as trivial.
- Refusing to consider alternatives.
- Reminding him that lots of kids do just fine at the state university and that he just needs to learn to adjust.
- Trying to make him feel guilty for choosing a more expensive college.

What You Need to Know

Studies show that students who feel at home at college are significantly more likely to remain in school, achieve, and graduate. Parents should not trivialize their child's desire to fit in and experience college with peers who share their values and goals. Colleges and universities have widely differing cultures and even students who think they have made a suitable choice during the admissions process often find out later that they would be happier at another school.

Students need to be prepared for "transfer shock," even if they are quite familiar with the new campus. They may feel confused and need time to find a niche. It's important that transfer students take care in choosing their housing. It's best if they can be housed initially with other transfer students or students their own age. It's also critical that your child has good advising from the beginning so that his academic progress won't be interrupted.

Each year there are students who transfer, thinking that this move will solve all their problems. Parents need to be attentive to a child's reasons for transferring and be ready to talk about their child's motivation in a nonjudgmental, but realistic, way. For example, there's a big difference between a child wanting to transfer because he feels smaller classes will benefit him and that he will have a better chance of being editor of the school's newspaper and a child who wants to transfer to avoid dealing with the stringent course requirements in his or her chosen major.

Taking Time Off

Your daughter has decided to take a semester off from school and work in the Bahamas at a resort. She says she's burned out after so many years in school and that she really needs a break.

What's on Your Mind

> Can she make enough money to support herself for a semester?
> What will happen to her financial aid package at school?
> What if she never goes back to school?
> Should we let her do this?

What's on Your Child's Mind

> I am so burned out with school. I need a break.
> This may be my only chance to do something fun for a while.
> I have it all figured out. I know I can get a good job.

What's Going On

Your daughter may need a break from the relentless demands of student life. Rather than just dropping out, she has a plan to do something productive with her semester off. In our experience, students who take time off for a semester or a year invariably come back to college refreshed and more motivated to tackle their college work. Moreover, it can be a real advantage for a student to live on her own, work, and get some job experience while she's in college.

As a parent, you may be used to things progressing in an orderly way and your daughter's decision to interrupt her education may worry you. Chances are good, however, that this break will give her a needed respite from college, and teach her some important things about living on her own in another culture and supporting herself. Remember that, in a few years, this will be remembered as an insignificant "blip" in her college years.

What to Do

- Try to listen to her desires.
- Support her in taking some time off.

- Ask her to give you a proposal for how she'll take care of herself.
- Make it clear that you expect her to return to school at an agreed-upon time.

What to Avoid

- Letting her know that you think this is a frivolous idea.
- Ridiculing her for being a "slacker."

What You Need to Know

Sometimes students who want to take a break from college are afraid to tell their parents for fear that they won't understand. Parents may be tempted to try to convince their child to stay in school. This often results in the child taking a break anyway. He or she may stop going to classes, neglect studies, get low grades, and eventually be forced to take a leave. It's important to listen carefully to your child and respect his or her needs.

You may have some pragmatic issues to deal with if your child decides to take some time off from college. While your daughter's financial aid package will probably not be affected by her decision to take a semester off, it is important that you look into her health insurance coverage. There may be stipulations that need to be addressed and resolved.

Dropping Out for Good

Your son is a mechanical whiz. He's decided to drop out of college and attend a trade school in your hometown. He says that he's always wanted to work with his hands and knows that he can get a good job following his training as an HVAC technician.

What's on Your Mind

I'm worried that his decision isn't a good one for the long term.
What if he regrets this choice later?
I know he's dazzled by the job prospects, but how secure is this choice?

What's on Your Child's Mind

Who needs college? I can make plenty of money if I get this technical training.
It's going to be so cool; after just a year of school, I'll be able to have my own apartment and a car.

What's Going On

Clearly, your son is intrigued with the idea of becoming self-supporting and learning a practical trade. While most students today see college as the ticket to a well-paying job in the future, he may be right that he can find a good job and create a satisfying life without having to complete a college degree.

What to Do

- Talk with him about the pros and cons of leaving school without a degree.
- Let him know that you support his right to make the choice, but share your concerns with him as well.
- Ask him if he has thought of a fallback plan if this training doesn't meet his expectations.

What to Avoid

- Preaching to him about the importance of a college degree. It will undoubtedly fall on deaf ears.
- Obsessing about all the things that could go wrong if he follows a different path.

What You Need to Know

A college degree, often touted as the route to upward mobility, is not the only path to a satisfying and financially productive career. For many college students today a college degree can mean crushing loan debt and slim job prospects upon graduation. Some students, having witnessed their parents and peers deal with a difficult job market, are opting to leave college and pursue a more practical course of study and training.

A recent headline in *The New York Times* announced, "Plan B: Skip College."[3] The writer states that, according to the Bureau of Labor Statistics, "Of the thirty jobs projected to grow at the fastest rate over the next decade in the United States, only seven require a bachelor's degree." Many economists and educators alike have been calling for increased opportunities for short-term vocational and apprenticeship training for young people to fill the jobs that will be in demand in the years to come. Earning a college degree may not be the best investment of time and money for your child, especially if he or she will be saddled with significant debt after graduation. It's possible that avoiding that debt burden could result in a happier, financially healthier life for your child over time.

While some students leave college each year, opting for study in technical vocational programs and go on to successful, fulfilling careers, it is certainly true as well that many college dropouts end up in low-paying, dead-end jobs. You can be an important consultant in helping your child research prospects for alternative programs and evaluating the possible outcomes. It's easy, in a culture that celebrates and reinforces the idea that the good life means having impressive academic credentials and a big salary, to be concerned if your child rejects a college degree for technical training that will place him or her in a so-called "blue collar" job. But there are many people who derive great satisfaction and a solid salary through technical or service career paths.

There is a big difference between the student who drops out and spends the next year idling on your sofa and the child who drops out and gets on with his life in productive ways. As a parent, you may be legitimately concerned if your child drops out of college but it's important to keep in mind that *your* dream of your child being a college graduate may not mesh with his interests and goals.

Plan B

When plans for earning a college degree are interrupted, it is usually an unsettling experience for students and parents alike. Whether your child leaves school voluntarily, is asked to leave, chooses to leave, or must leave due to financial circumstances, it is helpful to remember that there are alternatives to the traditional four-year residential college career.

Some students choose to enroll in a local community college for a couple of years before reapplying to a four-year institution, thereby saving a great deal of money. Others who have left college eventually earn a degree through an online university while holding down a job or decide to go to college later in life. Still others find a satisfying career, through vocational or on-the-job training, without the benefit of a college degree. Moreover, your son or daughter may have strong entrepreneurial and/or technical skills that could lead to the involvement with a start-up venture producing innovative goods or services.

When your child leaves college, for any reason, we urge you to think creatively about the options available; while it's never easy to let go of dreams and expectations, you can be your child's most valuable coach and adviser as he or she explores alternatives.

Chapter 12

Understanding Your Child's Postgraduate Choices

Graduate School or Job?

Four years ago when our daughter began college, all of us had great hopes for her future. She's now in her senior year with a degree in English and we're really worried about her job prospects. She wonders if she should just forget about trying to get a job and continue on to graduate school immediately. All of her friends who are graduating seem to be in the same boat, even those who have so-called "marketable" degrees such as engineering and computer science. We're pretty confused as to how to help her with the next chapter in her life.

Although at time of publication, there appears to be a slight recovery from the last two years' Great Recession, there is no doubt that we are facing an era of disturbing unemployment and underemployment. Don Peck, in his recent article, "How a New Jobless Era Will Transform America," argues, "This era of high joblessness will likely change the life course and character of a generation . . . in fact a whole generation of young adults is likely to see its life chances permanently diminished by this recession."[1]

The unemployment rate for young adults is high, even for the college-educated. According to the Bureau of Labor Statistics, the rate of unemployment for the eighteen to twenty-nine age group is nearly 14 percent, and another 23 percent are not even seeking a job, which puts the total at 37 percent, a number reminiscent of the Great Depression in the 1930s. As many young adults struggle to land that first professional job, they are either going home to live with their parents or taking short-term, temporary jobs, or both.

Young people today cannot, for the most part, expect to be gainfully employed in a job that offers a clear career trajectory and upward mobility upon graduation from college. This economic climate presents real challenges for students and their parents. In fact, this may be the most challenging transition in your child's life, a time when there is no clear road map to adulthood and independence.

The Winding Road to Adulthood

The so-called Millennial Generation of young people (those born between 1980 and 2000) has received an enormous amount of attention. They are described as special, sheltered, confident, optimistic, collaborative, pressured to achieve, overscheduled, and socially conscious. One characteristic that defies traditional notions of intergenerational relations is that they are uncommonly close to and respectful of their parents. This is a generation of college students that often maintains daily contact with their parents and relies on them for continual support, counsel, and emotional reinforcement.

While you may be justifiably proud of your good relationship with your young adult child, this extraordinary closeness could now get in the way of your child making the first moves, however tentative, to independence and self-sufficiency. This next stage of development in your relationship with your young adult child will bring new challenges that may test your capacity to step back and allow your child to navigate that winding road to independence without your constant vigilance and assistance.

The experiences and behaviors of this generation of young people have inspired the creation of a new stage in human development called "emerging adulthood." One of the reasons this new life stage has been identified is that the age of marriage, parenthood, and economic independence has risen dramatically in the last forty years. Instead of marrying and having children in their late teens or early twenties, most young people today now postpone these rites of passage until their late twenties. This allows for several years of exploration (and, yes, floundering) as they try out a variety of relationships and career paths before they become fully independent.

Jeffrey Arnett, who coined the phrase "emerging adulthood," and authored *Emerging Adulthood: The Winding Road from the Late Teens through the Twenties,* identifies five distinguishing features of emerging adulthood:

1. It is the age of *identity exploration,* of trying out various possibilities, especially in love and work.
2. It is the age of *instability,* of constantly shifting choices; exploration and instability go hand in hand.
3. It is the most *self-focused* age of life.
4. It is the age of *feeling in-between,* in transition, neither adolescent nor adult.
5. It is the age of *possibilities,* when hopes flourish, when people have an unparalleled opportunity to transform their lives.[2]

Surveys reveal that the majority of Americans believe that people between the ages of twenty and twenty-two should be finished with their education, working, and living on their own, but the reality is that many young people in their twenties and even early thirties have not yet reached those milestones of adulthood.

Add to this phenomenon recent brain research that identifies at least two areas in which the adolescent/emerging adult brain is different from the adult brain. We now know that the prefrontal cortex (the part of the brain that is active in planning, decision making, goal setting, and suppressing impulses) does not finish maturing until age twenty-five. The second finding from this research indicates that teenagers process emotions differently and more intensely than adults. While adults use their prefrontal cortex to process stimuli, adolescents tend to process stimuli in the amygdala (a more emotion-centered, instinctual part of the brain). The prefrontal cortex tempers emotional response. In an adolescent, the amygdala triggers a gut reaction that is less inhibited and less cautious than it would be if his or her prefrontal cortex were more fully developed and engaged.

As we learn more about this unique stage of human development and the implications of continuing brain research, perhaps we are on the cusp of needing to rethink our expectations of young people, even if we remove the obvious challenges and pitfalls of a profoundly troubled economic environment. And as the very idea of adulthood evolves, parents face unique and often daunting questions about how to support their "emerging adults" through this period of acclimation to the adult world.

If you've been an extraordinarily attentive and involved parent, this is the time for you to reassess your role. It may be difficult for you to imagine your son or daughter out there in the big, scary "real world" without your safety net, but this is the moment to take the leap of faith in your child's ability to handle the challenges of becoming (eventually!) an independent adult.

Graduation Looms Ahead

When graduation from college nears, and you anticipate what's next, you may be as worried and as uncertain as your child. After all, you've experienced the world of work for many years and you know how fragile economic stability and security can be.

You probably have at least as many unanswered questions as your child. Is it best to attend graduate school immediately after college? Or is graduate school simply a way to avoid trying to find that first job? Are unpaid or low-paying internships a viable option after spending so much money for a college education? What types of jobs are available for liberal arts graduates? Will a couple of years working as a barista affect your child's long-term career prospects? How much financial support will you be expected to provide after college graduation? What is your role as your child launches herself into the world after college?

Indeed, parents can play a significant role in helping their children make informed choices about life after college. Using your consulting skills and the information in this chapter, you can help your child assess his or her options and balance dreams with reality in this first step on the path to becoming a self-supporting adult.

Graduate School—Now or Later?

It can be tempting to encourage your child to go straight to graduate school, especially in a tight job market. In some fields this is a wise choice, while in others it's nearly impossible to gain admission to graduate school without some work experience. In the following scenarios, we will explore law school, medical school, business school, and other professional programs, as well as the traditional PhD program. In addition, we will help you assess whether your child's decision to apply to graduate school is a response to senior panic or the logical next step in a chosen career path.

Fear of Job Hunting

Your son, who is majoring in political science, comes home during fall break of his senior year and reports that he has decided to keep his options open by taking the admissions tests for business school (GMAT) and graduate school (GRE). He plans to apply to business school and to graduate school for a master's in political science. He says that he can't find a good job without a graduate degree; he's sure that he'll find a program that's right for him.

What's on Your Mind

> Does it make sense for him to take both of these admissions tests?
> How much will these tests and applications cost?
> Shouldn't he be more focused before he goes to graduate school?
> Maybe it's better for him to go directly to graduate school, given the lack of jobs.

What's on Your Child's Mind

> I am so confused.
> At least the process of applying to graduate school is clear; I don't have a clue about how to start looking for a job.
> If I go to graduate school, at least I won't have to take a low-level, boring job.

What's Going On

It's not unusual for college seniors to feel that they are the only ones who don't know what they want to do after college graduation. If a student's major has not prepared him for a specific career area, going to graduate school often looks appealing. School is familiar; he's spent his entire life in school. He knows how to take tests and fill out graduate school applications. He doesn't know how to look for a job, and he convinced that it's impossible to find a good one.

During the spring term of the junior year in college or early in the senior year, students come face-to-face with the scary question, "What's next?" It's not uncommon for panic to set in. For the first time in your child's life, he faces an uncharted future. Up until now, the next step has been relatively clear. But what now?

What to Do

- Listen to his fears about what he'll do after graduation.
- Remind him that it's natural to feel confused about what comes next.
- Ask him if applying to graduate school is what he really wants to do right now.
- Suggest that he talk to a career counselor at school who can help him determine whether graduate school is the best option.

What to Avoid

- Encouraging him to apply to graduate school, even if he's unclear about what he wants to do.
- Reminding him of how difficult it is to get a good job with just an undergraduate degree.
- Thinking that it's better to be in graduate school than floundering around in an uncertain job market.

What You Need to Know

It's normal for students, when facing this uncertainty, to want to avoid it by going to graduate school. This is usually not a good idea, especially if your child's graduate school plans are vague and fundamentally a response to "senior panic." For one thing, graduate school acceptance is based on evidence of a serious commitment to a field of study and graduate school admissions committees are fairly good at discerning who exhibits a true commitment to a particular course of study and who merely applies to delay the inevitable entry into the job market. In fact, most graduate business schools require their applicants to have a year or two of work experience before they will consider admitting them.

With a master's degree in political science he will not be any more qualified for jobs than he would be with a bachelor's degree in political science. If he wants a master's degree in order to work in government or public policy, it would make more sense for him to apply to one of a number of good graduate schools that award a professional (as opposed to a traditional academic) degree. There are schools that specifically prepare individuals for careers in government or public policy work.

Because the professional world is based on a system of credentialing, an advanced degree that offers specific training is a more practical choice in preparing for a career in a particular field. The degrees offered in a traditional academic area are usually an MA (master of arts) or MS (master of science), while professional degrees are highly specific: for example, an MPA (master of public administration); an MLS (master of library science); an MPH (master of public health); an MRP (master of regional planning); an MPS (master of professional studies in real estate, international development, or other professional areas); an MAT (master of arts in teaching); an MILR (master of industrial and labor relations); or an MEng (master of engineering) to name a few.

If your child wants a career in social service work, the master's degree in sociology (MS) will not provide credentialing to work in this area. He or she needs a Master of Social Work degree (MSW), which, after taking a licensing exam, will prepare him or her to hang out a shingle as a therapist or to work in a variety of social service organizations. Or if he or she wants to work in publishing, a master's degree in English (MA) is not the credential she needs. Although most editorial assistants obtain their jobs right out of college, some students enroll in one of several highly respected postgraduate certification programs in publishing from which many publishing houses recruit their entry-level employees. In short, a master's degree in any of the traditional academic areas (English, history, psychology, political science, biology, economics, sociology, etc.) will not move your child closer to the credential needed for work in a specific field, with the possible exception of teaching at the primary or secondary school level, but most teachers opt for the MAT (Master's in Teaching). The desire to get a master's degree in the traditional academic areas noted above is usually evidence of a lack of understanding of how graduate degrees translate into careers.

Delaying the Decision

Your son has decided that he's not going to take the LSAT and apply to law schools. He's going to take a year off and work in a ski resort in Colorado with a couple of his fraternity brothers.

What's on Your Mind

I've spent all this money on a college education and he wants to be a "ski bum"?
Is he copping out of the real world?

What's on Your Child's Mind

I can't face studying for the LSAT.
I can always go to law school later. What's the rush?

What's Going On

Your son may be afraid that he won't do well on the LSAT and wants to avoid having to worry about it in his senior year of college. It's also likely that he's sick of school and needs a break before going on to law school.

What to Do

- Listen to his fears and anxieties.
- Let him know that you're proud of what he has already accomplished in college.
- Be willing to accept his desire to have time off.
- Offer a compromise. Suggest that he ski during the season and consider getting a job at a law firm during the off-season. This may help him decide if law school is for him.

What to Avoid

- Accusing him of being a "slacker."
- Insisting that he explain why he's decided not to be a lawyer.
- Threatening him with stories of people who aren't motivated to do something meaningful with their life after college.

What You Need to Know

While this may be a surprising development for you, it's probably a good choice for him. It's not unusual for students to take time off between undergraduate studies and graduate school; by college graduation most students have spent a continuous seventeen or eighteen years in school and can benefit from a break. It's appropriate to suggest, however, that he get at least a temporary job that will help him decide if law school is for him. Working in a law firm or within the judicial or criminal justice system will not only give him an insider's view of the profession but it will help him when he's ready to apply to law school.

He can enhance his chances of admission to law school if he has some real world experience, especially if his time off includes a job in a related field. While it may be difficult for you to understand his desire to put off law school, this break could be a valuable and maturing experience for him and mean that he will be truly motivated to do well when he eventually becomes a law student. And it may be that he isn't ever motivated enough to go to law school. At that point, you can encourage whatever his interests are at the time.

What Graduate Program Would Be Best?

Your daughter, Bridget, is a junior in college and is trying to decide on graduate programs. When she was home over fall break, you had the following conversation:

BRIDGET: Mom, I really think I should be thinking about graduate school. If I want to go right after undergrad, I'll need to apply by next fall.

MOM: What programs are you thinking about?

BRIDGET: Well, I'm pretty sure I want to work with abused kids. I really love my volunteer work at the family and children's center. There are so many kids who need help.

MOM: I'm really proud of you for wanting to do such a difficult job, but are you sure that you will want to do it full time for the rest of your life?

BRIDGET: I think so. It's just amazing what the psychologists do with those kids. I want to be able to help, too.

MOM: Have you talked to any of the staff members there about what graduate degree you need to work with abused children?

BRIDGET: Yeah, but I get even more confused when I talk to them. One of them has a master's in social work and one has a PhD in clinical psychology. Both of them are really good with the kids, but I think the woman with the PhD gets to do more and makes a lot more money.

MOM: Well, maybe you should consider a PhD then.

BRIDGET: But, Mom, I've heard it's really hard to get into a PhD program in clinical psych and my grades aren't all that good. I'm pretty sure I could get into an MSW program though.

MOM: Is that what you really want?

BRIDGET: I don't know. I wish I knew if I could handle a PhD.

MOM: Could you talk to your faculty adviser about it? Or someone in the psychology department?

BRIDGET: I guess so, but I'm sure they're going to think I'm clueless.

MOM: Well, you do need some help figuring this out and they might be able to give you some advice.

BRIDGET: Yeah, maybe I'll talk to someone when I get back to school.

What's on Your Mind

I'm afraid Bridget is going to make this big decision without much information.

Isn't there someone who can give her solid advice about graduate school?

I wonder if she really understands what she's getting into, working with such depressing cases every day.

What's on Your Child's Mind

I really love working with these kids.

I think this is what I want to do for a career, but I'm not entirely sure.

How am I going to figure this out in time to apply to graduate school?

What's Going On

Bridget thinks she has found a career path that will be meaningful and rewarding, but she's not sure how to obtain the credentials she needs. She feels the pressure to apply to graduate school when she doesn't have enough information to make an educated choice of programs. And she's not sure she has the academic qualifications to be accepted to the most competitive and rigorous programs. It's common for juniors and seniors to begin to explore graduate programs and feel pretty confused about what to do next with their education.

What to Do

- Encourage your child to get as much information as she can in order to make an informed decision.
- Suggest that she talk to clinical psychologists and social workers on campus or in the community who can share their own graduate school experiences with her.
- Recommend that she talk to someone in the college's career center to get information on careers in both areas.

- Suggest that she talk to a faculty member in psychology about how she can get research experience, which will be important if she decides to pursue the PhD.
- Remind her that she may want to consider putting off the graduate school decision.
- Suggest that she could consider working in a center for abused children for a while after college to see if this is really what she wants to do.

What to Avoid

- Telling her how depressing this kind of work can be and how many people burn out after a short time.
- Suggesting that she settle for the master's in social work or insisting that she go for the more prestigious degree.
- Letting her know that you're frustrated with her indecision.

What You Need to Know

PhD programs in clinical psychology are among the most competitive. It is usually much easier to get accepted to a Master of Social Work graduate program. This doesn't mean that your child shouldn't try for the PhD. The key here is that Bridget doesn't appear to be prepared to make this big decision; she needs time to investigate her options, even if it means working for a year or two after college and applying to graduate programs later. This time might allow her to work in some capacity in the field that interests her and to make her decision based on experience.

Many students, given the tough job market, are choosing to work with AmeriCorps, AmeriCorps VISTA, City Year, or other community-based service organizations. These opportunities offer individuals a chance to gain skills and experience in a wide variety of public and community service projects. For example, Bridget could work as a tutor with disadvantaged youth, thereby giving her valuable experience to enhance her graduate school application, a subsistence salary, as well as a grant toward graduate school or to help her pay back her student loans.

Bridget may decide that working with abused children is not for her but that she wants to work in another one of the helping professions. Having some experience will undoubtedly help her get into graduate school eventually; it will also give her the distinct advantage of having focused her goals.

Graduate Business School

Your son has decided that he's going to apply to business schools to get an MBA and he wants you to pay for him to take an expensive course in preparation for taking the Graduate Management Aptitude Test (GMAT).

What's on Your Mind

He should have learned enough in college to prepare him for business school admissions
tests.
Am I going to have to pay for business school, too?

What's on Your Child's Mind

I really want to get an MBA. I need this degree to get ahead in business.
Dad doesn't understand how important the GMAT is.
I want to get into one of the top ten schools. Graduates from those schools get the best jobs.

What's Going On

Eager and motivated students usually want to go directly to graduate school, and they understand the importance of the graduate school admissions tests for helping them get into a top
school. It's usually a good idea to take these competitive examinations seriously; their specialized material does require additional study in order to achieve a good score. Students can prepare for these tests in various ways, and some of them are expensive. It's a good idea to be wary,
however, of the test courses that promise high scores and to investigate the reputation of any
organization offering test preparation. Students can receive advice on this issue at their college
career center.

What to Do

- Suggest that he investigate the test preparation courses available and give you some
  more information, especially if he's asking you to pay for it.
- Recommend that he talk to an adviser in the career center about applying to business
  school.
- Congratulate him on taking the initiative to explore his options for postgraduate
  study.

What to Avoid

- Telling him that you know he can do fine without the prep course.
- Refusing to discuss this option before you know what's involved.

What You Need to Know

While it might be a smart idea for your son to take a preparation course for the GMAT while he's still in college, chances are that he will not be accepted to business school right after graduation. Most of the top business schools require that students have at least one or two years of work experience before admitting them to the MBA program. If he takes the GMAT now, he can use his test score for five years; he won't have to take it again—unless he wants to—when he applies to business school later.

Most professional schools, such as law and business, do not offer assistantships or fellowships to cover tuition and expenses. These are expensive degrees and often leave graduates with a significant loan burden. But most lawyers and business people earn enough money to pay off their graduate education over time. A graduate degree in these areas is likely to be a good investment financially; however, advanced degrees in other less lucrative career fields can create a real financial burden following graduate school. Fields such as social work, architecture, library science, and teaching do not typically offer high enough salaries to easily pay off student loans. Students need to think carefully about how they will manage the costs of a professional master's degree.

Many organizations offer their employees tuition assistance and some even send their highest performers to graduate school and pick up the cost. It may be possible for your child to pursue a graduate degree part-time while employed, as many universities offer extensive night and weekend graduate degree programs.

PhD in Science

Your daughter is an outstanding physics student and has been encouraged by her professors to attend graduate school and earn a PhD in physics when she finishes her undergraduate degree next year.

What's on Your Mind

> Does she really need a PhD?
> What will she do with this degree?
> I don't have the money to put her through more school.

What's on Your Child's Mind

> I need a PhD in order to teach physics at a university.
> My professors think I can get accepted into a really good school.

What's Going On

Students who are seriously committed to a career in teaching and research in a college or university setting usually go directly to graduate school after college. If your daughter knows that she wants to be a college professor, there is probably no reason for her to delay going to graduate school. She will benefit most from her professors' interest and encouragement if she goes directly on to earn the PhD in her field.

What to Do

- Congratulate her on her outstanding academic career.
- Encourage her to get advice on which universities she should apply to from her current faculty members.
- Let her know that you are proud of her motivation and commitment to pursue such a difficult course of study.

What to Avoid

- Telling her that graduate school is too expensive.
- Encouraging her to be satisfied with teaching physics in a high school where she won't need the PhD.
- Reminding her of how hard it is to get a tenure-track faculty job today.

What You Need to Know

While obtaining entry-level positions as tenure-track assistant professors is very difficult in the current job market, it is not impossible, especially for the best students who graduate from prestigious universities and have the benefit of a network of respected scholars in the field. If your child is determined to make it in the academic world, she needs to have the best credentials possible. This usually means earning a PhD from a high-quality institution and where she has the support of faculty members who have confidence in her potential as a scholar and a teacher.

It used to be a given that a student accepted into a PhD program would be fully funded with assistantships and fellowships. While this still remains true in some academic areas, particularly in the sciences, some PhD programs no longer automatically provide financial assistance for every entering graduate student. These programs may require a student to assume the costs for a semester or a year so that the department can evaluate their academic performance before awarding financial support.

There are basically two types of aid: merit-based and need-based. Merit-based aid is awarded on the basis of academic accomplishment, talent, or promise. This type of financial aid comes in the form of grants, stipends, graduate assistantships, and/or fellowships. Assistantships are the most common type of graduate financial aid and usually translate into part-time teaching or research jobs. Students can investigate the availability of these types of aid before they formally apply to a particular graduate school. Fellowships are the most prestigious form of financial assistance at the graduate level. They are used by universities to attract students with the greatest potential. Most assistantships and fellowships will include full tuition coverage plus a modest stipend to cover living expenses. Grants are sums of money awarded for specific activities on a project basis and are usually funded by government agencies, foundations, or corporations.

In assessing financial aid, the university will calculate your child's need based on the difference between her total educational costs and his or her financial resources. In order to apply for this aid the student will need to fill out the Free Application for Federal Student Aid (FAFSA) form. Need-based aid programs include work-study programs, private and federal loans, grants, fellowships, and tuition remission programs offered to students by the graduate school.

All students attending graduate or professional school are considered financially independent by the Federal government; however, each year financial aid for graduate school becomes increasingly difficult to obtain. Applicants to graduate school need to be assertive in exploring all types of financial aid available and make sure that they have a good credit history before applying for assistance.

If your child is applying to graduate school, encourage her to visit her college career center early in the process for advice on graduate financial aid and to research sources of support. She should allow adequate time to explore the possibilities and to meet deadlines and application requirements.

Some students are intimidated by the PhD degree and decide to apply for a master's degree instead. In the traditional academic graduate programs, assistantships are not usually available for students earning the master's-level degree because the department will prefer to award support to students pursuing the PhD. Most academic counselors will encourage your child to apply for the PhD program directly instead of applying for the master's degree first. Students can always decide later if they want to complete their study at the master's degree, but the possibility of receiving financial aid increases dramatically when the applicant intends to pursue the PhD degree.

Applying to Law School

Your daughter, Jessica, is a junior in college and has done well in her major course of study—American history. She's beginning to think about going to law school. While home for fall break, she shared some of her plans with you.

JESSICA: I'm so excited about going to law school. Where do you think I should apply?

MOM: Well, I'm not sure, honey. It's been years since I went to grad school. Where would you like to go?

JESSICA: I went to the career center and they had all of this information about applying to law school; it's amazing how many good schools there are. I don't even know where to begin.

MOM: It's pretty confusing at this stage, I bet. Maybe it's helpful to think about the decision in the same way you chose which colleges to apply to. How did you make sense of all that college information?

JESSICA: Well, I had some help from the college adviser at school. He said I should apply to the most competitive colleges. I guess I just went where I felt the most comfortable when we visited.

MOM: So you had the college tour, and the advice of your high school counselor. Do you think the same kinds of things would help you explore law schools?

JESSICA: I don't know, Mom, I really don't have a lot of time to visit schools right now. I could ask my college adviser, but he's a philosopher and I think he got a PhD in grad school. I'm definitely not interested in getting a PhD!

MOM: So this is a different kind of decision, isn't it?

JESSICA: Yeah. It's so confusing and I have to make some decisions pretty soon. I also have to study and take the LSAT, probably over holiday break. I wish there was someone who could tell me what schools I should consider.

MOM: Your university has a law school, doesn't it?

JESSICA: Yeah, but I definitely don't want to stay there for law school.

MOM: That's understandable. I think it's smart to have another experience. I was just wondering if there was anyone else on campus you could talk to about law schools.

JESSICA: Yeah, maybe there is. Maybe I'll just go over to the law school and see if anyone there can help me. Maybe I could also go to the career center—I think there's a grad school adviser there who might know something about law schools.

MOM: Sounds like another good idea. I think you're on the way to finding out what you need to know to make this decision. Can I be helpful in any way?

JESSICA: Well, you could write my statement of purpose for the application! Just kidding! I know this is going to be a lot of work, but I'm really getting excited about going to law school.

MOM: I'm excited about it, too. You've worked hard in college and I'm sure it's going to pay off when you apply to law school. I'm really proud of you, Jess.

JESSICA: Thanks, Mom.

What's on Your Mind

I can't believe Jessica is thinking about law school already. It seems like yesterday when we dropped her off at college.

I'm flattered that she's asking my opinion, but I don't know anything about law schools.

I hope she can get some guidance from the university.

What's on Your Child's Mind

I have so much to do to get ready to apply to law schools.

How do I know which one is right for me?

This seems so much more serious than going to college.

What's Going On

Some students who are interested in a law degree go directly on to law school, while others decide to work for a year or two first. Although working can help students determine if they want a career in law, law schools typically don't require that their applicants have work experience.

In this dialogue, Jessica's mother used excellent consulting skills in guiding and supporting her daughter in this decision-making process. Although parents don't always have the specific answers, they can encourage their child, suggest how to gather information, and sometimes even connect their child with someone they know who has been to graduate school in the same field.

What to Do

- Listen to your child's dilemma.
- Ask open-ended questions, such as "How do you think you could get some advice on this big decision?"

- Remind her of situations in which she mastered a difficult decision and ask her to recall how she did it.

What to Avoid

- Cutting off the dialogue by telling her you don't know anything about getting into law school.
- Suggesting that she wait a couple of years because she's obviously not ready to make a decision.
- Asking why she doesn't ask her adviser at school. She'll probably just reply that her adviser doesn't know anything about law schools.
- Telling her it will all work out and to stop obsessing about it now.

What You Need to Know

With the increasingly high cost of a legal education and with the competitive job market that law school graduates face, it is important that your child thoughtfully determines if a law career is the right choice. Each year many students decide to apply to law school because they can't figure out what else to do. This can be a costly and time-consuming mistake.

Encourage your child to explore the field through his or her career center; it's likely that there will be someone on staff whose specialty is prelaw advising. He or she can also learn a lot about different schools by reading their Web sites. Any student interested in the law should talk to practicing lawyers to find out what they do on a daily basis, and to ask them about their satisfactions and dissatisfactions with their profession. It's also helpful to get a summer job or internship in a law office in order to observe the personal characteristics needed to succeed as a lawyer, as well as to experience what lawyers do in a typical day's work.

According to a 2009 study by the National Association for Law Placement (NALP), the overall median law firm starting salary has more than doubled in the last fourteen years, from $50,000 to $125,000. Even though overall employment rates are currently slightly lower for law school graduates and a significantly higher percentage of graduates are accepting part-time or temporary positions, the legal employment market remains relatively strong, considering the economic down turn.

Each year law schools graduate over 40,000 students and the job market continues to be competitive for entry-level law positions, especially with the largest, most prestigious firms. If your child aspires to a corporate law position, he or she needs to be aware that most corporate lawyers work long hours, six or seven days a week. Although the starting salary for these highly competitive positions may be in excess of $150,000 a year, most entry-level lawyers have to make significant sacrifices in their personal lives to be successful. If your child aspires to a public interest law position, the starting salary will probably be in the $35,000 to $45,000 range; this can be a rude awakening to a student who has accumulated significant debt to get through law school. Typically, law students do not receive assistantships or institutional financial aid, even if they need it; they usually have to take out loans to finance their law school education.

Medical School

Your son has wanted to be a doctor since he was a little boy. He's done well in college and, now, in his junior year, he's preparing to take the MCAT examination and apply to medical schools. He seems both excited and anxious about this process.

What's on Your Mind

> I'm worried about whether he will get into medical school.
> He has his heart set on being a doctor.

What's on Your Child's Mind

> I have to get into medical school.
> I know my grades are good enough to get in, but what if my MCAT scores are not high enough?

What's Going On

Some of the most driven and competitive individuals on campus are the premed students. They usually come to college committed to being doctors, or they decide early in their college years to apply to medical school. Knowing how difficult it is to be accepted to medical school, many students work hard and are extremely intense about doing everything they can to ensure they will be among the few that go on to medical school. Because of this strong commitment, many premed students do not want to consider alternatives and are devastated if they don't get in on the first try.

What to Do

- Empathize with your son's anxiety. Let him know you appreciate how hard he is working to get into medical school.

- Suggest that he think about a fallback position if he isn't accepted on the first try.
- Prepare yourself for the possibility that he might not get in right away, and be ready to deal with his feelings of disappointment.

What to Avoid

- Putting any more pressure on him to succeed.
- Dismissing his fears.
- Telling him you're sure he'll get in and to stop worrying about it.

What You Need to Know

Nationwide about 50 percent of first-time applicants to medical school gain admission. While application numbers may vary from year to year, the number of places in medical schools stays the same and, hence, the number of students accepted is fairly static. A key variable may be the type of college your child is attending and the quality of its premedical advising program. Prestigious colleges and universities that are well known for the high quality of their students and for their rigorous course of study, usually have acceptance rates significantly higher than the national average.

Some colleges have a formal premedical major and others do not. Medical schools do not require or even recommend any particular course of study, although they stipulate that certain courses, such as general and advanced biology, introductory and organic chemistry, introductory physics, English composition, and in some cases, mathematics, must be completed to be considered for admission. Medical school admissions committees overwhelmingly recommend that students select a major area of study primarily because it interests them, not because they feel a certain major will enhance their chances of acceptance.

Most colleges have a health careers program that provides information, guidance, and advice for students who want to go to medical school. Encourage your child to contact the school's health careers adviser as early as possible. They will be able to offer invaluable assistance as he or she experiences the complex and stressful process of preparing to apply.

Even if your child has a stellar academic and co-curricular record in college, there is still a chance that he or she won't be successful in gaining admission to medical school on the first try. As a parent, you can be extremely influential in helping your child consider alternatives to medical school. Your child will need all of your emotional support and thoughtful guidance during and after this process. There are many ways that he can use his time after college, and before applying to medical school again, to enhance the chances of getting accepted on the second try. A student can gain experience by working as a laboratory technician in a hospital, teaching biology or chemistry in a private school, or joining the Peace Corps as a health worker, to name a few possibilities. The health careers adviser may be able to suggest other options as well.

The First Job—and the Floundering Period—After College

Even in earlier more promising economic times, few students graduated from college with a job offer in hand. In fact, only about 20 percent traditionally had jobs upon graduation, but 95 percent were employed within a year of graduation. This picture has changed dramatically in the last few years. While it's true that some students (about 24 percent of 2010 graduates) leave college with jobs waiting for them, the prospects for students who are still looking after graduation are significantly dimmer. Students in preprofessional programs, such as engineering, nursing, or physical therapy, are more likely to find jobs before graduation than students whose college major has not specifically trained them for a particular job. There are also students in some specific liberals arts majors, such as economics and mathematics, who may have an easier time finding that first entry-level job.

All parents, especially those who have sacrificed financially to put their child through college, wonder how their college graduate will land that first job and be self-supporting. These scenarios will help you understand the job search process, why it may take your college graduate several years to land their first career-related job, and what you can do to help during this transition period.

Zero Prospects/Zero Ideas

Your son is a senior. Every time you ask him about his future plans, he says he doesn't want to think about it. It's clear that he doesn't have a plan and you're worried he might take up permanent residence on your couch after graduation.

What's on Your Mind

It's clear he's in denial; what are we supposed to do to help him?
He's got to find a job to start paying off his student loans soon.
I'm not opposed to him coming home for a while, but what will he do?

What's on Your Child's Mind

I don't want to think about what comes next.

I wish my parents would stop asking me what I'm going to do. I don't know!

What's Going On

It's very common for seniors to go directly into denial when facing life after college, especially as they witness their friends struggling to find direction. For the first time in their lives, it's not clear what follows and they are often embarrassed to admit that they're clueless.

With the job market so difficult, many students will return home to live with their parents after graduation. Although this is not a new trend, current college students may feel even more paralyzed by their lack of future prospects.

Some students need some gentle prodding to confront the first real job search of their lives. Students who haven't had internships or summer jobs to help them define their career interests, will need some counseling and support to search for that first job. Fortunately, colleges have career offices to assist in this effort, but students need to take the initiative in getting help.

What to Do

- Sit down with your son and have a frank conversation about your expectations if he plans to move home after college.
- Recognize that he may need a few weeks to regroup after graduation. Try to be patient.
- Urge him to make an appointment with the career center to get some counseling and prepare a résumé before he graduates.
- Talk with him about his options and offer to help him make contacts if you have friends or associates who can provide guidance.
- Let him know that you appreciate how scary and difficult this transition is, but remain firm in your expectation that he will eventually be able to find a job and support himself.

What to Avoid

- Criticizing him for being so disinterested in his future.
- Telling him he can't just come home and chill out until he "finds" himself.

- Taking on his sense of hopelessness.
- Accepting the fact that he'll be living with you for an indefinite period of time.

What You Need to Know

Many young people in this generation have been raised with the highest expectations to achieve and some are completely burned out after college, unable to generate any enthusiasm for the next chapter in their lives. A generation that has been raised to believe that they are special and destined for great things may have difficulty facing the harsh reality that college is over and their prospects are limited. Some will be eager to blame the economy and justify their lack of ambition to move ahead as a natural response to a bad situation. They may want to rely on their parents to sort out their circumstances, especially if their parents have shielded them from difficulties in the past and provided a comfortable place to land.

The transition from college to the first job is usually a stressful time for students and parents alike. This can be particularly confusing for students whose majors don't translate easily into a career area, or for students who are unfocused about what they want to do. This doesn't mean that your child will languish on your couch forever. It means that he needs to avail himself of the career services and advice he can receive while he's still on campus.

Students are often overwhelmed when they realize that seeking their first job requires extensive work and that staff members in the career center do not hand out jobs to seniors! In our experience, students who have developed job search skills during college find this process significantly less daunting than students who present themselves to the career office in a panic during their senior year. Your child is entitled to assistance and support from career office counselors, but he should not expect that counselor to find him a job.

Try to support any attempt he makes to deal with his prospects for employment. He may have to come home for a period of time after graduation to concentrate on his job search. In the meantime, it is entirely reasonable for you to insist that he get a job of some sort. Temporary agencies can offer short-term employment that will get him off the couch, engaged in work, and earning some money. And temporary jobs often lead to a permanent job later. He may need some time to sort through his options and earn enough money to be able to relocate to an area where jobs are available.

If he knows where he'd like to live and search for a job, he should check out employment agencies and internship possibilities in that area. It may mean that you have to partially support him while he gets his feet on the ground in another city, but that may be well worth your effort in the long run. Getting a child launched into the world of work, especially now, may require tremendous patience and understanding, as well as some temporary financial support.

Fortunately, part of the recent overhaul of the health insurance industry has guaranteed that your child can continue to be covered on your family health insurance plan until age twenty-six. This initiative can take some pressure off of the imperative to find a good job with health insurance benefits for new college graduates and can save you a significant amount of money providing health insurance for your underemployed child.

While there is no doubt that students today face formidable obstacles (most of them not of their own making), parents need to be vigilant in their responses to this transition. Although it may be hard for you, as a parent, to ignore your child's needs and desires, it is also critical that you don't facilitate your child's slide into "motivational paralysis." Your consulting skills may be more useful than ever after your child graduates from college.

Job Offer in Hand

Your daughter, a business major, is about to graduate and has received a great job offer from a large corporation. She was recruited through the campus career center and is excited that her new job is based in her home city. She recently announced that she wants to move back in with you and save some money before trying to get her first apartment in a year or two.

What's Going On

It's not unusual for students to come home after graduation and take some time to sort their things before getting settled into an apartment of their own. Many students, especially those who are beginning a first job in a large city, do not have the financial resources necessary to secure an apartment immediately. They may also feel the need to reconnect with family and have time to plan for the move.

What's on Your Mind

I thought she would be so eager to get her own apartment.
It's pretty expensive to get an apartment here, with broker's fees and security deposit.
I wonder how long she plans to stay with us before making the move.

What's on Your Child's Mind

I'm so excited about my new job.
It's great that I can live at home for a while.
I don't have the money to start out on my own right now.

What to Do

- Congratulate your daughter on the successful job search.
- Celebrate her achievement.
- Talk with her about her short- and long-term plans.
- Help her brainstorm ways to move toward her own apartment (i.e., you may be willing to let her live with you rent-free if she starts a savings account to facilitate her move to an apartment within a specified period of time).
- Let her know your expectations about her living at home (i.e., how will she participate in family life, what her responsibilities will be for keeping the household running, whether she will pay you rent, etc.).

What to Avoid

- Refusing to discuss the inevitable adjustments for all of you if she decides to move home after college.
- Making life at home so comfortable that she will have no desire to leave.
- Truncating her development by insisting that she move home and stay as long as she wants.

What You Need to Know

This is a good dilemma to have! A graduating child with a good job offer in hand is a cause for celebration.

Landing a first professional job is a big first step to launching your child on the track to independence but one that could easily be derailed if you are not vigilant about your expectations and responses. While it may be reasonable for your daughter to come home for a period of time in order to redirect her life, it is also reasonable that you have a serious discussion with her about this transition period and lay out some mutual ground rules for its duration.

Following Your Heart

Basketball has always been a great passion for your son. He played on the high school team, but realized he wasn't good enough to have a career in professional basketball. He decided to major in economics and has been a good student in college. He went to the career center to check out the job possibilities and the career adviser gave him a battery of skills and interests tests. Not surprisingly, he's still interested in sports, but he has also developed skills in math and analytical reasoning. He's wondering how he can put both his interests and skills to work after college.

What's on Your Mind

He's still as avid a basketball fan as ever.
It's too bad that he wasn't good enough to be a professional basketball player.
I wonder what he'll do with his economics degree.

What's on Your Child's Mind

I still wish I could have been a pro basketball player.
I can't see myself being a financial analyst, no matter how much money they offer me.
What am I going to do?

What's Going On

Many students have to come to terms with balancing their dreams with reality as they prepare for life after college. It's easy for students who have had limited "real world" experience or who have widely disparate interests and skills, to think there is only one predictable path for them to follow when looking for a job.

What to Do

- Encourage your son to return to the career center and have a counselor explore with him creative ways to combine his skills and interests.
- Recommend that he gather names of alumni who work in sports management and set up informational interviews with them.
- Suggest that he look into postgraduate internships that may be available with some of the major sports franchises.

What to Avoid

- Telling him that it's time to grow up and forget about a career in basketball.
- Suggesting that he should just accept the fact that he's probably going to have to work in a bank or financial services organization.

What You Need to Know

Many students find creative ways to combine their passions and skills when beginning their job search. While it's true that this student may have to give up his dream of being a professional athlete, it's not necessarily true that he will have to settle for a job with no connection to sports. He could potentially find a position in the financial division of the NBA.

One of the fastest growing sectors of the economy in the United States today is sports and entertainment. Students who have a strong interest in sports, film, television, theater, or music can often use their business and finance skills to find work in one of these industries. It simply takes some creative thinking about alternatives and the willingness to work hard to research and uncover possibilities.

Career center staff at most colleges can help your child explore ways to combine his dreams with the reality of finding an entry-level job. Skills and interest inventories can identify areas of strength, and contacts with alumni can provide useful advice and networking opportunities. If your child has a relatively unusual career objective, it's important that you encourage him to take advantage of the assistance he can receive while still in school.

Studies show that most people find jobs through personal contacts. Your child will need to become skillful at networking and informational interviewing to be able to find a job that combines his analytical skills with his love of sports. Contacting alumni of his college and setting up appointments to ask them questions about their careers in sports management is a good place to start. An alumnus may even agree to allow your son to spend a day or two with him at work, observing his daily activities and accompanying him to meetings.

While your son or daughter may have to abandon the dream of being the next Michael Jordan or Serena Williams, he or she doesn't necessarily have to give up a job in sports. There are jobs available for people with analytical and communication skills in sports administration, and behind-the-scenes work can be rewarding for individuals who have a passion for sports and entertainment.

Career Confident

Your daughter is an art history major, but has always had a great interest in journalism. She worked at the local newspaper last summer and really enjoyed getting to know the print news business. She's been discouraged, though, because she's sent out dozens of résumés to city newspapers across the country and hasn't received any positive response.

What's on Your Mind

I can't believe she wants to work in a newspaper. They're all cutting back and some are
  closing down completely.
What is she thinking?

What's on Your Child's Mind

I loved working at the newspaper last summer.
I know this is what I want to do after college.
I wonder if there are any jobs at newspapers anymore.

What's Going On

Although she doesn't have a journalism degree, she's convinced that she wants to be a newspaper
reporter. She is willing to take any job, even an unpaid internship, just to get her foot in the door
of a newspaper.

What to Do

- Suggest that she see a career counselor on campus to learn more about journalism as a
  career.
- Encourage her to try for an internship, even though it sounds like a dead end to you.
- Suggest that she talk to alumni who are journalists to find out more about this career
  path.

What to Avoid

- Discouraging her because you don't understand the field.
- Telling her that she should have majored in something more practical.
- Thinking that she's crazy to try to get a job in a dying industry.

What You Need to Know

As newspapers lay off people by the hundreds and the future of print journalism looks bleak, it
doesn't seem prudent to pursue a career in this field. It's difficult to know what the news busi-

ness will look like in five years but there are some things that students can do to enhance their odds of finding work in the newspaper business.

First and foremost is to get experience. Summer jobs and internships can pay off, especially if they've given a student the opportunity to write real stories and put together a clip portfolio. Writing for the college newspaper and working up to an editorial position is highly regarded by recruiters for newspapers. Students today also need to have technical skills; it's a good idea to learn layout software, Web design, and digital photography processes, and to take advantage of every opportunity to write including creating a personal blog.

Journalists are divided over the issue of whether a graduate degree is necessary to become a successful reporter at a prestigious newspaper. Most agree, however, that beginning journalists have to "pay their dues" in the profession by working in small markets and covering less exciting stories to gain the experience they need to move to the next level in the newspaper business. Most individuals spend several years with small and medium-sized newspapers before they are ready to apply for jobs in the bigger markets with large-circulation newspapers. This is usually the pattern in the fields of photojournalism and broadcasting as well.

Working Abroad

Your daughter is graduating with a major in European history and wants to live and work abroad for a couple of years. She spent a semester in Spain and thinks she can find a job there. She's willing to take practically any job in order to live in Spain again.

What's on Your Mind

How in the world does she expect to find a job in Spain?
I'm not even sure she can get a job here.
This idea seems so unrealistic.

What's on Your Child's Mind

I loved Barcelona and I want to go back.
I would take any job to get back to Spain.
I should go now before I have to settle down and find a real job or go to graduate school.

What's Going On

Many students who had a wonderful semester, summer, or year abroad want to go back there and live after college. They are convinced that they can get a job, but are unsure of how to go about doing an international job search.

What to Do

- Encourage her to talk to someone in the career center about her international job search.
- Listen to her dreams, but insist that she get some good advice.
- Offer to help if you have friends or associates who work abroad.

What to Avoid

- Telling her she's crazy to even think about working in Spain.
- Saying no to this idea before getting more information from your daughter.

What You Need to Know

An international job search is difficult at best. Most countries have legal requirements or ethical commitments to hire their own citizens; this can make it tough for a foreigner to obtain a work visa. There are programs, however, that do help American college graduates find jobs abroad. The Council on International Educational Exchange (CIEE) helps graduating seniors obtain jobs teaching English in Chile, China, the Dominican Republic, South Korea, Spain, and Thailand, and JET (The Japan Exchange and Teaching Program) places new graduates in English teaching positions in Japan. There are other organizations, as well, that focus on placing college graduates in short-term jobs abroad. If your child is determined to work and live abroad after college, it might be more realistic for her to join the Peace Corps or another type of international aid or nongovernmental organization that places people in foreign countries for a year or two after college. A Web search can give you more information on these opportunities.

In general, it is extremely difficult for students to work abroad for an extended period of time without extraordinary personal connections or qualifications. It is possible for some students to obtain placements abroad while working for an American company, but these assignments are usually reserved for employees who have some seniority or a special area of expertise.

Life in the Big City After a Trip to Europe

Your son is going to move to San Francisco at the end of the summer, but first he plans to travel around Europe for a couple of months. He doesn't have a job yet in San Francisco, but hopes to rent an apartment with three friends who already have good jobs in the Bay Area.

What's on Your Mind

Should he take this trip to Europe without a job?
I'm worried about him moving halfway across the country without a job.
How will he pay the rent and eat?

What's on Your Child's Mind

I really want to take this trip to Europe.
It will be so cool to live in San Francisco with my friends.
I'm sure I'll be able to get some kind of job when I get back from Europe.

What's Going On

Many students who can afford it, take the European tour during the summer after college. While he is more than ready to strike out on his own and move to the city with his friends, his youthful enthusiasm overrides any concerns he may have about whether he can find a job and support himself in San Francisco.

What to Do

- Encourage him to take the trip and enjoy his last summer of freedom from job responsibilities.
- Have a frank talk with him about how he plans to support himself in San Francisco.
- Take his plans seriously, but ask him to consider all of the possibilities before he makes the move, including a fallback plan if he's unable to find a job immediately.
- Find out what the costs will be and let him know if you are able or willing to help him with relocation money.
- Suggest that he visit the career center on campus to find out about the job market in San Francisco and get some counseling to focus his job search.

- Recommend that he gather names of alumni in the Bay Area that he can contact.
- Let him know that you are proud of his courage, even though you are concerned about the risks.

What to Avoid

- Telling him he can't go on the trip until he has a job.
- Refusing to help him relocate because you think this is a crazy idea.
- Letting him know you think he's incapable of taking care of himself.

What You Need to Know

Students who do not have job offers at graduation will probably not suffer from putting off their job searches until late summer or early fall. In fact, most organizations do little hiring during the summer. Late summer and early fall are far more productive times to begin a job search, and it's usually easier to find a job if a student has already relocated to his or her city of choice.

Although moving to a city without a job is frightening for parents who understand the risks, it is not uncommon for students to take this leap of faith when they graduate from college. And most learn a lot about themselves and benefit from having to cope on their own. Some students in this situation need a significant amount of support and financial assistance from parents. For example, in order to rent an apartment, he will probably need to come up with a chunk of money for his share of the security deposit and the first and last month's rent—and possibly even a broker's fee. This can amount to several thousand dollars, in addition to the money he will need to move and to take care of himself until he starts getting a paycheck.

There are various ways that students can produce the money they need to establish themselves. Some parents are able to give or lend their child the money; others insist that their child come home after college, get a job, and save the money necessary to relocate later in the summer or early fall. Some students, who don't have family resources, run up credit card debt or attempt to borrow money on their own. It can be tough on students who get themselves heavily indebted, especially if, six months later, they have to begin paying off student loans. It's important that parents take the initiative in talking about the costs involved, mapping out a plan, and then allowing their child to experience the consequences of his decisions.

Many of the national service organizations (such as AmeriCorps, City Year, VISTA, etc.) welcome college graduates for short-term employment in cities across the country. These opportunities can help students focus their career interests, maintain at least a subsistence standard of living, and provide valuable experience to bolster their application for more permanent employment or graduate school. Teach for America might also be a viable option if a student is willing to relocate to an area in need of teachers.

Some students get jobs when they move to a new area through a local temporary employment agency. Employing someone on a temporary basis gives the organization a chance to observe his or her work and make a decision on offering permanent employment later. Temp agencies (and employment agencies) usually specialize in a particular career area, such as public relations, marketing, sales, or advertising. If there is a good fit between the organization and the temp worker, that worker may receive a permanent job offer when the temporary work contract has been fulfilled. Even if this doesn't occur, your child will have gainful employment while he looks for a permanent position in another organization. Temporary jobs often allow flexibility in hours so that the employee can pursue a job search and coordinate job interviews elsewhere.

Web-Surfing for a Job

When you asked your daughter about her plans for finding a job after college, she said she had already found some leads through the Web and hoped that one of them would result in a job offer by graduation.

What's on Your Mind

> Can she really find a job through the Web?
> What ever happened to the face-to-face interview?
> I'm not sure this will work.

What's on Your Child's Mind

> It's so easy to find out about jobs on the Web.
> I think I'll have a job by graduation.
> One of my friends found a great job through the Web.

What's Going On

Students are used to getting all of the information they need through the Web. There are hundreds of job search sites and many students are discovering creative ways to use these sites to find a job. This can seem like a far cry from the traditional cover letter and résumé mailings that characterized a job search when you were graduating from college.

What to Do

- Ask your daughter to describe the search process she's using.
- Look at some of these sites.
- Congratulate her for taking charge of her job search.
- Suggest that she also talk to a career counselor for additional help.

What to Avoid

- Dismissing this method because you don't understand it.
- Insisting that you've never known anyone who got a job online.
- Discouraging this fledgling effort.

What You Need to Know

The Internet can be a wonderful resource for students looking for job prospects in preparation for the eventual face-to-face interview. But it can also be a passive medium, removing the all-important face-to-face contact that often carries more weight than an electronic exchange; hence, it may not be smart for a student to rely solely on the Internet to produce viable job prospects. All of the traditional job search strategies—utilizing alumni contacts, networking, researching prospective employers, conducting informational interviews, honing interview skills, and preparing the best résumé possible—should be employed when beginning this process.

Some of these traditional job search strategies can be significantly enhanced, however, through the use of media resources. LinkedIn, for example, offers very helpful ways to uncover networking possibilities through friends or friends of friends in specific companies, as well as the opportunity to connect with industry experts and insiders. Facebook offers a service called Simply Hired that facilitates a link between jobs in a variety of career areas and the organizations in which a job seeker may already have friends; hence, an applicant can use his or her social networking contacts to find inside leads in a specific company or organization. Internal referrals and contacts can be the key to uncovering a hidden job market, putting applicants in direct touch with people who have job openings. It's often the so-called distant contacts (those individuals who are friends of friends, or friends of friends of friends) that are most useful in building a professional network. These services can easily and quickly widen a job seeker's network of contacts and possibilities.

Twitter can also be used effectively to engage in conversations with individuals in a specific career area. The brevity of Twitter is particularly appealing to busy professionals who may be willing to take a few seconds to connect a job seeker to a promising lead on a job or refer him or her to someone else who can help.

While career office professionals can provide invaluable counseling to college students, most of them would agree that networking is a key strategy in a job search. In fact, most people get jobs through personal and professional networks. The vast array of technological services available can be enormously beneficial to a job seeker if those tools are used wisely and appropriately.

It's important to remember, however, that professional etiquette and ethical behavior need to be observed, even with these relatively informal exchanges. Contacts should be treated with respect and thanked for any assistance they provide. And it's good to remember, again, that everything posted on these Web services is public.

Your Son, the Banker

You were surprised and happy when your son, Marshall, called last night with the good news that he had received an excellent job offer as a result of interviewing with companies on campus.

MARSHALL: Hey, Dad, I've got some great news!

DAD: What's up, son?

MARSHALL: I just got a job offer.

DAD: Wow, that's great! What's the job?

MARSHALL: It's with Crouse and Barden.

DAD: So, what would you be doing?

MARSHALL: They offered me an entry-level analyst position and they have a great training program so I can learn all about the investment banking business.

DAD: Where is this job located?

MARSHALL: New York City. Isn't that cool, Dad? I'm going to live in the city. I can't wait.

DAD: This is such great news, Marshall. I'm really proud of you.

MARSHALL: The only problem is that I'm going to need serious money to live in the city. They offered me a good salary but New York City is expensive.

DAD: Well, that's for sure. It can really be expensive to get an apartment there.

MARSHALL: I've already decided to live with a couple of my friends. They're moving to the city, too. The three of us should be able to scrape up enough money for rent.

DAD: Sounds like you're already on your way.

MARSHALL: Yeah, I'm really psyched.

DAD: Your hard work has really paid off. Good for you.

What's on Your Mind

I can't believe it. Marshall has a job offer.
This is great. I'm so proud of him.

What's on Your Child's Mind

I am so excited to finish school and move to the city.
I can't believe I actually have a good job.
I'm really glad I majored in math.

What's Going On

Marshall is one of a relatively small number of students who will have a solid job when he graduates from college. Even in an uncertain economy, many banking and investment firms still travel to campuses each year to interview and choose outstanding students for entry-level training programs. Although this is not the typical experience for a college senior, Marshall has been diligent in researching opportunities and preparing for interviews, and now is in the enviable position of having an attractive job offer.

This is the kind of phone call that most parents would love to receive. It's a great relief to know that your child is on the way to becoming self-supporting in a career that offers financial rewards and growth potential.

What to Do

- Congratulate him on his job offer.
- Let him know how proud you are and that you have great confidence in his ability to succeed in this next phase of his life.
- Give yourself some credit, too, for all of the support and guidance—and perhaps, money—you've provided along the way.

What to Avoid

- Second-guessing the job offer he has accepted.
- Telling him that living in the city is going to be really hard and expensive.

What You Need to Know

Marshall is an example of a highly focused and confident student. His job offer was most likely the result of his participation in an on-campus recruiting program that coordinates interviews for jobs in areas such as banking, engineering, consulting, and insurance. His mathematics major and economics minor have prepared him to be a good candidate for a training program in investment banking.

There is significant support on most college campuses for students interested in participating in the on-campus recruiting program. Most career centers have staff members that help students make contact with hiring organizations and prepare for interviews. It is likely that Marshall registered early with the career center's recruiting program, attended preparation sessions, networked with alumni, and probably had some summer job experience that made him an attractive candidate.

Many students who are not in these highly sought-after fields of study don't realize how much they can gain from the services offered by their college career center. Parents can have significant influence by encouraging their children to take advantage of the services offered while they are still on campus. Most career centers have an array of helpful services, including a resource library and employer information, alumni databases, practice interview sessions, résumé referral services, on-campus recruiting programs, job listings, graduate and professional school counseling, individualized career advising sessions, interest testing and computerized career guidance assistance, internship programs, career fairs, and workshops on writing résumés and cover letters, networking, informational interviewing, interviewing skills, and negotiating job and salary offers.

Making Sense of Getting That First Job—Parent to Parent

Ken received a call last night from George, a friend whose child is graduating from college in the spring. George sounded pretty exasperated about his daughter's prospects:

> KEN: Hi, George. How's it going?
>
> GEORGE: Well, pretty good, Ken, but my daughter is making me crazy.
>
> KEN: Jenna? What's going on?
>
> GEORGE: She's decided that she's going to move to Washington, D.C., after graduation and take an internship at the Environmental Protection Agency that only pays her one hundred dollars a week! I don't think she has a clue about what it costs to live in a city.

KEN: Yeah, I remember those days of worrying about your kid's plans for after college. A few years ago, Meg told us she was going to move to Chicago after college and work at the Art Institute for seven bucks an hour. I thought she was nuts!

GEORGE: What happened?

KEN: Well, she moved to Chicago all right, and found out how hard it was to pay the rent on seven bucks an hour. I could have told her that, of course, but she had to find out for herself.

GEORGE: What did she do?

KEN: She found another job waitressing four nights a week. And she lived with six other girls in a run-down old house. It wasn't in the best neighborhood, but she didn't seem to mind. She was having a ball living in the city and she figured out how to make ends meet most months.

GEORGE: So, what's she doing now?

KEN: Well, it's taken a few years, but she just landed a great job in a community arts organization, and she's thinking of going to graduate school at night to get an MBA in arts administration. She has her own apartment now and she's doing fine. She seems really happy.

GEORGE: So, everything turned out all right for her, huh?

KEN: Yeah, sometimes you just have to let them do their thing, ya know? Jenna's a smart kid. She'll figure it out. It's you who's gonna suffer for a while!

GEORGE: Yeah, you're right about that!

What's on George's Mind

How is Jenna going to survive in the city?
I'm really worried about her.
Should we insist that she come home and work until she gets on her feet?

What's on Jenna's Mind

I am so excited about this internship and living in D.C.
I know I can find a place to live and take care of myself.
My parents are such worrywarts.

What's Going On

Jenna is excited about moving to Washington, D.C., and getting on with her life after college; her parents aren't so sure this is a good idea. They can't imagine her being able to support herself and they worry about her safety and security.

What to Do

- Talk to your child about the internship she wants to take.
- Let her know that you're proud of her taking charge of her life after college but that you're concerned about how she'll manage living in the city.
- Sit down with her and map out a plan for where she'll live and how she'll support herself on her internship salary.
- Suggest that she may have to get an additional job to make ends meet.
- Let her know to what extent you are able to help her financially.

What to Avoid

- Telling her she can't do this.
- Begging her to come home and work until she has enough money to move to the city.
- Assuming that she won't be happy unless she has a nice apartment and a car.

What You Need to Know

Many college students head off to a marginal job or low-paying internship in a city after graduation with great hopes and dreams of living on their own and being independent from their parents. Although you might consider this a risky proposition, your child probably sees it as a great adventure. It's hard to set aside your fears and believe that she can make it, but this is the beginning of her path to independence and that is an effort worth supporting. Many solid careers result from taking this first step, but the first year or two can be difficult for you. Launching a child into the real world means that you have to believe in her ability to cope with less-than-ideal living circumstances in order to make her way in her world.

This floundering period can take months or years, but very few college graduates, five years out, are living in marginal neighborhoods and subsisting on macaroni and cheese as they contemplate another day at a low-paying, dead-end job. This dose of reality can be a very positive experience that motivates your child to focus her goals and work to achieve them.

A few years out of college, most graduates are not doing anything related to their college major or their first job. In fact, the average person today will change careers many times in his or her working life. And those changes are likely to be most dramatic during the first ten years out of college. Most college graduates go through a floundering period during which they experiment with various vocational paths. This is a natural developmental process, even though it can be an unsettling and frustrating experience for you.

Hang in There!

Change is an absolutely predictable phenomenon in today's world of work. The days of accepting a job upon graduation, and sticking with it until retirement, are over. The challenges of the current economic environment can seem pretty overwhelming, particularly to a new college graduate with little experience. Even if the economy makes a dramatic recovery, it will take time to dig out of the enormous hole we've dug and it may be years before your college graduate settles into a rewarding job with a measure of security.

As your child ventures out into the challenging and ever-changing world beyond college, you can be an invaluable consultant and guide, offering support, encouragement, and unconditional love in the trials and triumphs to come. Your role will certainly change and evolve as your child continues along the path to fully independent adulthood. One of the great joys of parenting is observing your child on this journey and continuing to act as a trusted guide. We hope this book has helped you begin this journey and that you'll find yourself celebrating the many rewards and possibilities along the way.

Endnotes

2. The Electronic Umbilical Cord

1. Maggie Jackson, *Distracted: The Erosion of Attention and the Coming Dark Age* (Amherst, NY: Prometheus Books, 2008), 13.
2. Daniel de Vise, "Wide Web of Diversions Gets Laptops Evicted from Lecture Halls," *Washington Post,* March 9, 2010.
3. Mary Bart, "College Students Unplugged: 24 Hours without Media Brings Feelings of Boredom, Isolation, Anxiety," *Trends in Higher Education,* May 27, 2010.
4. Christine Rosen, "The Myth of Multitasking," *New Atlantic,* Spring 2008.
5. Matt Richtel, "Hooked on Gadgets and Paying a Mental Price," *New York Times*, June 6, 2010.
6. Nicholas Carr, "The Web Shatters Focus, Rewires Brains," *Wired Magazine*, May 28, 2010.
7. Richtel, "Hooked on Gadgets and Paying a Mental Price."
8. Nicholas Carr, *The Shallows: What the Internet Is Doing to Our Brains* (New York: W. W. Norton and Company, 2010), 120.
9. Ibid., 10.
10. Ibid., 116.
11. Ibid., 132.
12. Richtel, "Hooked on Gadgets and Paying a Mental Price."
13. Nicholas Carr, "Is Google Making Us Stupid?" *Atlantic,* July/August, 2008.

3. Getting Them Off to College

1. Ellen Goodman, "Parental Connections," *(Syracuse) Post-Standard,* September 19, 1997.

4. Roommates, Fraternity Parties, All-nighters, Changing Majors, and Hanging Out

1. Abigail Sullivan Moore, "Failure to Communicate," *New York Times Education Life,* July 25, 2010.

2. R. Hingson et al., "Magnitude of Alcohol-Related Mortality and Morbidity Among U.S. College Students Ages 18–24." *Annual Review of Public Health* 26 (2005): 259–79.

5. Is Your Child Confident, Confused, or Coasting?

1. James Marcia, "The Empirical Study of Ego Identity," in *Identity and Development,* eds. H. A. Bosma, T. L. G. Graafsma, H. D. Grotevant, and D. J. De Levita (Newbury Park, CA: Sage, 1994), 67–80.
2. Lyn Mikel Brown and Carol Gilligan, *Meeting at the Crossroads: Women's Psychology and Girls' Development* (Cambridge, MA: Harvard University Press, 1992).
3. S. Harter, P. Waters, N. Whitesell, and D. Kastelic, "Level of Voice Among Female and Male High School Students: Relational context, support, and gender orientation," *Developmental Psychology* 34, (1998): 892–901.
4. William E. Cross, Jr., *Shades of Black* (Philadelphia, PA: Temple University Press, 1991).
5. Diana Baumrind, "The Influence of Parenting Style on Adolescent Competence and Substance Use," *Journal of Early Adolescence* 11 (1991): 56–95; E. Maccoby and J. Martin, "Socialization in the Context of the Family: Parent-Child Interaction," in *Handbook of Child Psychology: Socialization, Personality and Social Development,* ed. E. M. Hetherington (New York: John Wiley and Sons, 1983).
6. Laurence Steinberg, *Adolescence,* 9th ed. (New York: McGraw-Hill, 2011).

6. Just When You Get Used to the Empty Nest, They're Back!

1. Salvador Minuchin and Michael P. Nichols, *Family Healing: Strategies for Hope and Understanding* (New York: Touchstone Books, 1993), 111.

7. Understanding the College Experience

1. Nicholas Carr, *The Shallows: What the Internet Is Doing to Our Brains* (New York: W. W. Norton and Company, 2010), 138.
2. John Palfrey and Urs Gasser, *Born Digital: Understanding the First Generation of Digital Natives* (New York: Basic Books, 2008), 197.

11. If They Leave College, Will They Ever Get Back on Track?

1. William Upski Wimsatt, "How I Got My Degree at the University of Planet Earth," *Utne Reader,* May–June 1998, 50.
2. Ibid.
3. Jacques Stein, "Plan B: Skip College," *New York Times,* May 16, 2010.

12. Understanding Your Child's Postgraduate Choices

1. Don Peck, "How a New Jobless Era Will Transform America," *Atlantic,* March 2010.
2. Jeffrey Jensen Arnett, *Emerging Adulthood: The Winding Road from the Late Teens through the Twenties* (New York: Oxford University Press, 2004), 8.

References

Arnett, Jeffrey Jensen. *Emerging Adulthood: The Winding Road from the Late Teens through the Twenties.* New York: Oxford University Press, 2004.

Bauerlein, Mark. *The Dumbest Generation: How the Digital Age Stupefies Young Americans and Jeopardizes Our Future.* New York: Penguin Group, 2009.

Bogle, Kathleen A. *Hooking Up: Sex, Dating, and Relationships on Campus.* New York: New York University Press, 2008.

Carr, Nicholas. *The Shallows: What the Internet Is Doing to Our Brains.* New York: W. W. Norton and Company, 2010.

Courtney, Vicki. *Logged On and Tuned Out: A Nontechie's Guide to Parenting a Tech-Savvy Generation.* Nashville, Tenn.: B&H Publishing Group, 2007.

Hofer, Barbara, and Abigail Moore. *The iConnected Parent: Staying Close to Your Kids in College (and Beyond) While Letting Them Grow Up.* New York: Free Press, 2010.

Jackson, Maggie. *Distracted: The Erosion of Attention and the Coming Dark Age.* Amherst, N.Y.: Prometheus Books, 2008.

Lanier, Jaron. *You Are Not a Gadget: A Manifesto.* New York: Alfred A. Knopf, 2010.

Levine, Madeline. *The Price of Privilege: How Parental Pressure and Material Advantage Are Creating a Generation of Disconnected and Unhappy Kids.* New York: HarperCollins, 2006.

Madison, Amber. *Talking Sex with Your Kids: Keep Them Safe and You Sane by Knowing What They're Really Thinking.* Avon, Mass.: Adams Media, 2010.

Marano, Hara Estroff. *A Nation of Wimps: The High Cost of Invasive Parenting.* New York: Random House, 2008.

Palfrey, John, and Urs Gasser. *Born Digital: Understanding the First Generation of Digital Natives.* New York: Basic Books, 2008.

Robbins, Alexandra, and Abby Wilner. *Quarterlife Crisis: The Unique Challenges of Life in Your Twenties.* New York: Penguin Putnam, 2001.

Seaman, Barrett. *Binge: What Your College Student Won't Tell You, Campus Life in an Age of Disconnection and Excess.* Hoboken, N.J.: John Wiley & Sons, 2005.

Stabiner, Karen. *The Empty Nest: 31 Parents Tell the Truth About Relationships, Love, and Freedom After the Kids Fly the Coop.* New York: Hyperion, 2007.

Strauss, William, and Neil Howe. *Millennials Go to College, Strategies for a New Generation on Campus: Recruiting and Admissions, Campus Life and the Classroom,* 2nd ed. Great Falls, Va.: LifeCourse Associates: 2007.

Tapscott, Don. *Growing Up Digital: The Rise of the Net Generation.* New York: McGraw-Hill, 1998.

Twenge, Jean M. *Generation Me: Why Today's Young Americans Are More Confident, Assertive, Entitled—and More Miserable Than Ever Before.* New York: Free Press, 2006.

———and W. Keith Campbell. *The Narcissism Epidemic: Living in the Age of Entitlement.* New York: Free Press, 2009.

Unell, Barbara C., and Jerry L. Wyckoff. *The Eight Seasons of Parenthood: How the Stages of Parenting Constantly Reshape Our Adult Identities.* New York: Random House, 2000.

Index

Index

About the Authors

Helen E. Johnson founded Cornell University's first parents' program and served as director of the parents' office at the University of North Carolina at Chapel Hill. She created the Gold Standard Model for Parent Relations and, as a consultant to higher education, she is widely recognized for her work in helping colleges and universities create outstanding programs and services for today's college parents. She earned a BA, summa cum laude and Phi Beta Kappa in communication theory from Wells College, and did graduate work in corporate communications at Ithaca College. She is the parent of two college graduates and resides in Chapel Hill, North Carolina.

Christine Schelhas-Miller is a faculty member in the Department of Human Development at Cornell University, teaching courses on adolescence and emerging adulthood. She also coordinates student advising as the assistant director of undergraduate studies. Previously she served as an associate dean of students at Cornell, responsible for programs for new students and their parents. For more than thirty years she has worked in higher education, teaching and providing academic, personal, and career advice to students. She consults with schools and parents on issues related to adolescent development as well as with universities on programs for first-year students. She earned a bachelor's degree from Bucknell University, a master's degree from Indiana University, and a doctorate in human development from Harvard University. She is the parent of two daughters who are enrolled in college and graduate school.